Religion and Contract Law in Islam

What is a contract in Islam? Is it an aspect of Muslim religion or of secular life? How much has it changed over the centuries? Undertaking a search that spans revelation, legal tradition, and the reality of the Muslim world, this book explores the Islamic contract (*'aqd* in Arabic) as a 'city' at the crossroads of convergent paths of translation, comparison, and law in context.

In particular, the book shows that only by re-orienting traditional categories of Western law-religion toward the East can an alternative path of discovery for the *'aqd* be advanced. Hence, through a fortuitous encounter with an *Arab Girl*, the reader will (re-)visit the Temple of Western modernity and explore a city ruled by Towers of dialectical forces, carrying a hermeneutical Ring that combines dialectics, Islamic studies, and media theory. This interdisciplinary approach will not only enrich our knowledge of the *'aqd* but also make it more understandable as a cultural and social construction to which both Muslims and non-Muslims have participated in forging its multiple representations. By inviting the readers 'to know who they are' while *looking at* her, the *Arab Girl* is already waiting for us to *listen to* the Islamic contract in a new way.

By applying a distinctive law and religion approach to the study of the contract in Islam, the book provides a comprehensive exploration of a topic that is of interest to legal and economic comparatists as well as to readers in anthropology, Islamic and cultural studies, and it is also of topical meaning for today's international lawyers and the operators of an increasingly multicultural and transnational market.

Dr Valentino Cattelan is Lecturer in Law at Birmingham City University, where he teaches contract law, EU law, and Islamic business law. He is specialised in comparative law and has published widely on aspects of Islamic law, economics, and finance.

ICLARS Series on Law and Religion

Series Editors:
Silvio Ferrari
University of Milan, Italy, Russell Sandberg, Cardiff University, UK
Pieter Coertzen
University of Stellenbosch, South Africa
W. Cole Durham, Jr.,
Brigham Young University, USA
Tahir Mahmood
Amity International University, India

The *ICLARS Series on Law and Religion* is a new series designed to provide a forum for the rapidly expanding field of research in law and religion. The series is published in association with the International Consortium for Law and Religion Studies, an international network of scholars and experts of law and religion founded in 2007 with the aim of providing a place where information, data and opinions can easily be exchanged among members and made available to the broader scientific community. The series aims to become a primary source for students and scholars while presenting authors with a valuable means to reach a wide and growing readership.

Other titles in this series:

Law, State and Religion in Bosnia and Herzegovina
Nedim Begović and Emir Kovačević

The Church and Employment Law
A Comparative Analysis of The Legal Status of Clergy and Religious Workers
John Duddington

Business, Religion and the Law
Church and Business Autonomy in the Secular Economy
Matteo Corsalini

Religion, Human Rights, and the Workplace
Judicial balancing in the United States Federal Courts and the European Court of Human Rights
Gregory Mose

Religion and Contract Law in Islam
From Medieval Trade to Global Finance
Valentino Cattelan

For more information about this series, please visit: www.routledge.com/ICLARS-Series-on-Law-and-Religion/book-series/ICLARS

Religion and Contract Law in Islam

From Medieval Trade to Global Finance

Valentino Cattelan

Routledge
Taylor & Francis Group
LONDON AND NEW YORK

First published 2024
by Routledge
4 Park Square, Milton Park, Abingdon, Oxon OX14 4RN

and by Routledge
605 Third Avenue, New York, NY 10158

Routledge is an imprint of the Taylor & Francis Group, an informa business

British Library Cataloguing-in-Publication Data
A catalogue record for this book is available from the British Library

ISBN: 978-1-138-50404-2 (hbk)
ISBN: 978-1-032-53914-0 (pbk)
ISBN: 978-1-315-14576-1 (ebk)

DOI: 10.4324/9781315145761

Typeset in Galliard
by Apex CoVantage, LLC

In memory of Prof. Francesco Castro,
Maestro di Diritto Musulmano

Contents

Figures and diagrams

Preface

The thoughts collected in this book belong to different periods of time and reflect different angles from which I have investigated Islamic contract law over the years.

Some of these thoughts (especially those in Chapter 3) date back directly to my Ph.D. research (Siena, 2009) and have been revisited in the light of a law-religion methodology (Chapter 1 and Chapter 2). The text also deals with issues of law in context (Chapter 4), cultural studies, Orientalism, dialectic, media theory, and the impact of our (non-)identity on the representation of the real (Introduction). In combining all these fields, I have tried to show the various ways through which the Islamic contract (*ʿaqd* in the Arabic language) has been *said* in space and time. By *listening* back to the *Arab Girl* (Conclusions) after having *seen* her (Introduction), I trust the reader will appreciate the consistency as well as the variations of meaning that the Islamic contract has experienced in relation to the diverse media of its representations.

Within this multidisciplinary frame, the manuscript develops around a single topic and three themes; namely, the meaning of the *ʿaqd* as manifestation of the revelation of Islam; as an aspect of cultural and intellectual history in the legal tradition; and as a fundamental element of market interaction in the socio-economic reality. More precisely, by carrying the 'One Ring' of non-identity (Chapter 1), the *ʿaqd* becomes, in this book, a means for comparing how law and religion interact in the East and the West (Chapter 2); Muslim jurisprudence (*fiqh*) within Sunnī orthodoxy provides the pathways to explore its meaning as a medium of legal tradition (Chapter 3); the continuity-in-change of this meaning – contextualized in the realities of the Muslim world, from medieval trade to the process of codification, and later, global finance – offers clues of socio- and anthropological reflections that complete the study (Chapter 4).

To cover all these interrelated dimensions, multiple layers of research have overlapped in the volume, for which I am indebted to many people and institutions.

In particular, in chronological order, I would like to acknowledge Prof. Francesco Castro (1936–2006), who first introduced me to Islamic legal studies at the University of Rome Tor Vergata in (the now distant) 2003, and to whose memory, for this reason, the volume is dedicated; the School of Oriental and African Studies of the University of London, where I met Prof. Werner Menski in 2008 (our engaging conversations about legal pluralism have continued over the years, from the time of my Ph.D. to the present), Nicholas H.D. Foster, and Dr Jonathan Ercanbrack; the Saudi Spanish Centre for Islamic Economics and Finance (IE Business School, Madrid), under the passionate guidance of Prof. Celia de Anca (with whom I have been in contact from 2011); the Oxford Centre for Islamic Studies of the University of Oxford (2013–2014); the Max Planck Institute for Social Anthropology in Halle (2017), where I received generous intellectual support and precious advice from Prof. Marie-Claire Foblets; the Käte Hamburger Centre for Advanced Study in the Humanities 'Law as Culture' in Bonn (2018). I also owe some of the contents of this book to my friends Anna and Doralice: their knowledge of mythology, the anthropology of the ancient world, and the history of religion have given special intellectual sustenance to my legal research.

This monograph has come into existence in inspiring research environments: the British Library in London; the Bodleian Library, the Sackler Library (where I could hide till late evening – a priceless benefit for a night owl), and the Middle East Centre (MEC) Library at St. Antony's College in Oxford, where I found in Maria Luisa temporary help and permanent friendship. Federica and Taidgh gave me accommodation many times in London, for which I am in debt. I also wish to thank Alison Kirk for her precious editorial assistance at Routledge Law and her patience in allowing me extra time to complete the manuscript, as well as Anna Gallagher, for her help in the final phases of production of this monograph. I am proud that the book has been accepted as part of the ICLARS Series on Law and Religion, and I would like to express my gratitude to the Series Editors and two anonymous reviewers for their initial feedback and suggestions about the original project and index of the manuscript. Christine Tracey revised the style of my English writing, which strongly improved the quality of the text.

The most special thanks go to my parents Agnese and Battista: without their constant support to my research work, this book could not exist.

At the same time of publication of this volume, another work on the contract in the Islamic legal tradition has become available to the public (Bantekas, I., Ercanbrack, J. *et al.* (2023) *Islamic Contract Law*. Oxford: Oxford University Press). Due to this concurrence, I could not have access to its contents and, for this reason, the work is only mentioned as a general reference in the Introduction. I trust that the reader will have the opportunity to take benefit from this reference, especially in relation to the topics covered in Chapter 3 of this book.

Acknowledgements

The artworks that appear in this monograph are not simply a support to the contents; they are themselves content.

For this reason, I would like to acknowledge here the people and institutions that have made possible their reproduction in the volume by granting copyright permissions. My gratitude goes first to the private owner of the Najd Collection for the image of Gérôme's *The Almeh with Pipe* (Figure 0.1), and to the owner and managing director of Mathaf Gallery London, Mrs Gina MacDermot, who kindly provided the picture from the Gallery's original catalogue. Both the reproduction of El Greco's *Christ Cleansing the Temple* (Figure 1.1) and Utagawa Hiroshige's *Sudden Shower over Shin-Ōhashi Bridge and Atake* (Figure 4.1) have been permitted by the open access policy respectively of the National Gallery of Art, Washington DC, and the Metropolitan Museum of Art, New York. As far as Figure 2.1 is concerned, it brings me back to a distant period of study of Arabic in Cairo (where I took the picture while sitting in the Mosque-Madrassa Sultan Hassan in 2009): it was at that time that I started thinking about the echo of the divine Word in the tradition of *fiqh*, surrounded by the beauty of Islamic architecture.

My writing has also been inspired by two exhibitions that I visited in 2019 at the Bodleain Library in Oxford; namely, *Babel. Adventures in Translation* (displayed 15 February – 2 June 2019) and *Talking Maps* (in programme 5 July 2019–8 March 2020), whose influence on this work can be clearly seen in the Introduction, Chapter 2, and Chapter 3.

In Chapter 3 and Chapter 4, I broadly draw from three articles – namely, 'Property (*māl*) and credit relations in Islamic law: an explanation of *dayn* and the function of legal personality (*dhimma*);' 'Between theory(-ies) and practice(s): legal devices (*ḥiyal*) in classical Islamic law;' and '*The Typewritten Market*: Shari'ah-compliance and securitisation in the law of Islamic finance' – that I published respectively in 2013, 2017, and 2021. I am thankful to the *Arab Law Quarterly* for their permission to reproduce content.

Introduction

Ways of *seeing* an *Arab Girl*

This book attempts to explain to as wide a readership as possible what a contract is in Islam; how some qualities of the Islamic contract (*ʿaqd* in Arabic) can be deemed consistent within a great synchronic and diachronic variation of contexts; and why this unity-in-diversity (continuity-in-change) can be coherently linked to the interaction between law and religion in Muslim jurisprudence as part of the intellectual, cultural, and social history of Islam.

The book claims that certain features of the Islamic contract, perhaps the most controversial for Western scholars, but at the same time, the most revealing of its nature, cannot be properly understood unless their rationales are located within the religious background of Muslim juristic discourse. Accordingly, by departing from many valuable works of legal scholarship already available on the subject, it looks at religion and law as co-determining factors in the construction of the *ʿaqd* both as part of divine revelation (Chapter 2) and as a human enterprise of intellectual/social nature that has developed in the legal tradition (Chapter 3) and in the reality of the Muslim world, within a theory-practice interplay (Chapter 4).

Within this framework, the essential theoretical stance of this volume is that a full understanding of the *ʿaqd* cannot be achieved without embracing a dialectical relation between the Occident and the Orient in the definition of what-is-law and what-is-religion, with the subsequent need to revisit how the *ʿaqd* has been constructed in Western literature through comparative methodology, also in the light of media theory (Chapter 1).

More broadly, the book employs the contract as a medium to investigate the Islamic *nomos*. Thus, the *ʿaqd* will become, in these pages, a vehicle of legal meaning that is not only particularly useful, as we will see, for shedding light on the interface between the secular and the religious in the normative universe of the Muslim world, but also for disclosing how the nature of the contract, so familiar to legal scholars, has been considered differently in the Western and Islamic legal traditions and how its rules (part of mutable social contexts, where the experience of every individual's life subsists) have been exercised differently in space and time.

DOI: 10.4324/9781315145761-1

In brief, by devoting its contents to the contract in Islam, the aspiration of this work is to say something valuable about the Muslim world as well as about contract law as a fundamental aspect of human life in any society. Accordingly, it will show how the study of the *ʿaqd* can contribute as much to a better understanding of law and religion in the East and the West as to the cultural relation between the Orient and the Occident, and ultimately, to its re-orientation.

From archetypes to *corpora iuris*

Two caveats are needed before starting this study.

First, this book does not argue (even remotely) that a general and uniform idea of contract belongs to Islam as a sort of archetype spanning the whole history of the Muslim world.

Presenting the *ʿaqd* (lit. 'tie,' 'bond,' pl. *ʿuqūd*; from the Arabic root *ʿ-Q-D*, 'to tie, to knit,' 'to bind,' 'to gather,' hence, 'to conclude a contract:' Wehr, 1979) as a consistent subject of research does not imply here a claim for any trans-historical and trans-geographical univocal identity. In fact, insofar as the multiple rules of the *ʿaqd* that can be found in Muslim jurisprudence (Chapter 3) have combined elements of doctrine interlinked with changeable factors of social reality, so its practice has always been affected by a variety of local customs and has entered into contact with other legal systems and traditions. In brief, the *ʿaqd* has never been a uniform entity, since, like any other legal institution, it has never existed in a vacuum. Rather, it has always experienced multiple formulations and contaminations from the time of its origins to the modern period and present times (Chapter 4). A dialectic of non-identity (Chapter 1) will constantly support this approach to the *ʿaqd* through the pages of this work.

Nevertheless, a key assumption of this book is that a specifically *Islamic* meaning has always underpinned the multifaceted nature of the *ʿaqd*: in other terms, the *ʿaqd* has maintained within its transformative praxis some constant elements (a unity-in-diversity, a continuity-in-change) that can be recognised in the diverse range of human contexts of the Muslim world as related to the religion of Islam. It has enjoyed a continuity *in practice*, despite the changeable and plural nature of its *theories and practices*: a continuity whose rationales, as this book will try to show, can be coherently linked to the core postulates of Islamic religion (Chapter 2). It is in this sense that the *ʿaqd* will become, for us, a precious tool of enquiry of the rich and diverse normative universe of Islam; a source of information about how the secular and the religious interact in the Muslim world; a vehicle of legal meaning within a 'unity of diversities,' whose rationales have to be studied in a dialectical perspective with Western law and religion, in order to be properly understood.

Second, and as a direct corollary of what has just been said, a core argument of this book is that the deepest meaning of the unity-in-diversity of the *ʿaqd* cannot be fully appreciated unless studied in a comparative approach with the tenets of Western religion (Chapter 2) and law (Chapter 3).

If the plurivocal discordance and disagreement of rules (in Arabic *ikhtilāf*) within the literature of *fiqh* – Islamic classical law in the sense of Muslim jurisprudence – certainly conflicts with the doctrinal archetypes of Western legal tradition, which is grounded on principles of systematic and general normativity within a coherent *corpus* – a 'body of law' – the apparent Western incoherence of these rules will prove to be the major proof of Islamic coherence of the *'aqd* in a methodological framework grounded on its non-identity with the West (Chapter 1). In fact, this *absence* of a unified *corpus* for the Islamic contract departs both from the style of civil law (grounded on the *droit académique* of European conceptual jurisprudence)[1] and common law (where cases follow precedents according to the *stare decisis* principle). Scattered in a myriad of rules presented in a casuistic style, although the *'aqd* constitutes a substantial topic of *fiqh al-mu'āmalāt*,[2] it has no 'legal body' in the *eyes* of Western jurisprudence – it has no *corpus iuris*:[3] a body for the *'aqd* cannot be *seen* when Western standards are applied.

This book will therefore try to demonstrate that, far from being a sign of incoherence, this is, in fact, evidence of the deep-rooted coherence of *fiqh*. As noted by Norman Calder, a systematic organisation of the contents could not belong to Muslim jurisprudence *for the very reason that* Muslim scholars never aimed for this. On the contrary, 'its variation, its complexity, its extravagant exploration of detail, its constant citation of different authorities, its apparent irrelevance, sometimes, to practice, its cunning and witty accommodation, sometimes, to practice: all these things . . . will alert . . . readers to the fact that "a valid and sensible corpus of laws" is not quite what . . . [Muslim] jurists had in mind' (Calder, 1996, p. 979).

It is from this *absence* of a valid and sensible *corpus* of laws that our voyage of discovery can start – together with the consideration that, in modern times, through the colonisation process and the transplant of Western legal culture, the *presence* of the Occident has somehow been able to 're-clothe' the Islamic contract with a *corpus* 'in its own image and likeness' – to paraphrase the Bible, Genesis 1:26–27. The recognition of this co-existence of *absence* and *presence* in the story of the *'aqd* provides precious material for further reflection at the beginning of our journey.

Representations, meaning, and signifying practices: the riddle of the Sphinx

Although, in Muslim jurisprudence, a unified *corpus iuris* for contract law does not exist, as stated previously, the *'aqd* has been 'clothed' according to Western standards in modern times, providing it with some sort of body, even though this may be considered artificial. More precisely, the *'aqd* has been rendered more *visible* to Western *eyes* both through the process of codification in Muslim countries (e.g. the celebrated Majalla of the Ottoman Empire, enacted between 1869–1876; or the Egyptian Civil Code, 1949, conceived by the great Egyptian jurist 'Abd al-Razzāq al-Sanhūrī: see Chapter 4) and important doctrinal works, both by Arab (notably Chafik Chehata in his *Théorie Générale de l'Obligation en Droit Musulman Hanéfite*, 1969) and non-Arab authors (for instance: in English, Rayner, 1991; Vogel, 2006; in French, Linant de Bellefonds, 1965; in Italian, Santillana, 1926, 1938). The most recent volume about Islamic contract law in the English language is by Bantekas, Ercanbrack *et al.* (2023).

But, if these works of legal scholarship have solved the interpretative issues of the *'aqd* by *translating* them (on the problem of translation, see Chapter 2) into Western jurisprudence, many riddles have remained: metaphorically speaking, if the 'Sphinx' has been tamed by 'clothing' it in a Western fashion, its wildest and most inner nature has remained mainly unchallenged. As is well-known, in ancient Greece, the Sphinx was a mythical beast with the body of a lion, the head of a woman, and wings of a bird. According to Greek mythology, a Sphinx, which guarded the entrance to the city of Thebes, asked travellers a riddle before allowing them to pass, devouring those who were unable to reply: 'What walks on four feet in the morning, two in the afternoon and three at night?' The legend tells that Oedipus solved the riddle with the correct answer: 'Man – who crawls on all fours as a baby, then walks on two feet when an adult, and later uses a walking stick in old age.' Certainly, travellers in foreign lands always face challenges – and looking for the meaning of the contract in Islam is precisely the challenge that this book dares to take on. Fortunately for us, this voyage appears less dangerous than Oedipus' meeting with the Sphinx of Thebes – although not without its own risks.

When starting a journey, a general outline of the itinerary is always needed. Travellers may well already imagine their destination as it has been previously represented to them: Thebes, with its Sphinx, was extremely popular in ancient Greece; *mutatis mutandis*, today, for instance, the beauty of Rome is linked, in tourists' minds, to the image of centurions standing close to the Colosseum or that of Tosca flinging herself for love to her death over the edge of Castel Sant'Angelo. What is certain is that neither the centurions nor Tosca depict Rome *as-it-is*: rather, they represent the city in a way which is attractive for visitors, and the success of their narratives undoubtedly contributes to the appeal of Italy as a popular tourist destination. However, any *representation*, as a *signifying practice*, 'depends on a difference between what presents and what is presented,' 'for . . . representations . . . frequently fail to mirror in any direct way the complex world beyond the texts in which they appear' (Cooper, 2011, p. 5, referring to Eagleton, 1991, p. 213). The inherent distance between what is *absent* and what is *present* unveils the intrinsic dialectic that belongs to any representation (from the Latin *re-ad-praesentare*, literally 'to present again,' 'to make something present,' or better, 'to make something which is distant in time or space, and hence *absent*, *present* in the here-and-now'). The point is highlighted in a famous article by Roger Chartier.

> [O]n the one hand, the representation makes visible an absence, that which supposes a clear difference between what represents and what is

> represented; on the other, the representation is the display of a presence, the public presentation of a thing or a person. In the first sense, the representation is the instrument of a mediated knowledge that makes visible an absent object by substituting it with an "image" capable of reminding (the viewer) of it and of "portraying" it as it is.
>
> (Chartier, 1989, p. 1514; author's translation)[4]

Any mediated knowledge selects certain qualities of the referent while marginalising others, frequently by using some 'codes' that are shared between the speaker (the person representing the referent) and the addressee (the receiver of the representation). Natural languages are themselves codes that represent reality where words, both written and oral, are a medium for communication, and are, in fact, our mediated knowledge of what-is-real. Fellow citizens use the same language (English, French, Arabic, Finnish . . .) to communicate, and by doing so, they share a common national and cultural identity. In the same way, images, as representations, implicitly hold messages with a certain meaning. With regard to natural languages, issues of meaning can generally be solved by a process of *translation*: 'ciao' in Italian means 'hello' in English. But many aspects of human life necessarily require an effort of *comparison* to reveal unexpected nuances of meaning behind the translation. 'Ciao,' the most common informal greeting in Italian, comes from the Venetian dialect *s-ciao*, *s-ciavo*, literally '[I am your] slave, servant' (from the late Latin *sclavus*), as used by peasants to greet their landowner, and became part of Italian language only in the 20th century. This is a story of meaning that is completely different from the English 'hello,' which dates back to the early 16th century as an order to stop, from the French *holà*: *ho* 'whoa' + *là* 'there.' Alongside this comparative study, to reach the full understanding of their story or stories, words must also be put in *context*, since their meaning is immersed in social reality, and so, subject to their presence in-time; nobody today would mistake 'ciao' for 'your slave.'

Just as any word (and any city) has a story, so the *'aqd* as a vehicle of legal meaning of Islamic *nomos* will be studied in this book according to the 'stories' of three overlapping layers that are related respectively to the *translation* of the revelation of Islam (Chapter 2), the *comparison* between the Islamic and the Western traditions of contract law (Chapter 3), and the *contextualisation* of the Islamic contract in the changing social realities of the Muslim world (Chapter 4). In doing so, the study will also directly subscribe to the nature of *fiqh* in terms of 'a conceptual replica of social life, . . . balanced between revelation, tradition and reality, all three of which feed the discussion and exemplify the concepts' (Calder, 1996, p. 981: see more specifically section 1.4), and in this way, issues of hermeneutics (the theory of language and interpretation) will be linked to fundamental problems of epistemology (the theory of knowledge) in dealing with Muslim *fiqh*.

With this aim in mind, before entering more details about the methodology underpinning our comparative study of religion and contract law (Chapter 1), some additional considerations are needed regarding the semantic power of representations, whether in the form of natural languages, mythology, and visual images of a city or legal categories (such as the *ʿaqd*) translated from Islam to the West. Specifically, we cannot avoid at this point a reference to the practice of Orientalism.

Imaginative geographies of Orientalism: *The Almeh* and the city of the *ʿaqd*

Representations are tools through which we know; to wit, the *medium* of our knowledge. As means of communication, they do not respond to parameters of absolute truth but to criteria of mutual understanding; a collective signifying practice is 'real' on the grounds of its shared representation within a certain community. Moving back to the example given before, centurions and Tosca are not the 'truth' of what-Rome-is; rather, they mirror the collective perception of how-Rome-is-known in the world; in brief, they are 'real' as representations in terms of collective knowledge.

When speaking of legal archetypes, *corpora iuris*, and intelligible representations in connection to the plan of exploring unknown places, the previous pages have referred to images taken from ancient Greek mythology (Oedipus and the Sphinx); figures related to Rome (centurions, Tosca); as well as words from the Italian language ('ciao'). Although these references may appear, at first glance, detached from a study of law and religion, they can be functional to introduce the topic of this book, whose specific project can be metaphorically described as an attempt to understand better the 'land' of Islam by exploring the 'city' of the *ʿaqd* and the life of its 'inhabitants' – the Muslim believers practising Islamic contract law. The research will show how the normative world of this town has been conceived by Muslim scholars, the experts of *fiqh* (Chapter 3), in accordance with the postulates of Islamic law and religion (Chapter 2), and how the rules of the *ʿaqd* have changed in the market as a space of social interaction over time, in mutable historical scenarios (Chapter 4). Chapter 1 will outline more in depth the research methodology according to the general objectives outlined at the beginning of this Introduction, both in relation to what a contract is in the Western and Muslim legal traditions (as different signifying practices); how the interaction between law and religion in the West has represented and 'codified' the *ʿaqd*; and why this representation does not fully shed light on certain 'features of Muslim juristic discourse, those perhaps which are most revealing of its nature and its intentions' (Calder, 1996, p. 979).

While still at the entrance of our allegorical city, the quest for the *corpus* of Islamic contract law returns. I have already pointed out that, although this body has been represented by modern elaborations of Western scholarship and codified in the legislation of Muslim countries, a coherent system and a general theory of the *ʿaqd* is *absent* in classical *fiqh*. In the end, it was the Western representation of Islamic law that made visible (*present*) an *absence* (see Chartier, in a foregoing quotation). While dealing with this issue, we are fortunate that, at the gate of the town, it is an Arab girl and not a Sphinx who is waiting for us, and both for reasons of courtesy and intellectual curiosity, we can no longer put off a meeting with her (see Figure 0.1).

The Almeh with Pipe (oil on canvas, 1873; also known as *Arab Girl in a Doorway*; Najd Collection/Mathaf Gallery London) is a painting by the

Figure 0.1 *The Almeh with Pipe* (also known as *Arab Girl in a Doorway*; oil on canvas by Jean-Léon Gérôme, 1873; courtesy by Najd Collection/Mathaf Gallery London)

French artist Jean-Léon Gérôme (1824–1904),[5] completed after his visit to Cairo.[6] In the foreground of the picture, a young woman poses seductively looking at the visitor; in the darker background, another figure (we can reasonably assume an older woman) stands, wrapped in a heavy cloak – seemingly moving towards us. We do not know anything about the girl's personal life, but the image suggests that she is waiting for some company, and some malicious eyes could charge her with soliciting from the street.[7] In fact, her physical beauty is shadowed by a sense of moral decay which is materially carved in the broken, patterned grille over the doorway. All the visual elements of *The Almeh*'s representation[8] bear witness to the triumph of Neoclassicism, of which Gérôme was a great master. By blending the French *art académique* with the romanticised appeal of a cultural re-elaboration of the Muslim world, Gérôme's paintings were extremely popular during his lifetime. The 'improper body' of *The Almeh*, with her lascivious figure, greatly appealed to the eyes of his Western public in the 19th century. However, in his representation, Gérôme did not falsify reality; rather, the depiction of *The Almeh* as a concubine, in the figure of a sensual belly-dancer, easily matched the Orientalist imaginary of the Europeans of his time. Western travellers often misapplied the term *almé*[9] to young females of an inferior class who performed erotic dances that were, in fact, prohibited by the Egyptian government, while, on the contrary, as Edward William Lane carefully reports in his famous *Account of the Manners and Customs of the Modern Egyptians*,[10] *'awálim* (pl. of *almeh*) were often female professional singers of high social status. The name *almeh* actually means 'learned woman.'

Beyond this historical reality, the mischievous representation of the *Arab Girl* was shared between Gérôme and his public as if it was the 'real' Orient (although 'fail[ing] to mirror in any direct way the complex world beyond the . . . [paintings] in which they appear:' see Cooper, quoted previously in this Introduction). Moving from the past to present times, one can arguably note how a common destiny of decadence and misinterpretation, although in different forms, associates the contemporary representations of centurions and Tosca in Rome, as they appear to the eyes of foreign travellers to Italy, with Gérôme's learned women to the eyes of 19th-century Europeans. Reflecting both an appeal of cultural re-elaboration and appropriation, they select and emphasise (not completely innocently) certain characters of the referent to shape the ultimate meaning of its depiction.

At this point, I would like to explain how I met Gérôme's *Arab Girl* and why I believe she is so important to the search for Islamic contract law.

Many beautiful things occur by serendipity, and while I was looking for bibliographical sources at the Middle East Centre (MEC) Library of St Antony's College in Oxford, *The Almeh* appeared in front of me as the cover illustration of Maxime Rodinson's *Europe and the Mystique of Islam* (1988) (English version of the original French *La Fascination de l'Islam*, 1980). Captivated as I was by her appeal (probably just as Oedipus was intrigued by the riddle of the

Sphinx), so my attention was immediately struck by the powerful impact of Gérôme's Orientalism, and how it certainly nourished the European image of Islam in the 19th century. Not by chance, *La Fascination de l'Islam* deals with Western views of Muslim civilisation and underlies how much '[a] knowledge of Islam and the images of Islam . . . [is] an important key to the understanding of this world' (Rodinson, 1988, p. xiii). Certainly, the representation of the Orient by means of 'imaginative geographies' (according to the concept popularised by Edward Said in his *Orientalism*, 1978) has been a powerful instrument of knowledge construction and cultural domination by the West. Significantly, the cover of the first edition of Said's book itself is another painting by Jean-Léon Gérôme, *The Snake Charmer*, ca. 1879. As mentioned previously, representations, as collective signifying practices, are 'real' as a space – an 'imaginative geography,' created through imagery, texts, and/or discourses. But, to quote Edward Said,

> none of this Orient is merely imaginative. The Orient is an integral part of the European *material* civilization and culture. Orientalism expresses and represents that part culturally and even ideologically as a mode of discourse with supporting institutions, vocabulary, scholarship, imagery, doctrines, even colonial bureaucracies and colonial styles (Said, 1978, p. 2). . . . Thus the Orient acquired representatives, so to speak, and representations, each one more concrete, more internally congruent with some Western exigency . . . (*ibidem*, p. 62). Imaginative geography . . . legitimates a vocabulary, a universe of representative discourse peculiar to the discussion and understanding of Islam and of the Orient (*ibidem*, p. 71).

It is in this regard, I believe, that the image of the body of *The Almeh*, by mediating *our* understanding of the Orient, can offer a preliminary interpretative key to enter the city of the contract in Islam.

In fact, just as the 'proper body' of Lady Justice powerfully represents the Western trust in the moral virtue of *its own* legal and judicial system (*we* imagine *Iustitia* as a dignified, blindfolded woman holding scales and a sword, allegorically personifying equity, order, and the rule of law, and her statue proudly stands in many halls of justice and town squares),[11] the 'improper body' of Gérôme's *Arab Girl* can tell us much about *our usual* (mis?)*representation* of Islamic law; hence, indirectly, about how Western legal scholars have imagined the space of the contract in Islam. And if all 'narratives, . . . texts, images, spectacles, events; cultural artifacts . . . "tell a story"' (Bal, 1997, p. 3), the (re-)interpretation of the 'story' of the Islamic contract in the West and how it has been translated, compared, decodified, re-codified, and then re-contextualized, can offer valuable insights in the processes through which any culture constructs its own *nomos* – its normative universe in dialectical terms – i.e. by opposing (and re-affirming) its identity to another.

As each *nomos* defines the 'legal reality' of a certain culture (e.g. Lady *Iustitia* in the West), it also affects the perception, and so too, a possible misperception, of the normative universe of the culture of *others*. Hence, as Jean-Léon Gérôme was extremely successful and influential during his lifetime, so in the circle of Islamic legal studies was Joseph Schacht (1902–1969), whose *Introduction to Islamic Law* (first edition in English, 1964) has been, for decades, one of the most authoritative references in the field.[12] I am not contesting that Schacht's *Introduction* is a masterpiece of Western scholarship on Islam; in fact, what I argue is that this masterpiece contains essential elements of *cultural (re-)elaboration* of Muslim *fiqh* when it describes '[t]he sacred Law of Islam [a]s an all-embracing body of religious duties, the totality of Allah's commands that regulate the life of every Muslim in all its aspects . . . [since] it comprises on an equal footing ordinances regarding worship and ritual, as well as political and (in a narrow sense) legal rules' (as the volume significantly begins at p. 1). A 'religious body' that '[i]n the vast field of the law of contracts and obligations . . . had to resign an ever-increasing sphere to practice and custom. The theory of the sacred Law did not fail to influence practice and custom considerably, albeit in varying degrees at different places and times, but it never succeeded in imposing itself on them completely' (1964, p. 77). Hence, according to Schacht's *representation* of the 'sacred Law of Islam' (in the form of religious law *corpus iuris*; on the point, see Chapter 2), '[a]t the very time that Islamic law came into existence, its perpetual problem, that of the contrast between theory and practice, was already posed' (*ibidem*, p. 209), to the extent that 'Islamic law . . . [,] conscious of its character as a religious ideal . . . [,] believes in a continued *decadence* since the time of the caliphs of Medina . . . and it takes the *corruption* of contemporary conditions for granted' (*ibidem*, p. 199; italics added). In brief, the sacred Law of Islam was-not-law in contractual affairs, due to the unbridgeable gap between its religious *ideal* and the secular *real* of commercial practice.[13]

The reader may already have noted the extent to which this decadent scenario of the corrupted body of Islamic contract law shows noteworthy resemblance to Gérôme's *Almeh* and how much Schacht's *droit académique* (see endnote 1 in this chapter) equals Gérôme's *art académique* – a point that fully confirms the importance of the *Arab Girl* for our study. Of course, Gérôme's paintings and Schacht's scholarship were *not* falsifications of the 'true' Muslim world; on the contrary, they were 'real' imaginary spaces built by Europeans in *thinking* the Orient. A cultural construction that, as argued by Said, has functioned to make the Orient subservient to the Occident.[14] In the same way that *The Almeh* was not a respectable learned girl, so Islamic law was-not-law in contractual affairs, and a final sentence was given by Orientalists: the *nomos* of the Islamic contract was mainly *un*-present in the social reality of the Muslim world.

Looking at normative worlds; listening to the language of Islam

Along with the issues related to Orientalism, the providential meeting with the *Arab Girl* at the gate of the city can contribute to our itinerary even in a more radical way, giving *The Almeh*, I would say, the role of protagonist of this book as an allegory of the Islamic contract as represented by Western scholarship.

We have already noted the commonalities between the hidden ideologies[15] of Gérôme's paintings and Schacht's scholarship and how much (Lady *Iustitia*'s) proper and (*The Almeh*'s) improper bodies mirror the positive Western bias towards the *corpus* of its own legal tradition and the negative bias towards that of *fiqh* jurisprudence – with its assumed gap between ideal theory and real practice. In addition, *The Almeh* may also draw critical attention to some deeper Western assumptions when *looking at* Islamic law.

In this regard, the reader can agree with me that

> *seeing comes before words*. . . . It is seeing which establishes *our place* in the surrounding world. . .. Yet this seeing which comes before words, and can never be quite covered by them, is not a question of mechanically reacting to stimuli . . . *We only see what we look at. To look is an act of choice*. . . . We never look at just one thing; we are always looking at the relation between things and ourselves. Our vision is continually active, continually moving, continually holding things in a circle around itself, *constituting what is present to us as we are*. . . . [A]ll images are man-made.
> (Berger, 2008, pp. 7–9; italics added)

Ways of Seeing was a famous television series by John Berger and Mike Dibb, broadcasted on BBC Two in 1972, and later, adapted into a book of the same title, from which the foregoing extract is taken. The back cover of the volume tells us that 'when we see, we are not just looking – we are reading the language of images' (Berger, 2008) – a statement to which I totally subscribe.

But what if jurists' normative world (i.e. *their* way of conceiving the law) is constructed *not* by *looking at* words which are graphical/visual but by *listening to* words which are prophetic/phonetic? What if, in radical opposition to the foregoing extract, *words come before seeing*, so that these words and *not* human eyes (which hold implicitly a human centrality in the understanding of reality) define the *place* of men in the surrounding world? Is *listening to* these words, when visual references are lacking, an act of choice, as it is when we decide to *look at* something (which implies putting man's eye at the centre of the scene), or isn't the attempt to understand their meaning more an act of intellect aimed at *constituting what we are as those words present us*?

It is by replying to these interrelated questions, I believe, that a *new way of listening to* (rather than *looking at*) Islamic law, and subsequently, the *'aqd* as a vehicle of Islamic *nomos*, can be pursued. This is a new way of listening that may overcome much prejudice towards the *Arab Girl* and her improper *corpus* – metaphor of a negative bias towards Islamic contract law by Western jurisprudence – by adhering conceptually to the language of Islam as the revelation of God's Word. If (God's) *Word comes before* (human) *seeing* in Islam, as I am assuming here, this must necessarily re-define the *place* of men in the surrounding world (see Berger, previously quoted): it is precisely by re-orienting our perception *from looking to listening* that our research on the Islamic contact can be re-contextualised in a Muslim universe of sense.

With this specific aim, my suggestion is that our normative language must move from a *visual* to an *acoustic space*, by following the differentiation made by Canadian philosopher and media theorist Marshall McLuhan (1911–1980) (see section 1.3.3). This implies, as McLuhan proposes (1989), a radically different way of *thinking* the man-space relationship, so that the human search for meaning also follows other cognitive ways of understanding.[16] Regarding our journey, as we will see, it is by substituting our *looking at* the *corpus* of the Islamic contract with the Muslim *listening to* the plural meanings of the revealed Word in *fiqh* legal texts that the choice of following *Šarīʿah* when performing the contract can help discover the unity of its *own* Islamic meaning. This is an Islamic meaning that will appear connoted by elements of *non-identity* in a dialectical relation with Western *visual* jurisprudence, as well as governed, in its own *acoustic* coherence, by aspects of differences, divergences, and even contradictions. Chapter 1 will highlight this point in relation to Roy Bhaskar's philosophy of dialectics (1993; see section 1.3.1) and Shahab Ahmed's scholarship (2016; section 1.3.2).

As previously announced, to facilitate the reader in the search for the meaning of the *ʿaqd*, the book will adopt the image of an allegorical city, at whose gate the *Arab Girl* is standing, waiting for us, and whose inhabitants 'can be understood . . . only because the law as a particular manifestation of the divine Word constitutes them *by way of word*' (Stelzer, 2008, p. 169; italics in the original text). It is a city deprived of strict linearity, as we will discover, lacking in any systematic topography and without codified borders in the form of a 'body,' but whose 'map' can be reconstructed by following the literature of *fiqh* tradition (Chapter 3) in echoing the divine revelation (Chapter 2) and by locating its rules in the history of Muslim social reality (Chapter 4). Departing from the narrative through which Western legal scholarship has represented the *ʿaqd* as a *place* of its *own* imaginative geography requires a paradigm shift (Kuhn, 1962) in 'practising the trade' of legal comparison. This paradigm shift will be advanced in Chapter 1 by dealing with methodological issues related to the *non-identity* of law-religion by borrowing, in particular, fundamental aspects of Roy Bhaskar's philosophy of dialectic.

Our meeting with *The Almeh* has not revealed the hotspots of the journey yet, nor has it provided solid ground for our enterprise. It has raised, on the contrary, some fundamental questions about the traditional perception, interpretation, and representation (misrepresentation?) of Islamic law as a religious *corpus* (Schacht's 'sacred Law of Islam') that this book will try to overcome – so as to avoid being devoured by the Sphinx while attempting to solve the riddles regarding the normative world of the *ʿaqd*.

Moving in-between the normative wor(l)ds of the Occident and the Orient as co-existent in the story, or (better) stories of the *ʿaqd*, a final remark should be added: by undertaking this journey, we must be conscious that, here and there, in the East as in the West,

> law and narrative are inseparably related. Every prescription is insistent in its demand to be located in discourse – to be supplied with history and destiny, beginning and end, explanation and purpose. And every narrative is insistent in its demand for its prescriptive point, its moral. History and literature [as well as art] cannot escape their location in a normative universe, nor can prescription, even when embodied in a legal text, escape its origin and its end in experience, in the narratives that are trajectories plotted upon material reality by our imaginations.
>
> (Cover, 1983, p. 5)

Since we always 'inhabit a *nomos* – a normative universe' (*ibidem*, p. 4) and our imagination shapes our *nomos* as much that of the others, by visiting the city of the *ʿaqd* in this book, it is my purpose to show how the *ʿaqd*, like the contract in any other society, can be a topic which is *bonne à penser* (to borrow Lévi-Strauss' famous phrase) to deal with law and religion in a comparative perspective, by navigating in between the spiritual and the material; the sacred and the profane; the religious and the secular.

In this sense, as highlighted at the beginning of this Introduction, not only will the relevance of the *ʿaqd* as a religious, legal, and social category of Muslim jurisprudence be disclosed along the journey but additional understanding of Western law and religion will also be achieved along the way. Discovering much more about *our*-selves by *listening* to the *Arab Girl* (see Conclusions), will be, I believe, the real surprise which this voyage will bring us all.

Notes

1 I use here the phrase *droit académique* to describe the civil law tradition as a jurisprudential model that conceives the law as a system of concepts related one to the other, leading inescapably to the formalisation and systematisation of norms. This style found one of its highest expressions in the German *Begriffsjurisprudenz* of the 19th century. In this regard, European civil law is certainly more dogmatic (and, in this sense, 'more academic' in terms of abstraction and theorisation) than English common law, which is grounded on cases and judicial precedents.

2 *Fiqh al-muʿāmalāt* can be translated as 'the law of worldly dealings' or, better, 'jurisprudence of human interactions;' Hans Wehr describes this field as the rules of 'human relations, conduct of people among themselves . . . in contrast to [*fiqh al-*] *ʿibādāt*, conduct of men towards God' (Wehr, 1979).

3 The crucial symbolism of the 'body' in Western tradition is well illustrated in the title of the *Corpus Iuris Civilis* (lit. 'Body of Civil Law'), the collection of fundamental legal texts issued by order of the Roman Emperor Justinian from 529 to 534 AD. This 'ordered body' still belongs to the style of the *droit académique* in continental Europe (see endnote 1). In addition, it can be argued that this body of 'living laws' brings to mind, in some way, the 'living flesh' of Jesus as 'body' of

Christianity – an aspect of interdependence between law and religion in the West on which Chapter 2 will elaborate.

4

> On the one hand the 'representation' stands in for the reality that is represented, and so evokes absence; on the other, it makes that reality visible, and thus suggests presence. Moreover, this opposition can easily be reversed: the representation is present in the former case, even if only as a surrogate; in the latter case it ends up recalling, in contrast to itself, the absent reality that it is intended to represent.
>
> (Ginzburg, 2001, p. 63; see also Ginzburg, 1991)

5 Caroline Juler, the compiler of the book dedicated to the *Najd Collection of Orientalist Paintings*, describes Gérôme as follows:

> he became the most famous in his lifetime. He travelled frequently in the Near East and, though less often, in North Africa, maintaining his zest for long journeys until he was nearly eighty. His view of Arab and Turkish society was as romantic as that of any of his predecessors. The themes he chose often emphasized traditional aspects of life in Muslim countries with which the European public was already familiar, but his pictures appeared more realistic because of his precise, so-called 'clinical' technique. In fact, Gérôme was a photographer and used his own and other people's photographs when working on compositions in his studio.
>
> (Juler, 1991, p. 126)

6

> Gérôme studied the Egyptian dancing girls . . . on his visit to the Fayoum oasis in 1868. Though the name 'Almeh' actually means 'learned woman', they earned their living by entertaining soldiers and were banned from southern Egypt in the mid-19th century. . . . 'The Almeh' [*with Pipe*] (1873) is one of several paintings in which Gérôme depicted a woman in . . . dancing girls' clothes . . . The Almehs had already been banished in Cairo when Gérôme visited Egypt and though he met a group of them further South in 1868, the models used for these paintings were probably French dancers dressed up for the occasion in his studio. This one leans alluringly against a wall, holding a long wooden 'shibuk' against her hip. Behind her a veiled figure can be seen outlined in the dark passageway. But Gérôme has concentrated on the loose folds and decoration of the woman's silk crimson trousers and, the way her skin shows through her thin blouse.
>
> (Juler, 1991, p. 141)

7 In fact, everything about her representation (from her enchanting gaze to the lascivious pose, as she leans against the stone doorway; from her semi-naked belly and breast to the arm cushioning her head, semi-concealed by veils of green and dark chiffons) may lead the visitor to think about her as a prostitute. This lures the imagination of the observer towards the dark passage behind, with the older woman probably being the procuress.

8 Such as: the architecture; the location of the model in a clearly delimited space; the meticulously painted costume; the naturalistic realism of the voluptuous belly; the ethnographic mannerism of the bracelet, the necklace, the shoes, and the long pipe. . . .

9 In fact, the term *almeh* was primarily used in 19th-century Egypt for courtesans and female entertainers, usually well-educated and of good social standing, trained in dancing, singing, and poetry, who performed behind a screen or from another room at weddings and other respectable festivities.

10 Lane gives full details about

> female professional singers . . . called ''Awálim;' in the singular, ''Ál'meh,' or ''Álimeh;' an appellation . . . literally signifying 'a learned female;'. . . . The 'Awálim are often hired on the occasion of a fête in the ḥareem of a person of wealth. There is generally a small, elevated apartment, called a 'tuḳeyseh,' or 'mughannà,' adjoining the principal saloon of the ḥareem, from which it is separated only by a screen of wooden lattice-work; or there is some other convenient place in which the female singers may be concealed from the sight of the master of the house, should he be present with his women. But when there is a party of male guests, they generally sit in the court, or in a lower apartment, to hear the songs of the 'Awálim who, in this case, usually sit at a window of the ḥareem, concealed by the lattice-work. Some of them are also instrumental performers. I have heard the most celebrated 'Awálim in Cairo, and have been more charmed with their songs than with the best performances of the 'Aláteeyeh [male professional musicians], and more so . . . than any other music that I have ever enjoyed. They are often very highly paid. I have known instances of sums equal to more than fifty guineas [local Egyptian currency] being collected for a single 'Ál'meh from the guests at an entertainment in the house of a merchant, where none of the contributors were persons of much wealth. . . . There are, among the 'Awálim in Cairo, a few who are not altogether unworthy of the appellation of 'learned females;' having some literary accomplishments. There are also many of an inferior class, who sometimes dance in the ḥareem: hence, travellers have often misapplied the name of 'almé,' meaning ''ál'meh,' to the common dancing-girls . . . or they may have done so because these girls themselves occasionally assume this appellation, and generally do so when (as has been often the case) the exercise of their art is prohibited by the government.
> (Lane, 1860, pp. 355–356)

11 I would like to acknowledge here my intellectual debt to Dr. Valérie Hayaert for our conversations about law, symbolism, and the allegory of Lady *Iustitia* during my stay as a Fellow at the Käte Hamburger Centre for Advanced Study in the Humanities 'Law as Culture' (Bonn, April–September 2018).

12 Schacht's *Introduction* discloses, in a compact size, an undoubtedly complex subject, from the chronological development of *fiqh* to the intricacies of Islamic family law, property law, obligations and contracts, criminal law, and judicial procedure.

13 As we will see in Chapter 4, Schacht consequently interpreted the use of *ḥiyal* ('legal devices') in Muslim medieval trade as evidence of this disconnection between theory and practice; ideal and real; religious and secular (all pairs that will later be discussed as expression of the binary code of Western modernity in Chapter 2). 'The legal devices represented a *modus vivendi* between theory and practice: the maximum that custom could concede, and the maximum (that is to say, formal acknowledgement) that the theory had to demand' (Schacht, 1964, p. 80).

14 On the genesis of Islamic law (in a sense mirroring Western legal theory and practice), important considerations have been recently advanced by Léon Buskens and Baudouin Dupret. They argue that 'the notion of "Islamic law" is a scholarly and social construct' (2015, p. 31) and that this category was 'invented' by Western legal scholarship during the Western colonial domination: 'not only in the epistemological innocent sense of "discover," . . . [since] we also intend to stress the constructive character of the category "Islamic law"' (2015, p. 31, note 1). One of the first protagonists of this invention was the Dutch Arabist Christiaan Snouck Hurgronje (1857–1936; *ibidem*, p. 34). Buskens and Dupret stress how

> Snouck Hurgronje's 'deontological' conception of Islamic normativity was spread by his two main pupils, the German (and later British) Arabist Joseph

> Schacht (1902–1969) and the French sociologist Georges-Henry Bousquet (1900–1978), neither of whom were jurists by training either. However, they both used the term 'Islamic law' in the titles of their manuals and essays.
> (*ibidem*, p. 38)

Additional comments on the invention of Islamic law (in relation to the Western conception of law as *corpus iuris*) will be advanced in this book at section 4.3.1.

15 The notion of ideology relates to categories of true or false cognition; meaning, signification but also illusion; distortion; representation; mystification; (pre-)assumption and understanding, just to name some of them. All these concepts characterise ideology also in terms of shared signifying practices (on which this Introduction has focused): please refer to Eagleton on the subject (1991).

16 With regard to the visual space as the predominant symbolic form of Western culture, a list of terms that we commonly use in social research relates in fact to *looking at* something: 'paradigm,' 'worldview,' 'point of view,' 'perspective' (from the medieval Latin *ars perspectiva*, the 'science of optics,' and the verb *perspicere*, 'to look through'). All of them witness a primacy of visual metaphors that is distant from Muslim culture, where the normative knowledge (*fiqh*) comes, in contrast, from *listening to* God's Word. These problems will be linked in Chapter 1 and Chapter 2 to what Martin Jay defines as the 'scopic regimes of modernity' in European culture (1988). For a fascinating reconstruction of the birth of visual metaphor in Western modernity, from Machiavelli to Descartes and Leibniz (the first philosopher to use the phrase 'point of view' from a cognitive approach), see Ginzburg, 2001, pp. 139–156; for a history of seeing and visual technologies, Denham Wade, 2019.

References

Ahmed, S. (2016) *What Is Islam? The Importance of Being Islamic*. Princeton and Oxford: Princeton University Press.

Bal, M. (1997) *Narratology: Introduction to the Theory of Narrative*, 2nd ed.; 1st ed. 1985. Toronto, Buffalo and London: University of Toronto Press.

Bantekas, I., Ercanbrack, J. *et al.* (2023) *Islamic Contract Law*. Oxford: Oxford University Press.

Berger, J. (2008) *Ways of Seeing*. London: Penguin (originally published in 1972, London: BBC, Penguin).

Bhaskar, R. (1993) *Dialectic: The Pulse of Freedom*. London: Verso.

Buskens, L., and Dupret, B. (2015) The invention of Islamic law: a history of Western studies of Islamic normativity and their spread in the orient. In: Pouillon, F., and Vatin, J.-C. (eds.) *After Orientalism: Critical Perspectives on Western Agency and Eastern Re-Appropriations*. Leiden and Boston: Brill, pp. 31–47.

Calder, N. (1996) Law. In: Leaman, O., and Nasr, S.H. (eds.) *History of Islamic Philosophy*. London and New York: Routledge, pp. 979–998.

Chartier, R. (1989) Le monde comme représentation. *Annales: Economies, Sociétés, Civilisations*. 44(6), pp. 1505–1520.

Chehata, C. (1969) *Théorie Générale de l'Obligation en Droit Musulman Hanéfite: Les Sujets de l'Obligation*. Paris: Éditions Sirey.

Cooper, L.H. (2011) *Artisans and Narrative Craft in Late Medieval England*. Cambridge: Cambridge University Press.

Cover, R.M. (1983) The Supreme Court, 1982 term – Foreword: *nomos* and narrative. *Harvard Law Review*. 97(1), pp. 4–68.

Denham Wade, S. (2019) *As Far as the Eye Can See: A History of Seeing*. Cheltenham: The History Press.

Eagleton, T. (1991) *Ideology: An Introduction*. London: Verso.

Ginzburg, C. (1991) Représentation: le mot, l'idée, la chose. *Annales: Economies, Sociétés, Civilisations*. 46(6), pp. 1219–1234.

Ginzburg, C. (2001) *Wooden Eyes: Nine Reflections on Distance* (trans. by Ryle, M., and Soper, K. (1998) from the Italian original version *Occhiacci di Legno: Nove Riflessioni sulla Distanza*. Milano: Feltrinelli). New York: Columbia University Press.

Jay, M. (1988) Scopic regimes of modernity. In: Foster, H. (ed.) *Vision and Visuality*. Dia Art Foundation – Discussions in Contemporary Culture Number 2. Seattle: Bay Press, pp. 3–23.

Juler, C. (1991) *Najd Collection of Orientalist Paintings*. London: Mathaf Gallery & Manara.

Kuhn, T. (1962) *The Structure of Scientific Revolutions*. Chicago: Chicago University Press.

Lane, E.W. (1860) *An Account of the Manners and Customs of the Modern Egyptians*, 1st ed. 1836. London: Charles Knight.

Linant de Bellefonds, Y. (1965) *Traité de Droit Musulman Comparé, Vol. 1, Théorie Générale de l'Acte Juridique*. Paris and La Haye: Mouton & Co.

McLuhan, M. (1989) Visual and acoustic space (from McLuhan, M., and Powers, B.R., *The Global Village*. New York: Oxford University Press). Reprinted in Cox, C., and Warner, D. (eds.) (2004) *Audio Culture: Readings in Modern Music*. New York and London: Continuum, pp. 67–72.

Rayner, S.E. (1991) *The Theory of Contracts in Islamic Law: A Comparative Analysis with Reference to the Modern Legislation in Kuwait, Bahrain and the United Arab Emirates*. Arab and Islamic Laws Series. London, Dordrecht and Boston: Graham & Trotman.

Rodinson, M. (1980) *La Fascination de l'Islam* (trans. into English by Veinus, R. (1988) *Europe and the Mystique of Islam*. London: I.B. Tauri). Paris: François Maspéro.

Said, E.W. (1978) *Orientalism*. London and Henley: Routledge & Kegan Paul.

Santillana, D. (1926) *Istituzioni di Diritto Musulmano Malichita con Riguardo Anche al Sistema Sciafiita*, Vol. I. Roma: IPO.

Santillana, D. (1938) *Istituzioni di Diritto Musulmano Malichita con Riguardo Anche al Sistema Sciafiita*, Vol. II. Roma: IPO.

Schacht, J. (1964) *An Introduction to Islamic Law*. Oxford: Oxford University Press.

Stelzer, S.A.J. (2008) Ethics. In: Winter, T. (ed.) *The Cambridge Companion to Classical Islamic Theology*. Cambridge: Cambridge University Press, pp. 161–179.

Vogel, F.E. (2006) Contract law in Islam and the Arab Middle East. In: Von Mehren, A. (ed.) *International Encyclopedia of Comparative Law, Vol. VII, Contracts in General*. Tübingen: Mohr Siebeck; Dordrecht, Boston and Lancaster: Martinus Nijoff, pp. 1–77.

Wehr, H. (1979) *A Dictionary of Modern Written Arabic (Arabic-English)* (ed. by Cowan, J.M.), 4th ed. Wiesbaden: Harrassowitz.

1 Expelling the merchants from the Temple

Methodology and the contents of this book

In the Introduction, I argued that, alongside the history of the Muslim world, the *ʿaqd* has maintained, 'a continuity *in practice*, despite the changeable and plural nature of its *theories and practices*: a continuity whose rationales . . . can be coherently linked to the core postulates of Islamic religion.' I also added that the deepest meaning of the *ʿaqd* 'cannot be fully appreciated unless studied in a comparative approach with the tenets of Western religion . . . and law.' It is now time to provide the reader with more details about why, to understand the *ʿaqd*, the law and religion of Islam must be put in a comparative perspective with the West, within a dialectical framework that this chapter will clarify.

Dealing with the nature of representations as signifying practices when looking at Islam as *other* than the West, there is no doubt that the imaginative geography of the *ʿaqd* is worth a visit. In fact, if the *Šarīʿah*, the Right Path to be followed by Muslim believers, considers the market, like any other place of social interaction, a space of ethical behaviour, the *ʿaqd*, as an essential landmark of this space, offers a privileged angle from which to examine the interaction between law and religion in Muslim societies. In particular, it is by showing 'the mutually constitutive relationship between Islam and Muslims: . . . how Islam makes Muslims as Muslims make Islam' (Ahmed, 2016, p. 543; see later, section 1.3.2) that this book will investigate the unity-in-diversity of the *ʿaqd*, both in the literature of *fiqh* and in its transformative praxis.

At the same time, the *ʿaqd* can also provide significant points of reflection in its comparative analysis with Western contract law, especially when located, as a topic of research, between the religious and the secular realm of human actions.

Within this background, fundamental issues related to the conceptualisation of law and religion in the East and the West will emerge – something that has already led our study towards a critique of the Orientalistic representation of the Muslim world that the Occident has fostered. The Introduction has specifically focused on this aspect by imagining a meeting with Gérôme's *Almeh* at the gate of a city that we will metaphorically visit as we proceed with our investigation. This chapter is dedicated to illustrating the methodological approach that we will follow during our visit by looking for the meaning of the *ʿaqd* not only as a relevant aspect of the revelation of Islam, the Muslim legal

DOI: 10.4324/9781315145761-2

tradition, and the social life of Muslim people but also in a dialectical perspective with the West from the perspective of law and religion.[1]

1.1. One Ring, some daemons, and Jesus Christ: the non-identity (1M) of law and religion

The core methodological assumption that animates this work (one could say, taking inspiration from Tolkien's *Lord of the Rings*, 'the One to rule all its contents') is that the Orient-Occident dialectics cannot be solved unless dealing with the couple law-religion both **(a)** as a culturally-oriented pair that affects the conceptual construction of *our* normative world and the *nomos* of Islam, and **(b)** as a topic of Orient-Occident comparative research. If the Western representation of what-is Islam has always been affected by its *own* conception of law-religion, venturing to the land of Islam requires precedent awareness of how Western people practice *their own* affairs within *their own* law-religion. In fact, it is by moving from the *non-identity* of law-religion in the Occident and the Orient that our journey will be able to render the 'visible' image of the *'aqd* (reduced to a decadent *Almeh* in Schacht's interpretation: 1964, p. 199) more 'audible' to Western observers/listeners (section 1.3.3).

But how should we proceed in this direction? Are we fated to be devoured in this adventure by a Sphinx, unable to solve its riddles? Or to be intrigued by Gérôme's *Almeh*?

Some clues for a safe, or at least less risky, study of the Islamic contract have already been given in the Introduction. The most attentive traveller may have noted that, just before meeting Gérôme's *Arab Girl*, I referred to the need for a preliminary dialectical engagement with 'what a contract is in the Western and Muslim legal traditions (as different signifying practices).' It is this dialectical approach that allows us to investigate 'how the interaction between law and religion in the West has represented and "codified" the *'aqd*; and why this representation does not fully shed light' over the most distinctive qualities of the Islamic contract – certain 'features of Muslim juristic discourse, those perhaps which are most revealing of its nature and its intentions' (Calder, 1996, p. 979).

Those hints pointed to what the ancient Greeks efficaciously summarised under the famous maxim 'know thyself' (*gnōthi seauton*), inscribed in the pronaos of the Temple of Apollo in the city of Delphi. In brief, the Western explorer should, firstly, 'know his *own* law-religion' by dealing with the daemons (from the Greek *dáimōn*, 'god-like' entities) that dominate the Temple of Western thought, prior to investigating the meaning of the *'aqd*. We need, somehow, to take a step back from the preliminary meeting that we had with the *Arab Girl* at the entrance to the Oriental city. In fact, in the attempt to 'know ourselves,' we must radically change the starting point of our search before entering the space of Islamic revelation (Chapter 2). But worry not: we will meet again the *Almeh* at the beginning of Chapter 3, when we will be much more prepared to *listen to* her voice; she will wait patiently for us to come back.

Then, let's assume that our journey starts from the Occident; more precisely, from a city whose inhabitants, we suppose, are mainly Christian. These people must have clear in their mind one of the most famous events in the life of Jesus: 'And said unto them [the merchants], It is written, My house shall be called the house of prayer; but ye have made it a den of thieves' (Matthew 21:13, King James Version). Reported in all the four canonical Gospels of the New Testament (Matthew 21:12–17; Mark 11:15–19; Luke 19:45–48; John 2:13–16), not only is *The Cleansing of the Temple* narrative well-known among Christian believers but it is also a common motif in Christian art. There are numerous artists – from Giotto to Scarsellino and El Greco, to name but a few – who have represented the vigorous impetus of Jesus Christ beating traders and money-changers to expel them from the Temple. Human bodies, the *corpora* of Christ and the merchants, are located in the same *visual* space, in a scene which is explicitly aimed at separating the spiritual good from the material bad: Christ casts away sinners desecrating the Temple, setting boundaries between the religious and the secular; the divine and the worldly; the sacred and the profane. The visual power of Christ purifying the Temple by beating the merchants is a scene that may appear violent to most eyes; canonised in the Christian collective imagery, this violence becomes a warning for the observer. It is notable that the image probably has no equivalent in other religions and has certainly no counterpart in Islam: the representation of the human body, and living beings, in general, is condemned; above all, no *corpus* separating the religious and the secular can be found in Islamic visual art.

Significantly for our reasoning, the etymology of 'visual' comes from the Latin *visus* ('sight') and *videre* ('to see'). In the early 15th century, the term *visualis* pertained to the faculty of sight; at that time, a beam of light proceeding from the eye of the person to the object was believed to make vision possible. Today, in many languages derived from Latin, the 'face' of the person – in Italian, *viso*; in French, *visage* – continues to reflect the primacy of knowing the world by sight for the human observer.

In contrast, both the *corpus* and the *visus* are traditionally 'foreign' to Islamic visual art; the rare depictions of the Prophet are faceless, or the Prophet is depicted with a covered face. More precisely, to the extent to which Islamic art has reached its highest expressions through the art of calligraphy, by making visible the *verbal* words of the revelation, the *visus*, as the faculty of sight, plays a marginal role, if any, in this. It is by *hearing* and reciting the Word that the Message was transmitted to the Prophet, and though Him to all Muslim believers, *not* by *looking* at it, as it was in the Christian tradition, through the *corpus* of Jesus Christ.

Let us focus on this role of the *corpus* in Christian art by referring to one of the number of versions that El Greco (1541–1614) painted of *Christ Cleansing the Temple*. This artwork is today displayed at the National Gallery of Art, in Washington D.C. (Figure 1.1).

Figure 1.1 *Christ Cleansing the Temple* (oil on canvas by El Greco, around 1570; National Gallery of Art, Washington DC)

The website of the National Gallery highlights how in this

> tempestuous scene, El Greco depicted an angry Christ . . . [and] portrayed partially draped women and bare-chested men writhing and twisting to escape the blows of Christ's scourge, emphasizing the agitation of the participants and exaggerating their irreverence. The setting is one of classical grandeur, more reminiscent of an Italian Renaissance than of the sacred precincts of the Temple of Jerusalem.
>
> (NGA, 2019)

While admiring El Greco's *Christ*, the reader should compare this 'classical grandeur . . . reminiscent of an Italian Renaissance' with the decadent atmosphere where Gérôme located the *Arab Girl* – at the gate of her Oriental city (Figure 0.1; Introduction). The urban architectures of the two paintings may well exemplify the meaningful distance that subsists between the 'proper body' of Western law and the 'corrupted body' of Islamic law, where the ideal theory is corrupted by legal practice, according to Schacht's interpretation. The architecture displayed in Gérôme's *Arab Girl* reflects a feeling of decadence just as, conversely, Jesus's Temple transmits an idea of 'proper order' in a visual construction grounded on the Renaissance perspective (see later, section 1.3.3).

Furthermore, as noticed previously, the theme of the cleansing of the Temple – a visual space embedding the separation between the secular and the religious – is totally *absent* in Islamic visual art. This suggests that we must depart from Western law-religion – the conceptual framework underlying that separation – in order to explore the Islamic Temple of law-religion. Accordingly, the way through which we perceive our 'body of rules' must change for the Occident and the Orient to be put in a dialectical perspective.

With this in mind, a principle of *non-identity* – a conceptual category that I borrow from Roy Bhaskar: see later section 1.3.1, where the marker '1M,' used in the title of this section, will find full explanation – should be embraced. This non-identity of law-religion relates, for instance, to the lack of separation between 'secular law' and 'religious law' in Islam, where the realm of *fiqh al-muʿāmalāt*, the 'jurisprudence of human interactions,' turns out to be as lego-religious as that of *fiqh al-ʿibādāt*, the 'jurisprudence of the conduct of men towards God.' But it also implies the awareness that it is impossible to understand Islamic contract law *within* a conceptual Temple grounded on the dichotomy secular vs religious; Islam removes *ab initio* this spatial separation, and different 'daemons' rule trade inside the mosque.

Considering all this, how can the Islamic contract be (re-)*present*ed to a Western audience, while Western forms of representation (the visual separation between the secular and the religious; the *corpus* of contract law; the primacy of the *visus*) are *absent* in Islam?

Carrying the One Ring of non-identity, between what is (re-)*present*able and what is *absent* in the Orient, this book moves from the Christian town and its Western Temple towards the city of the *ʿaqd*. Its purpose is precisely to (re-)orient the reader from the signifying practices underlying Western contract law to those of Islamic law – using the *ʿaqd* as a medium, a vehicle of legal meaning, and a conceptual tool of discovery.

By departing from the Temple and expelling the daemons of the Western pairing of law-religion as a conceptual background, the One Ring can help us to remove some pre-assumptions in the practice of legal comparison, so as to understand how Muslim jurists and believers have practiced their trade in their *own* world through the *ʿaqd*. Accordingly, our journey will deal both with the religion of Islam (Chapter 2) and Muslim jurisprudence (Chapter 3), following an itinerary that will later contextualise the *ʿaqd* in the social realities of the Muslim world (Chapter 4). But, in order to carry the Ring safely, as we know from the epic of *The Lord of the Rings*, supportive fellowship is needed; in particular, before approaching the city of the *ʿaqd*, some further reflections are required about the idea of non-identity and its implications.

1.2. The problem at the heart of this book

In any journey, there are moments of peril (that are not necessarily as dangerous as Oedipus's meeting with the Sphinx or Frodo's fight against Lord

Sauron) when not only is the help of fellow travellers strongly desirable but guidance from masters becomes compelling. In this regard, when dealing with categories of law and religion as signifying practices between what-it-is and what-we-know (see Introduction), some support can be found in Ludwig Wittgenstein's *Tractatus Logico-Philosophicus* (1922), whose contents identify the relation between reality (what-it-is) and language, and how human comprehension (what-we-know) stems from their connection. It is not the content of the *Tractatus* per se that is of direct relevance for the aims of this volume; rather, it may induce some preliminary clarifications about the contents of its research. Introducing the *Tractatus*, Bertrand Russell warns the reader that '[i]n order to understand Mr Wittgenstein's book, it is necessary to realize what is the problem with which he is concerned' (Russell, 1922, p. 7). Stranded between the Occident and the Orient (a sort of Middle-Earth), while we have not yet left Jesus's Temple and the *Almeh* is standing at the gate of her Oriental city waiting for us, it is now appropriate to disclose more in depth the problem that we face; that is to say, how to understand the *'aqd* **(a)** in the intersection between law and religion, and **(b)** from an Orient-Occident dialectical perspective.

This problem can be clarified through five interrelated points.

First, the phrases (i) 'Islamic contract' and (ii) 'contract in Islam' are used as equivalent in this book to remark the 'mutually constitutive relationship between Islam and Muslims' (Ahmed, 2016, p. 543). In this sense, to the extent to which the 'Islamic contract' defines Islamic religion as background for Muslim orthopraxis, the 'contract in Islam' correspondingly entails 'how Islam makes Muslims as Muslims make Islam' (*ibidem*) in the social reality of the Muslim world. As mentioned in the Introduction, this does not imply the claim of an autonomy of the *'aqd* from a myriad of other non-Islamic components, from local customs to the impact of Western transplants in modern and contemporary times; nor does it lead to the assertion that the religion of Islam should be regarded as the only determinant of the Islamic contract. Rather, the problem of this book consists in explaining how the meaning of the *'aqd* requires us to investigate its theories and practices in relation to the revelation of Islam (Chapter 2); how the variety of its rules exists, in practice, through a continuity with its theories (Chapter 3); and how its practices, moving from the unity of God's Word to the diversity of its wor(l)dly manifestations, echo Islamic law and religion in a transformative praxis that is distinctive to the Muslim world (Chapter 4).

The second point is that it is precisely in this sense that looking for the meaning of the *'aqd* can become a precious *medium* to understand the religion of Islam: a subject that is *bonne à penser* for a readership beyond the circles of lawyers and comparatists, extending its hermeneutical values towards religious studies, sociology, anthropology, but also semiotics, cultural studies, and media theory. For instance, if no contract law *corpus* exists in the Islamic legal tradition, this *absence* will raise in the book further questions about how to 'place,' 'frame,' and 'map' the *'aqd* in Muslim jurisprudence (see sections 3.1 and 3.2).

Thirdly, the attempt to understand the meaning of the Islamic contract in both its theories and practices will lead our investigation to span both Muslim intellectual[2] and social history. Hence, on the one hand, we will refer to the *'aqd* in Muslim jurisprudence (Chapter 3) as the product of an intellectual élite (the experts of *fiqh*) devoted to give body (rectius, *wor(l)d*) to the divine Word. On the other hand, we will put legal texts in the context of a changing social reality, from medieval trade to the modern state and contemporary global finance – so as to deal 'with texts' (*cum*-texts) in their own contexts (Chapter 4).

The fourth point is that, although the understanding of the *'aqd* will necessarily lead our attention to the literature of *fiqh*, this book does not implicitly subscribe to an idea of Islamic law as 'the epitome of Islamic thought, the most typical manifestation of the Islamic way of life, the core and kernel of Islam itself' (Schacht, 1964, p. 1).[3] The experts of *fiqh*, in fact, have always constituted a privileged and relatively small community composed of literate people of higher lego-religious education and social authority. If the textual polity of *fiqh* (on the notion of textual polity, see Messick, 1989, 1993), by channelling the normative impact of the revelation, has always affected Muslim social realities, legal scholars have, themselves, been part of these social realities. In this light, it is not by considering *fiqh* the 'core and kernel of Islam,' but rather, by contextualising Islamic law in the history and sociology of the Muslim world ('from medieval trade to global finance,' as the subtitle of this book recites) that the meaning of the '*aqd* can be fully understood in its transformative praxis.[4]

Last but not least, the One Ring of law-religion non-identity will raise some other fundamental issues about the way in which law and religion are *thought of/conceived/imagined* as spaces of social interaction in the West and the East; how visual boundaries deeply influence their construction in the former; and how these borders become less relevant (or even irrelevant) in the latter, where the divine Word makes intellectual rationales of interpretation more 'acoustic' than 'visual' by defining the human being *by way of word*.

In summary, in order to 'say' the *'aqd* correctly (see Conclusions), we need to change our way of 'practising trade' when dealing with Islam; the problem this book is concerned with, then, becomes how to *listen to* its Wor(l)d.

1.3. Some conceptual help from three companions

Before entering the first proposition of his *Tractatus* ('The world is everything that is the case'), Wittgenstein remarks that his book will 'be understood by those who have themselves already thought the thoughts which are expressed in it – or similar thoughts' (1922, p. 27). The reader must have already noticed the extent to which the investigation of the *'aqd* can raise a myriad of issues and much broader questions about the representation of the Orient by the Occident: the *Almeh* as allegory of an improper *corpus iuris*; the separation between the secular and the religious, as in El Greco's *Christ*

Cleansing the Temple; the conceptualisation of the relation between the human and the divine in different cultures and how it can be linked or not to a visual imagery; how the interaction between law and religion can emerge from the practice of trade; and so on. While carrying the One Ring, the absence of a 'valid and sensible corpus' (Calder, 1996, p. 979) for contract law in the tradition of *fiqh* constitutes another challenge in the reconstruction of the *ʿaqd* in Muslim jurisprudence. It seems as if the riddles of the *ʿaqd* are multiplying; as if Oedipus could never escape from the Sphinx.

These and other similar thoughts in dealing with the One Ring of **(a)** law and religion, **(b)** in an Orient-Occident comparative approach, suggest that, to proceed in our travel, we should ask for the help of other 'companions' to better clarify the methodology of this volume.

With this in mind, I will refer in the following pages to three questions that closely relate to the aspirations, contents, and objectives of our research journey: how can we compare the *ʿaqd* in a frame of *absences*? (section 1.3.1); what is Islam? (section 1.3.2); and how should we deal with law and religion in Islam, beyond the Western secular-religious Temple? (section 1.3.3). These queries and their answers are going to be respectively linked to the scholarships of three great thinkers; namely, the philosopher Roy Bhaskar (1944–2014) and his dialectical critical realism as overarching 'philosophy of philosophy' (Bhaskar, 1994, p. xi); the Islamic scholar Shahab Ahmed (1966–2015), with his manifesto about how to tackle Islam as a category of thought (*What Is Islam?*, 2016); and the media theorist Marshall McLuhan (1911–1980), through his differentiation between conceptual patterns of visual divide or acoustic overlap.

1.3.1. How to compare? Non-identity, dialectic, and transformative praxis (Bhaskar)

Our attempt to understand the meaning of the *ʿaqd* necessarily raises one initial question about how to compare contract-*s* as legal categories that exist between doctrinal elaboration (where they stand as archetypes of human interactions) and actual social practice (with the concrete manifestation of those interactions). Indeed, the issue of 'how to compare,' which is already problematic within the Western legal tradition of common and civil law, becomes even more challenging when dealing with Islam, when interpretive concerns enter the discussion regarding the law-religion relationship. In the Introduction, I have already stressed the nature of legal categories, both as abstract constructions, 'archetypes,' and material bodies, '*corpora*,' of intellectual elaboration; moving from theory to practice, socio-legal studies similarly refer to the distance between the black letter of written law, 'the law in the books,' and the substance of living law, 'the law in action.' At the same time, when we look at the contract as an entity that belongs to the reality of human life, the elaborations of legal scholars themselves are constantly influenced by this reality too. It is this interdependence between theory and practice, within the multiplicity of human life, that now requires further elaboration in the dialectical comparison between the Islamic *'aqd* and the Western contract.

To cope with all this, the fundamental reference for this volume lies in the teachings (and in the terminology which has already been used, without mentioning it explicitly) by philosopher Roy Bhaskar, especially in quest for *non-identity* when dealing with law-religion. Bhaskar's dialectics, in fact, can help us to move beyond what-it-is, according to the daemons of the Western Temple, towards what-it-is-not in Islam; hence, the occurrence of *absences* – of visual representations, of a valid *corpus* of law, etc. – when dealing with the Islamic contract. Correspondingly, through his approach, the *'aqd* can become in our journey a tool to expel some Christian-rooted assumptions about the practice of trade from the hermeneutical Temple of legal comparison in a process of symmetrical reflexivity (see later section 1.4).

In the 1970s, Roy Bhaskar was the initiator of the movement of 'critical realism' in the philosophy of the being, ontology, and social sciences. The term 'critical realism' was not originally used by Bhaskar himself, who first dedicated his attention to 'transcendental realism' (*A Realist Theory of Science*, 1975; see also Archer, Bhaskar *et al.*, 1998) and later moved towards what he defined 'critical naturalism' (*The Possibility of Naturalism*, 1979) in relation to human sciences. 'Critical realism' is an elision between the former and the latter (Collier, 1994, p. xi) that has come to indicate Bhaskar's philosophical movement in the form of a major renewal in social scientific method, occurring by the rejection of both the couple positivism/empiricism and the postulates underlying post-structuralism, relativism, and interpretivism. In the quest for a radical renovation in the philosophy of social sciences, a key advance was further made by Bhaskar through what he named 'dialectical critical realism,' as initiated by his *Dialectic: The Pulse of Freedom* (1993), whose principal themes were resumed later in *Plato Etc.: The Problems of Philosophy and Their Resolution* (1994).[5]

Bhaskar explains how the core objective of his dialectic relates to a totalising critique of Western philosophy,[6] arguing that '*determinate absence* was the void at the heart of the Western philosophical tradition; that it was this concept that was crucial to dialectic, a concept which in the end Hegel could not sustain' (Archer, Baskhar *et al.*, 1998, p. xix; italics in the original text). Consequently, he advances 'a real definition of dialectic as the *absenting of constraints* (which could be viewed as *absences*) on *absenting absences or ills*, applicable quite generally, whether in the epistemic, ethical or ontological domains' (*ibidem*). Within this overarching model, Bhaskar explores fundamental issues in dealing with the one and the other, the changeable yet the same (hence continuity and transformation), and so, the nature of human praxis as transformative agency. By radically redefining the inter-relation between being (ontology) and knowing (epistemology), in *Dialectic* (1993), he advances a renewal of Western philosophical thought and social science methodology which challenges the distance between theory and practice, both located in the dyad unity/diversity. It is the concept of polyvalence (that embraces both presence, what-it-is, and seeming absence, what-is-not) that links absence and change, as well as continuity and transformation, in Bhaskar's 'four-dimensional analysis for classifying and resolving the problems of philosophy' (Bhaskar, 1994, p. 11): (1M) non-identity; (2E) negativity; (3L) totality; and (4D) transformative praxis.

Bhashar's dialectics of non-identity, in my opinion, can address and provide meaning to the *absences* (what-is-not in the polyvalent relation with what-is present in the Western tradition) that have been already mentioned regarding the law-religion of Islam and the *'aqd*.

In particular, what is important for the purposes of this book is the primary attention given by Bhaskar to the first moment of dialectics (1M), in terms of *non-identity* and *absence*, that allows us to recognise 'the unity of theory and practice in practice' (*ibidem*, pp. xix-xx), where it is human agency – as made possible by social structures, themselves made possible by the reproduction of human agencies – that defines its own (self-)transformative praxis by connecting permanence and change within a general frame of alterity. Indeed, 'absence is ontologically prior to, and the condition for, presence or positive being. . . . Moreover, it opens up . . . the critique of the fixity of the subject, in . . . the "identity thinking" of the "analytical problematic"' (Archer, Baskhar *et al.*, 1998, p. xxii). Moving through a (2E) second dialectical edge of *negativity* or *negation*, analogous to Hegel's second stage of antithesis, and a (3L) third level of *totality*, not, however, comparable to Hegel's idea of synthesis,[7] the whole circle of dialectical critical realism is closed – and unified, while kept open to change – in the (4D) fourth dimension of (self) *transformative praxis*, where the human sphere implies and reconciles the other three moments in social life *qua* totality of action, constituted by 'four dialectically interdependent planes: of material transactions with nature, interpersonal relations, social structures and the stratification of the personality' (*ibidem*, p. xxiii). Here, 'the moral evolution of the species, like the future in general, is conceived of as open. Its dialectics are the site of ideological and material struggles, but also of absolute reason (the unity of theory and practice in practice) and it incorporates DCR [dialectical critical realism]'s dialectic of desire to freedom' (*ibidem*).

The reader can recognise in the previous lines important concepts that have been already mentioned in the Introduction to this book, such as non-identity, unity of theory and practice in practice, agency, and transformative praxis, in accordance with Bhaskar's terminology. These concepts can be related, for instance, to the interplay between legal theory and practice in the unity of social agency; the transformative nature of this interplay in time and space; as well as to a postulate of non-identity of law-religion in the dialectical relation between East and West. Within this general conceptual framework, the concepts of negativity (2E), totality (3L), and transformative praxis (4D) will reappear as essential conceptual tools respectively in Chapter 2, Chapter 3, and Chapter 4.

But, when we assume a unity-in-diversity of the *'aqd* that 'can be coherently linked to the core postulates of Islamic religion' (see the beginning of this chapter), what do we mean by 'Islam'? Which idea of Islam are we going to embrace on our journey? In this regard, a second milestone must be added to the methodology of this book.

1.3.2. What is Islam? Unity as plurality in the Muslim world (Ahmed)

As we have noted, in any community, representations play the role of signifying practices by fostering truths which can project underlying ideology.[8] For instance, a certain representation of Islam was implicit in the portrait of Gérôme's *Almeh*. With regard to the imaginative geographies of Orientalism (Said, 1978), we also referred in the Introduction to Schacht's scholarship as a paradigmatic example of the assumption of a divergence between the sacred Law of Islam and Muslim social reality, where '[a]t the very time that Islamic law came into existence, its perpetual problem, that of the contrast between theory and practice, was already posed' (1964, p. 209). As remarked, a common fate of decadence and corruption (*ibidem*, p. 199) seems to associate here the destiny of the *Arab Girl* and the 'scholarly and social construct' of Islamic law (Buskens and Dupret, 2015, p. 31), where an ideal Islam was detached from the reality of the Muslim world – against the tenets of the 'unity of theory and practice in practice' that belongs to Bhaskar's dialectics (see previous section).

'[T]hose who have themselves already thought the thoughts which are expressed' (Wittgenstein, 1922, p. 27) in the previous lines may find, at this point, a second core reference in Shahab Ahmed's *What is Islam? The Importance of Being Islamic* (2016). With an all-embracing critique, Ahmed puts under review widespread assumptions in representing Islam (both in non-Muslim and Muslim contexts) and their underlying ideologies. By means of a wide-ranging landscape of materials which cover both popular references and erudite sources, he radically revaluates an array of suppositions applied in interpretative and social sciences in thinking Islam. Monolithic categories like 'religion,' 'culture,' 'law,' and 'civilisation,' in Ahmed's opinion, are all unable to recognise intrinsic diversities in the unity of Islam. To describe this unity, I would use the formula 'Islam-Muslim-world' (an expression that I will repeat in Chapter 4), so as to reflect the persistent continuity *in practice* of Islam, despite the *non-identity* (hence, change) of (Islamic) theories and (Muslim) practices.

What is of particular significance for our research is Ahmed's pursuit of a conceptualisation of Islam both as a theoretical object and an analytical category of analysis

> that maps meaningfully onto Islam as a human and historical phenomenon – a human and historical phenomenon characterized and constituted, not merely by immense variety and diversity, but by the prodigious presence of outright contradiction. [Previous] . . . existing conceptualizations of Islam – whether as religion, as culture, as civilization, as discursive tradition, as core beliefs, as whatever-Muslims-say-it-is, as a

> law-centered phenomenon, as so plural and various as to be "islams-not-Islam," *etcetera* – have in various ways failed to convey the fullness of the reality of what it is that has actually been (and is) going on in historical societies of Muslims living *as Muslims.*
>
> (Ahmed, 2016, p. 542)

The fundamental support that Ahmed can provide to our research lies in his radical invitation to look at (or rather, to *listen to*, as I will propose in section 1.3.3) the unity of the Muslim world, not despite, but *through* its diversity and plurality; in brief, to look at the unity of Islam as plurality in terms of the Islam-Muslim-world. With this in mind, Ahmed, in his book, gives profound semantic value to the inherent diversity and outright contradictions of Islam *as Islam* in order to proceed in its reconstruction 'not by elimination of difference but by inclusion of difference' (2016, p. 542).

> In seeking to conceptualize Islam in terms that map onto the human and historical reality wherein Muslims have authored and lived with contradiction *as Islam*, . . . [his] book has sought to locate the logic of difference and contradiction as coherent with and internal to Islam – that is, to provide a coherent account of contradiction in and as Islam (*ibidem*, p. 542) [. . .] [by drawing] attention to . . . the mutually constitutive relationship between Islam and Muslims: on how Islam makes Muslims as Muslims make Islam (*ibidem*, p. 543).

By fully recognising the plural contradictions co-existing in the unity of Islam (a unity-of-diversities that corresponds to its continuity-in-change), Ahmed departs from the self-feeding depiction of Islam as 'religion,' 'culture,' 'law,' or 'civilisation.' All these archetypes are unable to convey the fullness of human realities where, precisely, 'Islam makes Muslims as Muslims make Islam.' In this regard, I subscribe to Aaron W. Hughes's opinion that Ahmed's early death in 2015 was

> a tragedy for the field in that he was one of the few scholars . . . to take seriously the concept that the study of Islam is not an insider club, but must illumine and be illumined by relevant cognate fields. This . . . will be its legacy providing, of course, that scholars of Islam pay attention to it and not simply pick-and-choose what is important for their own particularist purposes, to wit, to show how Islam is somehow unique or sui generis.
>
> (Hughes, 2017)

Ahmed's fundamental legacy for our journey lies precisely in the recognition that, only by carrying the One Ring of the dialectics law-religion in a conceptual frame of Islam-Muslim-world and its intrinsic non-identity, can we unveil 'what a contract is in Islam; how some qualities of the Islamic contract . . . can be deemed consistent within a great synchronic and diachronic variation of contexts; and why this unity-in-diversity (continuity-in-change) can be coherently linked to the interaction between law and religion in Muslim jurisprudence as part of the intellectual, cultural, and social history of Islam' (see the beginning of the Introduction to this volume).

We have already embraced Hughes's suggestion that the study of Islam 'is not an insider club' and that the understanding of the *'aqd* cannot be pursued 'for its own particularist purpose,' to show how the Islamic contract 'is somehow unique or sui generis.' In contrast, by moving from a much broader landscape and referring to apparently distant images and fields of studies (from the Sphynx to Rome; from the *Arab Girl* to *Christ Cleansing the Temple* as metaphors of Orientalism), the purpose of this book is to move towards the *'aqd* as something whose rationales can be disclosed only by 'knowing ourselves' (see section 1.1); that is to say, by means of a dialectical engagement between the Occident and the Orient in the frame of non-identity. At this point, to better disclose 'the mutually constitutive relationship between Islam and Muslims,'[9] a third fellow must join our enterprise, so that we can better 'know ourselves' by broadening our view towards sociology and media studies in the cognitive perception of the world by the modern West.

1.3.3. How to deal with law-religion in Islam? Visual vs acoustic space (McLuhan)

In the final section of the Introduction, while commenting on the nature of normative worlds, this book pointed to some underlying issues in the Western way of *looking at* Islam by noting how '[s]eeing comes before words. . . . We only see what we look at. . . . In the end, all images are man-made' (Berger, 2008, pp. 7–9). The construction of *our* world is grounded on representations as signifying practices that also define, by opposition, the world of others – i.e. its *alterity*. In this regard, two visual images (Gérôme's *Almeh* and El Greco's *Christ Cleansing the Temple*) have already been used to illustrate the cultural construction of Islamic law as decadent and corrupted,[10] as opposed to the Western *corpus iuris* of Lady *Iustitia* and the Renaissance buildings.

We have already seen, in section 1.1, how visual representations are generally absent in the Muslim tradition and how this *absence* should be interpreted in the light of the non-identity between Western/Islamic law-religion (in a reflexive frame), through Bhaskar's dialectics.

But can this *visual absence* also be related to 'the logic of difference and contradiction as coherent with and internal to Islam' (Ahmed, 2016, p. 542)? In other terms, can the visual absence find its *own* meaning as interdependent with a logic of differences and divergences that belongs internally to Islam? And, accordingly, can this shed further light on the nature of *fiqh*, by acknowledging 'the fact that a valid and sensible corpus of laws . . . [was] not what . . . [Muslim] jurists had in mind' (Calder, 1996, p. 979)?

As this volume will try to explain by the investigation of the *ʿaqd*, within Islamic law-religion the human being seems to 'inhabit a *nomos* – a normative universe' (Cover, 1983, p. 4) where 'looking at' as an *act of will* (a choice reflecting the centrality of man's visuality) is replaced by 'listening to' as an *act of intellect* in the form of understanding God's Word (see Chapter 2).

This paradigm shift (Kuhn, 1962) from a *visual* to an *acoustic* cognitive space may be better clarified by an image taken directly from the Arab world. Let us, therefore, imagine ourselves alone in the desert, after we have strayed away from the path that would have led us to an oasis and provided us with fresh water. Dunes of sand make the landscape nearly identical in all directions – a scenario that was certainly part of the collective imagination of pre-Islamic Arab peoples. Our *sight* is practically useless in such a situation: no territory borders, no street boundaries can help our itinerary; even worse, we cannot *choose* an itinerary, since we cannot *see* any. It is precisely at this point, when our life seems at stake, that a Word descends to give orientation and provides the Right Path (*Šarīʿah*) to salvation. For the Message to be comprehended, we need to *listen* carefully for a correct understanding (*fiqh*) of the Path. Here, *choosing* is no longer an option (salvation depends solely on listening to the Message); instead, human *intellect* is asked to discern the Word properly. The Path may look distant; sometimes practicable other times impracticable; viable while requiring effort. In the attempt to understand it, not only do different opinions about its meanings become legitimate but they are also beneficial to enrich the construction of a collective *nomos* that aims to echo the *Word* to provide Guidance to the Muslim community in the *world*.

Concordant and discordant rules overlap as coexistent *words* that can contribute to the understanding of the Message of the only *Word*. As different surfaces echo the same voice with different intensity and tone, so the route to salvation is offered to the believer according to different legitimate interpretations. The image of a consistent *corpus iuris* (in visual terms) is then replaced by overlapping *iurisdictiones*, from the Latin *ius dicere*, in acoustic terms. *Ius-dicere*, 'to say the law,' in the law-religion of Islam, embodies the echo of the *dictum* of the revelation; it is by *listening to* the revealed *Word* that Muslim *iurisprudentia*, *fiqh* as the 'science of law,' operates in social reality by 'echoing' divine transcendental rules, *aḥkām*, pl. of *ḥukm* (see section 2.4.5 on this specific point).

The suggestion to move from *looking at* our normative world to *listening to* the language of Islam was already mentioned at the end of the Introduction by referring to the distinction between visual and acoustic space by the influential media theorist Marshall McLuhan (1989).

In his research, McLuhan examines the way in which visuality comprehensively affects human subjectivity, community, and understanding in the West. Below the surface of Western culture, the visual space lies as the dominant symbolic form; not by chance, terms that are commonly used in social research imply an action of 'looking at' (e.g. 'paradigm,' 'worldview,' 'point of view,' 'perspective:' see Introduction, endnote 16) and witness a primacy of visual metaphors that cannot render the meaning of the normative knowledge (*fiqh*) of Islam coming, in contrast, from 'listening to' God's Word.

The deep interconnection between Western rationality and the *ars perspectiva* (the 'science of optics') emerges also from the seminal work of Erwin Panofsky (*Perspective as Symbolic Form*, 1991; original German version, 1924),[11] one of the most widely commented essays in 20th-century aesthetics with regard to art theory, Renaissance paintings, and Western modern codes of depiction.[12] Panofsky highlights how '[i]n order to guarantee a fully rational . . . space, . . . "central perspective" makes . . . rather bold abstractions from reality' (1991, pp. 28–29) in a geometrical visual space that depends on the *eye* of the beholder. This implies a *choice* of 'looking at' as an act of will, expression of human autonomy; not by chance, El Greco's *Christ* follows the rules of the *ars perspectiva* precisely in depicting Christ's action in a space that is dependent on the *eye* of the spectator. Rationality, abstraction, and geometrical visual space, all reflecting the centrality of human eyes and autonomy, combine in El Greco's *Christ*, whose setting is a Western Temple ruled by what Martin Jay defines as the 'scopic regimes of modernity.'

> The modern era . . . has been dominated by the sense of sight in a way that set it apart from its predecessors. . . . Beginning with the Renaissance[13] and the scientific revolution, modernity has been normally considered resolutely ocularcentric. The invention of printing, according to the familiar argument of McLuhan and Ong,[14] reinforced the privileging of the visual abetted by such inventions as the telescope and the microscope. . . . [T]he visual has been dominant in modern Western culture in a wide variety of ways. Whether we focus on "the mirror of nature" metaphor in philosophy with Richard Rorty or emphasize the prevalence of surveillance with Michel Foucault or bemoan the society of spectacle with Guy Debord, we confront again and again the ubiquity of vision as the master sense of the modern era.
>
> (Jay, 1988, p. 3; on the primacy of 'visual culture' in the West see also Mitchell, 1994)

Accordingly, as McLuhan remarks, '[t]he rational man in our Western culture is a visual man' (McLuhan and Fiore, 1967, p. 45); to the extent to which visuality and rationality become interchangeable in this cognitive frame, '[v]isual space is uniform, continuous, and connected' (*ibidem*). The ordered body of law in the Western tradition necessarily assumes norms to be inter-connected in a uniform and continuous *corpus iuris*: in a nutshell, in a visual-rational *perspectiva* about law. The scopic regime of modernity lies *a priori* in the power of graphical words as verbal images; the alphabet as 'a construct of fragmented bits and parts which have no semantic meaning in themselves, and which must be strung together in a line, bead-like, and in a prescribed order' (McLuhan and Fiore, 1967, p. 44). The definition of borders, their criteria of separation as well as connection, delimitation, regulation, and certainty of boundaries in the graphical alphabet as the language of *our* world, impose 'a medium that depends solely on the eye for comprehension' (*ibidem*); a paradigm of knowledge and understanding grounded on *looking at* the world/*reading* the law. As a result, *our* normative world is a construct of the mind where *we choose what to see* too.[15]

In contrast, moving from a completely different rational setting, being stranded in the desert necessarily entails a paradigm shift where '[t]he dominant organ of sensory and social orientation' (McLuhan and Fiore, 1967, p. 44) becomes the *ear*. The world of the eye, which is fully ordered according to human *will*, is substituted here by the primacy of the divine Word, a realm of understanding that is inaccessible to the sight (whose 'neutral world,' shaped around human rationality, is useless; in the desert, on the contrary, 'hearing . . . [is] believing': *ibidem*).[16] Within this acoustic space, information spreads with no boundaries, within no defined borders, and human *intellect* is asked to understand the revelation.

> What do you mean by "acoustic space"? I mean space that has no center and no margin, unlike strictly visual space, which is an extension and intensification of the eye. Acoustic space is organ and integral . . . whereas "rational" or pictorial space is uniform, sequential and continuous and creates a closed world with . . . [no] resonance . . . the ear, unlike the eye, cannot be focused and is synaesthetic rather than analytical and linear. Speech is an utterance, or more precisely, an outering . . .; the auditory field is simultaneous, the visual successive.
>
> (McLuhan, 1969)[17]

The desert – a space with no centre and no margin – asks the believer to rely on the verbal language, the utterance, the outering of the revelation; the human being is asked to choose to *hear* (this is the only option for salvation) and then to *listen to* – hence, discern carefully – the *Word* in its potentially indefinite echo. It is the *totality* (3L, in Bhaskar's terms) of this echoing, with no boundaries and no centre, its own discontinuity, replication, non-linearity, overlapping, and superimposition, that defines a unity made of differences and contradictions (Ahmed) beyond the absence (2E, *negativity*) of the Western, rational visuality. Embracing this totality entails an effort (*ijtihād*) to understand the divine revelation, an act of devotion that belongs to the core of Muslim agency in its *transformative praxis* (4D).

In summary, the non-identity of law-religion in the Occident and the Orient, defined through the four dimensions of Bhaskar's dialectics, requires a departure from a praxis grounded on a visual space towards a praxis *echoing* the acoustic space of the *Word* in the social reality of the Muslim world. It is only within this paradigm shift that 'the mutually constitutive relationship between Islam and Muslims' (Ahmed, 2016, p. 543) can define what Islam-Muslim-world is by *listening* to the language of Islam.

1.4. Carrying the One Ring in the practice of trade: revelation, tradition, and reality

Western and Muslim jurists, respectively immersed in the *nomos* of their *own* distinct spaces, may appear 'proponents of competing paradigms [that] practice their trades in different [normative] worlds.' This paraphrase of a passage from *The Structure of Scientific Revolutions* by philosopher Thomas Kuhn (1962, p. 150) can help to summarise the contents of this chapter regarding the methodology that we will adopt to explore the city of the *ʿaqd* – a methodology that is grounded on the philosophical, cognitive, and epistemological inputs by Bhaskar, Ahmed, and McLuhan, to which the previous sections have referred.

The metaphor of the One Ring, representing the interpretive challenge related to the *non-identity* of law-religion in the West and Islam, has initially led our attention towards the need to 'know thyself' (*gnōthi seauton*) of the Temple of Apollo and its daemons; hence, towards the cognitive construction of a normative world that separates the secular from the religious, as in the visual display of El Greco's *Christ Cleansing of the Temple.*

The problem this book is concerned with (how to understand the *ʿaqd* **(a)** in the intersection between law and religion and **(b)** in an Orient-Occident comparative perspective) requires us to expel the Western 'dominance of the visual' as standard 'practice of trade' when dealing, dialectically, with Islam. This chapter has tried to explain precisely how to proceed towards this aim. If Western comparatists may naturally tend to (re-)view Islamic *fiqh* as an improper *corpus iuris* by *looking at* it through the perspective of their own visual space, it is, on the contrary, by following Bhaskar's four-dimensional dialectic (section 1.3.1) that *non-identity* can emerge as a conceptual pre-condition to understand the law-religion of *others* – i.e. its alterity. At the same time, it is the logic of diversity and plurality that belongs to the mutually constitutive relationship between Islam and Muslims (Ahmed, section 1.3.2) that suggests approaching Islamic law-religion according to an *acoustic*, rather than visual, space (McLuhan, section 1.3.3). In this context, while *looking in* a direction in the desert may be of no help, it is by *listening to* God's Word that its understanding (*fiqh*) can provide the Path (*Šarīʿah*) to salvation.

Within this conceptual background, the One Ring of *non-identity* will accompany us while we try to proceed towards the city of the *ʿaqd*. A journey in which the *ʿaqd* itself, as a vehicle of legal meaning, will become an instrument to shed light over the *totality* (3L) of the Islamic *nomos*, both in its constitutive and *transformational* relationship with Muslim *praxis* (4D) and in its dialectics with the Western legal tradition, by *absenting* the latter from the former (2E of *negativity*).

This methodological path, grounded on the tenets of alterity, totality, and transformative praxis, finds a corresponding outline in the contents of this book. With regard to the destination of our journey, in fact, the pursuit of *listening to* the language of Islam involves the need to 'present Islamic [contract] law in such a way as to demonstrate its values rather than the values of the [Western] observer' (Calder, 1996, p. 979), in a space where

> [t]he centripetal (if rather distant) focus of scholarly comment was revelation. That consideration suggests a preliminary definition of Islamic law: it is a hermeneutic discipline which explores and interprets revelation through tradition. The last two words of that definition are the most important. For the most obvious shaping factor, in any work of Islamic law, is its engagement with the past of a particular tradition, and its loyalty to it. So much is this true that . . . Islamic law is a discipline that explores tradition, and uses tradition to discover (and limit) the meanings of the revelation.
>
> (Calder, 1996, p. 980)

Within this background, moving from an assumption of ***non-identity*** of law-religion (1M), this book will investigate firstly the meaning of the *'aqd* by adhering to the religious background of *fiqh* juristic discourse as ***absent*** in the West (2E). The ***theories*** of this juristic discourse will be examined in their internal relationality and mutual differentiation as ***totality*** (3L). Finally, their ***practices*** in the Muslim reality, as grounded 'on the mutually constitutive relationship between Islam and Muslims' (Ahmed, 2016, p. 543), will be set in the ***transformative praxis*** (4D) of Islam-Muslim-world. In doing so, we will follow Calder's interpretation of *fiqh* in terms of a juristic discourse consisting in an

> activity of exploration, interpretation, analysis and presentation of the law. [...] . . . There are two major types of *fiqh* literature, that known as *furūʿ al-fiqh* (branches) and that known as *uṣūl al-fiqh* (roots). The former sets out . . . concepts and rules that relates to conduct . . . [from] acts of worship (*'ibādāt*) . . . [to the domain of human relations, *mu'āmalāt*]. The whole is a conceptual replica of social life, not necessarily aspiring to be either complete or practical, but balanced between revelation, tradition and reality, all three of which feed the discussion and exemplify the concepts. The literature of *uṣūl* identifies the divinely revealed sources of the law (Qur'ān and *Sunnah*), auxiliary sources (like consensus, *ijmā'*), and the hermeneutics disciplines that permit the complex intellectual cross-reference between revelation, tradition and reality which is exemplified in a work of *furūʿ*.
>
> (Calder, 1996, p. 981)

By interconnecting revelation (Chapter 2), tradition (Chapter 3), and reality (Chapter 4) in the study of the *'aqd*, this book aspires to depict the tradition of Muslim *fiqh* as 'a conceptual replica of social life,' whose diversities, differences, and pluralities have been never represented in Islam by means of 'a valid and sensible corpus of laws.' By ***absenting*** this representation in a dialectical perspective, the *'aqd* will be ***presented***, on the contrary, in accordance with the acoustic space of the revelation of Islam.[18] A space that *negates* Western visual rationality (Chapter 2 = 2E) in a *totality* of unity-in-diversity of the Islamic legal tradition (Chapter 3 = 3L) that has connoted the reality of Islam in its *transformative praxis* as the Islam-Muslim-world (Chapter 4 = 4D).

More in detail, to maintain the 'cross-reference between revelation, tradition and reality' while moving from the normative world of Western law-religion to the *nomos* of Islam, Chapter 2 will discuss some fundamental aspects of cognition (about what-is-known and how-to-know) in relation to the language of Islamic law as part of the religion of the revealed Word. Here, preliminary issues of *translation* will be addressed from a semiotic perspective – where the Latin *translatio* highlights the link to the verb *transferre* ('to carry [meaning] from one place to another') as a process aimed at *negating* the language-source within the language-target, so as to reconcile them in the *totality* of meaning that can be derived. The transfer of meaning of the contract from the visual space of the Occident to the acoustic space of the Orient will be the first challenge of our journey towards the land of Islam (the biblical Tower of Babel mimicking the insidious traps of Lord Sauron's Tower: see section 2.1).

After these first steps into the *nomos* of Islamic law, Chapter 3 will investigate the Muslim *fiqh* of contract, in *comparison* to the Western legal tradition. By re-framing the place of the *'aqd* in 'crafting' an imaginary city within the universe of Islam, the book will present the various *theories* of the Islamic contract (a *totality* of stratification and differentiation) as 'echoed' by classical juristic schools (*madhāhib*, pl. of *madhhab*: in the Sunnī universe, Ḥanafī, Mālikī, Šāfi'ī, and Ḥanbalī schools) in the *absence* of a unique *corpus iuris*. In the frame of the acoustic space of Islam, these concepts will be related to the internal and external dimensions of the action of Muslim believers with regard, respectively, to the psychological formation (section 3.4) and the material occurrence (section 3.5) of the *'aqd*.

To conclude this tripartite study, Chapter 4 will then *contextualise* the *'aqd* in the realities of the Muslim world in relation to the textual polities (Messick, 1989, 1993) that Islamic law has experienced over the centuries within its own *transformative praxis*. This effort of contextualisation of the Islamic *nomos* (so as to put its theories and practices *into practice*) will lead our analysis not only to *listen to* the language of Islamic law but also to examine the legal reality(*-ies*) of its 'speakers;' that is to say, how Muslim merchants – the 'inhabitants' of the *'aqd* – have practiced their trades throughout the centuries and so, how their city has changed historically, within Islam-(as)-Muslim-world. In particular, the study will differentiate three moments of continuity-in-change of the *'aqd* under the labels of *Verbal Trade*, *Codified Norm*, and *Typewritten Market*, highlighting how the evolution of the latter two has been related to the encounter of the Muslim world with the modern West.

By identifying the continuity of the *'aqd* within a synchronic and diachronic transformative praxis, our journey will terminate with final considerations about the meaning of *saying* the *'aqd* (instead of 'seeing it' from the perspective of the scopic regime of Western modernity). As we will find, the destination of our journey will no longer be the discovery of the 'place' of the Islamic contract, but rather, a new way of 'seeing,' *rectius* 'saying,'[19] it – by listening back to *The Almeh* within the acoustic space of Islam.

Notes

1 Law and religion studies have grown in recent decades as a distinctive field of research, after the seminal contribution by Harold J. Berman's book *Law and Revolution. The Formation of the Western Legal Tradition* (1983) (see also Berman 1974, 1986, 2008). In relation to the topic of this volume, a chapter of *Law and Revolution* deals precisely with 'Mercantile law' (pp. 332 ff.), with a discussion on the interaction between religion and the rise of capitalism and the new system of commercial law in the West. Regarding the development of law and religion studies, see also John Witte, Jr. (1997, 2006) and Witte and Alexander (2008). For a useful introduction, see Sandberg (2011).

2 As a domain of global intellectual history, *fiqh* can certainly be described as a '*monument de l'esprit humain digne de la plus entière admiration*' (Linant de Bellefonds, 1965, p. 18).

3 Schacht's words are mirrored in French scholarship by Bousquet and Bercher in saying that '*le Fiqh, c'est la quintessence de l'Islam, sa création la plus personnelle*' (as reported by Linant de Bellefonds, 1965, p. 17, note 18).

4 This perspective shares great similarities with the opinion expressed by Laoust in introducing his translation of the work by the Ḥanbalī jurist Ibn Qudāma:

> *la méditation des traités de Fiqh qui ont formé des générations de fidèles, loin d'être une vaine discipline, comme des jugements trop superficiels peuvent le laisser croire, est indispensable à quiconque porte quelque curiosité à une étude historique ou sociologique des peuples musulmans, à plus forte raison quand de tels traités conservent une indéniable valeur d'actualité.*
>
> (Laoust, 1950)

5 Valuable guidelines to Bhaskar's dialectics can be found in the collection of essays *Critical Realism: Essential Readings* (Archer, Bhaskar *et al.*, 1998) as well as in Norrie, 2009. Regarding the concepts of 'absence' and 'negativity' see also sections 2.3 and 2.5 in this book. For an attempt to rethink Islam and Muslims in a multi-faith world according to Bhaskar's philosophy, see Wilkinson, 2014.

6 'The net project of *Dialectic* and *Plato Etc.* is to attempt an anti-Parmenidean revolution, reversing 2,500 years of philosophical thought' (Bhaskar, 1994, p. xi).

7 Bhaskar's third level must be intended as a more open totality than Hegel's closed synthesis, so to allow an in-depth awareness of continuity in/of change. Bhaskar's totalit-*ies* are internally connected but also open to interact with other totalities (hence, they recognise intrinsically their pluralities being 'one and the other') – e.g. (total) Islam occurs in (individual) Muslims, (collective) peoples, (Western) representations, as well as the (global) world.

8 On the meaning of ideology, see Eagleton, 1991; see also endnote 15 of the Introduction.

9 This passage, I believe, reveals a deep intellectual connection between the thoughts of Ahmed and those of Bhaskar in conceiving 'how Islam makes Muslims as Muslims make Islam' within a *totality* that embodies a continuity in/of change open to other totalities: individual Muslims, collective peoples, others' Western representations, and the global world too (see endnote 7 in this chapter).

10 According to Schacht's representation, as highlighted in the Introduction, 'Islamic law is conscious of its character as a religious ideal; it believes in a continued *decadence* from the time of the caliphs of Medina, 'the caliphs who followed the right course', and it takes the *corruption* of contemporary conditions for granted' (Schacht, 1964, p. 199; italics added).

11 Neher (2005) shows how the idea of symbolic form was taken over by Panofsky from Ernst Cassirer's philosophy of culture. A passage from Panofsky's essay is particularly explanatory:

> if perspective is not a fact of value, it is surely a fact of style. Indeed, it may even be characterised as (to extend Ernst Cassirer's felicitous term to the history of art) one of those 'symbolic forms' in which 'spiritual meaning is attached to a concrete, material sign and intrinsically given to this sign.'
>
> (1991, pp. 40–41)

12 Panofsky specifically links the invention of *ars perspectiva* to modern Western Renaissance (1991, p. 27). In wondering 'whether and in what way antiquity itself might have developed a geometrical perspective' (*ibidem*, p. 37), Panofsky compares modern *perspectiva* to Vitruvius' *scenographia* ('the perspectival representation of a three-dimensional structure on a surface': *ibidem*, p. 38) but admits that 'not a single surviving antique painting possesses such a unified vanishing point' (*ibidem*). In contrast, McLuhan attributes an intrinsic visual nature to all the Western construction of space: 'since the collapse of the oral tradition in early Greece, before the age of Parmenides . . . [s]uch is the power of Euclidean or visual space that we can't live with a circle unless we square it' (McLuhan, 1989, p. 68). It is significant to note here how this is precisely what one of the most famous drawings of the Italian Renaissance, Leonardo da Vinci's *Vitruvian Man* (circa 1490; preserved today at the Gallerie dell'Accademia, Venice), reminds us: an ideal representation of the human body (hence, of Western man) in geometrical proportions, where the body (not by chance) is inscribed both in a circle and a square.

13 Jay makes explicit the interconnection between modernity, visual space, and the *ars perspectiva* in the light of

> an immense literature on the discovery, rediscovery, or invention of perspective – all three terms are used depending on the writer's interpretation of ancient visual knowledge – in the Italian Quattrocento. Brunelleschi is traditionally accorded the honor of being its practical inventor or discoverer, while Alberti is almost universally acknowledged as its first theoretical interpreter. From Ivins, Panofsky, and Krautheimer to Edgerton, White and Kubovy, scholars have investigated virtually every aspect of the perspectival revolution, technical, aesthetic, psychological, religious, even economic and political.
>
> (Jay, 1988, p. 5)

14 The impact of printing, with the domination of graphical over phonetic words, represents a core element in the investigation of communication technology and the role of media in the construction of our cognitive space by Marshall McLuhan. On the topic, see, in particular, his *Understanding Media: The Extensions of Man*, 1964, and *The Medium is the Massage: An Inventory of Effects*, 1967, written in collaboration with graphic designer Quentin Fiore (the title is a play on McLuhan's motto 'the medium is the message,' re-adapted to denote the 'massage' effect of each medium on the human sensorium).

15

> To summarize, visual space structure is an artefact of Western civilization. . . . It is a space perceived by the eyes when separated and abstracted from all other senses. As a construct of the mind, it is continuous, which is to say that it is

> infinite, divisible, extensible, and featureless. . . . It is also connected (abstract figures with fixed boundaries, linked logically and sequentially but having no visible grounds), homogeneous (uniform everywhere), and static (qualitatively unchangeable).
>
> (McLuhan, 1989, p. 71)

Correspondingly, in Western civil codes, the contract is an abstract form, with fixed boundaries in its theoretical elaboration, while linked logically and sequentially with the theory of obligations, homogeneous in all its aspects and static, as its definition is assumed unchangeable over time. The visual-rational nature of the Western contract perfectly reflects, in the end, McLuhan's paradigm.

16 In this sense, tribal societies of the past certainly shared an acoustic space of social knowledge by means of oral transmission.

> The dominant organ of sensory and social orientation in pre-alphabet societies was the ear – 'hearing was believing.' The phonetic alphabet forced the magic world of the ear to yield to the neutral world of the eye. Man was given an eye for an ear.
>
> (McLuhan and Fiore, 1967, p. 44)

17 'Acoustic space structure is . . . both discontinuous and nonhomogeneous. Its resonant and interpenetrating processes are simultaneously related with centers everywhere and boundaries nowhere' (McLuhan, 1989, p. 71; please compare this description with that of the visual space in endnote 15 in this chapter).

18 This remark about the *presentation* of rules in Islamic law through a cognitive process of (acoustic) simultaneity will be elaborated in Chapter 2.

19 I have readapted here, indirectly, a famous quote from Marcel Proust: 'My destination is no longer a place, rather a new way of seeing' ('*Ma destination n'est plus un lieu, mais une nouvelle façon de voir*'). The quote is actually a shortened version of the citation source of Proust's *Remembrance of Things Past* (1922–1931) (from the original French version *À la Recherche du Temps Perdu*, 1913–1927), volume 5 (*The Captive*, 1923) where the narrator is commenting at length on art, rather than travel:

> The only true voyage of discovery, the only fountain of Eternal Youth, would be not to visit strange lands, but to possess other eyes, to behold the universe through the eyes of another, of a hundred other, to behold the hundred universes that each of them beholds, that each of them is; and this we can contrive with an Elstir, with a Vinteuil [i.e. with great artists]; with men like these we do really fly from star to star.
>
> (Proust, 2006, p. 657; on this point, see also the Conclusions of this book)

References

Ahmed, S. (2016) *What Is Islam? The Importance of Being Islamic.* Princeton and Oxford: Princeton University Press.

Archer, M., Bhaskar, R. *et al.* (eds.) (1998) *Critical Realism: Essential Readings.* London and New York: Routledge.

Berger, J. (2008) *Ways of Seeing.* London: Penguin (originally published in 1972, London: BBC, Penguin).

Berman, H.J. (1974) *The Interaction of Law and Religion.* London: SCM Press Ltd.

Berman, H.J. (1983) *Law and Revolution: The Formation of the Western Legal Tradition.* Cambridge, MA and London: Harvard University Press.

Berman, H.J. (1986) The religious sources of general contract law: an historical perspective. *Journal of Law and Religion.* 4(1), pp. 103–124.

Berman, H.J. (2008) The Christian sources of general contract law. In: Witte, J. Jr., and Alexander, F.S. (eds.) *Christianity and Law: An Introduction*. Cambridge: Cambridge University Press, pp. 125–142.
Bhaskar, R. (1975) *A Realist Theory of Science*. London: Verso.
Bhaskar, R. (1979) *The Possibility of Naturalism: A Philosophical Critique of the Contemporary Human Sciences*. Brighton: The Harvester Press.
Bhaskar, R. (1993) *Dialectic: The Pulse of Freedom*. London: Verso.
Bhaskar, R. (1994) *Plato Etc.: The Problems of Philosophy and Their Resolution*. London: Verso.
Buskens, L., and Dupret, B. (2015) The invention of Islamic law: a history of Western studies of Islamic normativity and their spread in the Orient. In: Pouillon, F., and Vatin, J.-C. (eds.) *After Orientalism: Critical Perspectives on Western Agency and Eastern Re-Appropriations*. Leiden and Boston: Brill, pp. 31–47.
Calder, N. (1996) Law. In: Leaman, O., and Nasr, S.H. (eds.) *History of Islamic Philosophy*. London and New York: Routledge, pp. 979–998.
Collier, A. (1994) *Critical Realism: An Introduction to Roy Bhaskar's Philosophy*. London and New York: Verso.
Cover, R.M. (1983) The Supreme Court, 1982 term – Foreword: *nomos* and narrative. *Harvard Law Review*. 97(1), pp. 4–68.
Eagleton, T. (1991) *Ideology: An Introduction*. London: Verso.
Hughes, A.W. (2017) *What Is Islam? The Importance of Being Islamic* – Book Review. Available at: https://readingreligion.org/9780691164182/. Accessed 18 March 2019.
Jay, M. (1988) Scopic regimes of modernity. In: Foster, H. (ed.) *Vision and Visuality*. Dia Art Foundation – Discussions in Contemporary Culture Number 2. Seattle: Bay Press, pp. 3–23.
Kuhn, T. (1962) *The Structure of Scientific Revolutions*. Chicago: Chicago University Press.
Laoust, H. (1950) *Le Précis de Droit d'Ibn Qudāma – Jurisconsulte Musulman d'École Hanbalite*. Beirut: Institut Français d'Etudes Arabes.
Linant de Bellefonds, Y. (1965) *Traité de Droit Musulman Comparé, Vol. I, Théorie Générale de l'Acte Juridique*. Paris and La Haye: Mouton & Co.
McLuhan, M. (1964) *Understanding Media: The Extensions of Man*. New York: McGraw-Hill.
McLuhan, M. (1969) The Playboy interview: Marshall McLuhan. *Playboy*. March, pp. 26–27.
McLuhan, M. (1989) Visual and acoustic space (from McLuhan, M., and Powers, B.R. *The Global Village*. New York: Oxford University Press). Reprinted in Cox, C., and Warner, D. (eds.) (2004) *Audio Culture: Readings in Modern Music*. New York and London: Continuum, pp. 67–72.
McLuhan, M., and Fiore, Q. (1967) *The Medium Is the Massage: An Inventory of Effects*. New York: Bantam Books; London: Penguin Books.
Messick, B. (1989) Just writing: paradox and political economy in Yemeni legal documents. *Cultural Anthropology*. 4(1), pp. 26–50.
Messick, B. (1993) *The Calligraphic State: Textual Domination and History in a Muslim Society*. Berkeley and Los Angeles: University of California Press.
Mitchell, W.J.T. (1994) *Picture Theory: Essays on Verbal and Visual Representation*. Chicago and London: The University of Chicago Press.

National Gallery of Art, Washington (NGA) (2019) *Christ Cleansing the Temple*. NGA. Available at: www.nga.gov/collection/art-object-page.43723.html. Accessed 1 August 2019.

Neher, A. (2005) How perspective could be a symbolic form. *The Journal of Aesthetic and Art Criticism*. 63(4), pp. 359–373.

Norrie, A. (2009) *Dialectic and Difference: Dialectical Critical Realism and the Grounds of Justice*. London: Routledge.

Panofsky, E. (1991) *Perspective as Symbolic Form* (trans. by Wood, C.S. (1927) from the original German version published as Die Perspektive als 'symbolische form'. In: *Vorträge der Bibliothek Warburg 1924/25*. Leipzig and Berlin: Teubner, pp. 258–330). New York: Zone Books.

Proust, M. (2006) *Remembrance of Things Past* (trans. by Moncrieff, C.K.S., and Hudson, S), Vol. 2. Ware, Herts: Wordsworth Editions.

Russell, B. (1922) Introduction. In: Wittgenstein, L. (ed.) *Tractatus Logico-Philosophicus*. London: Routledge & Kegan Paul, pp. 7–23.

Said, E.W. (1978) *Orientalism*. London and Henley: Routledge & Kegan Paul.

Sandberg, R. (2011) *Law and Religion*. Cambridge: Cambridge University Press.

Schacht, J. (1964) *An Introduction to Islamic Law*. Oxford: Oxford University Press.

Wilkinson, M.L.N. (2014) *A Fresh Look at Islam in a Multi-Faith World: A Philosophy for Success Through Education*. London and New York: Routledge.

Witte, J. Jr. (1997) *From Sacrament to Contract: Marriage, Religion and Law in the Western Tradition*. Louisville, KY: Westminster John Knox Press.

Witte, J. Jr. (2006) *God's Joust, God's Justice: Law and Religion in the Western Tradition*. Cambridge: William B. Eerdmans Pub.

Witte, J. Jr., and Alexander, F.S. (eds.) (2008) *Christianity and Law: An Introduction*. Cambridge: Cambridge University Press.

Wittgenstein, L. (1922) *Tractatus Logico-Philosophicus*. London: Routledge & Kegan Paul.

2 The revealed Word in translation

The space of law and religion in Islam

Carrying the One Ring of non-identity, Chapter 1 has endorsed *The Fellowship* of three great thinkers: Roy Bhaskar, Shahab Ahmed, and Marshall McLuhan. It has also subscribed to Calder's portrayal of Islamic law as 'a conceptual replica of social life, not necessarily aspiring to be either complete or practical, but balanced between revelation, tradition and reality' (1996, p. 981). This chapter focuses on the first of these three elements. More precisely, by investigating how differently religion relates to law in the Occident and the Orient, it will try to *translate* the *space* of the revelation of Islam to the Western explorer.

Thus, departing from the Temple that we have previously visited, we can imagine we are now in a sort of Middle-Earth, where, as Sauron's fortress starts to become visible, with its Eye watching over Mordor from the top of Barad-dûr, the Ring becomes more difficult to carry.

2.1. Babel, languages, and the sacred law of Islam

Whether or not Tolkien took inspiration for his masterpiece from sacred texts, one is immediately struck by the similarity between Barad-dûr, the Dark Tower, and a well-known symbol of evil in the Bible; namely, the Tower of Babel. According to the Bible, the city of Babel[1] united all of humanity, where a single language was spoken; but the inhabitants decided to build an immense tower ('whose top may reach unto heaven:' Genesis 11:4) for the glory of man. The Lord punished their arrogance, giving each person a different language and scattering the people throughout the Earth. In the *Foreword* to the book complementing the exhibition *Babel. Adventures in Translation* (Bodleain Library, Oxford; 15 February – 2 June 2019), Richard Ovenden observes how

> [t]he biblical myth . . . tells us that humankind has long dreamed of a shared 'perfect' language. . . . But the myth also highlights an even more fundamental feature of human communication: 'language' exists only in the form of specific 'languages'. . . . Translation builds bridges between [these] languages . . . [and] permits and encourages adaptation to new cultural contexts and needs: it changes languages as it bridges them.
>
> (Duncan, Harrison *et al.*, 2019, p. 7)

DOI: 10.4324/9781315145761-3

Thus, if Babel is a curse for the interpreter, the practice of translation becomes a blessing when it allows peoples of different lands to communicate and to merge the spaces of their cultures. The bridge of translation is never built on a shared perfect language; on the contrary, it is by transferring the complex systems of the interrelated meanings of which each language is made that intercultural communication can possibly occur. For this reason, following the teachings by Umberto Eco (2003), translation never happens 'word by word,' but 'world to world;' for a good translation to emerge, words must be located within their *own* encyclopaedia (Eco, 1999, p. 226) – i.e. the world of meaning(-s) that belong to their own cultural setting.

Profound encyclopaedic issues can indeed arise when one questions whether 'religion' and 'law' mean the same thing in the Western and Islamic legal traditions. In fact, as noted by Giovanni Sartori, 'words are tools of thinking (not merely of communication), and are by no means neutral, for they powerfully orient, in and by themselves, our perceptions and interpretations' (Sartori, 1975, p. 13). If different law(s)-religion(s) do not share a uniform space but *co-exist* in the bridge of *non-identity* (Bhaskar, see section 1.3.1), how should/could we translate their wor(l)d(s)'s meanings while crossing the bridge? Should we assume, for instance, that Islamic law is inherently religious? And, if so, which kind of secular law (if any) can describe the *'aqd* in the Muslim world – the one of customary business practice?[2] A fortiori, which is the implicit meaning of 'religious' and 'secular' that we are applying?

To reply to all these questions, one should preliminarily consider the status of the Qur'ān by comparing the centrality of God's Word in Islamic religion to that of Christianity. The New Testament reads: 'In the beginning was the Word, and the Word was with God, and the Word was God' (John 1:1); here, 'the Word' translates the Greek *logos*, widely interpreted in Christian religion as referring to Jesus (the 'Word made flesh' who 'dwelt among us:' John 1:14). There are two remarkable differences between this *logos* and that of Islam, and so too, their respective normative worlds. First, the Christian *nomos* has been shaped in Western modernity according to a binary code that separates the religious of *Corpus Christi* from the secular of the *Corpus Iuris Civilis* (see here section 2.2; see also endnote 3 of the Introduction). Second, if the Christian 'Word made flesh' has led to the translation of the Bible from Greek and Latin and, later, to modern languages (the sacred Word being embodied in Jesus, and not in the texts of the Gospels), the *logos* of Islam attributes to the Word of Allāh and to His *nomos* quite a different status.

> The Qur'an stands in contrast to . . . Christian linguistic veils and layerings. . . . [It] was revealed word by word to Muhammad through the intermediary of the angel Jibril (Gabriel): in consequence, it is 'inimitable'. This does not mean that the Qur'an is not allowed to be translated; but it does change how the translations are used and understood. Muslims must get to know the Qur'an in Arabic, and (unless they are unable to do so) use the Arabic text for religious purposes. . . . A translation

> could not take place of the sacred book, as translations of the Christian Bible have done in hundreds of languages.
>
> (Reynolds, 2019, p. 63)

Of course, although the sacred Qur'ān cannot be translated, its meaning can be explained from Arabic to other languages so as to carry its Message to all of humanity. This precisely reflects the etymology of 'translation' as derived from the Latin *translatio* and the verb *transferre*, 'to carry from one place to another' (Reynolds, 2016, p. 14). Translation can be rendered in Arabic with *naql* (verb *naqala*), whose root, *N-Q-L*, means 'to transfer,' 'to shift,' 'to move from one place to another,' and so 'to move from one language to another.' A second word is *tarjama* (root *T-R-J-M*), which stands for 'interpretation' and 'explanation,' from which derives *tarjumān*, meaning 'translator,' in the sense of 'explainer of speech in another language.' The word entered European languages during the Middle Ages, from the Medieval Latin *dragumannus* to the Old French *drugeman*, the Italian *dragomanno* and the English 'dragoman' to indicate, from the 16th to the 20th century, the person acting as official interpreter and guide between Turkish, Arabic, and Persian-speaking countries and European kingdoms.[3] Dragomans were mediators and important actors in Orient-Occident political relations – a connotation that underlines how 'all translations involves diplomacy' (Reynolds, 2016, p. 6).

Moving from one legal world to another, without the good training of a dragoman, legal scholars may keep their *own* meanings when dealing with semantic worlds that are very distant from their own paradigms,[4] making wrong evaluations and coming to erroneous conclusions. Referring to the concept of encyclopaedia, Eco provides two remarkable examples of cognitive misperceptions that may be helpful to illustrate which kinds of risks are always involved in the practice of translation, when no immediate equivalent can be found from the language-source (that of the speaker) to the language-target (the one that the speaker wishes to translate). The first misperception was experienced by the Italian explorer Marco Polo (1254–1324) when he arrived in the island of Java.

> Often, when faced with an unknown phenomenon, we react by approximation: we seek that scrap of content, already present in our encyclopaedia, which for better or worse seems to account for the new fact. A classic example of this process is to be found in Marco Polo, who saw what we realize were rhinoceroses on Java. Although he had never seen such animals before, by analogy with other animals he was able to distinguish the body, the four feet, and the horn. Since his culture provided him with the notion of a unicorn – a quadruped with a horn on its forehead, to be precise – he designated those animals as unicorns . . . [which appeared] rather strange – not very good examples of the species, we might say – given that they were not white and slender but had "the hair of the buffalo" and feet "like the feet of an elephant."
>
> (Eco, 1999, p. 57)[5]

The second case relates to the meeting of the first Australian colonists with the platypus, a 'strange animal' which seems to 'have been conceived to foil all classification, be it scientific or popular,' by qualities that belong either to 'a beaver, a duck, or a fish' (*ibidem*, p. 58).[6]

> The first Australian colonists to see the platypus found themselves in the same quandary: they saw it as a mole, and in fact they called it the "water mole," but this mole had a beak, and therefore it was not a mole. Something perceptible outside the "mold" supplied by the idea of mole made the mold unsuitable – because to recognize a beak as a beak we would have to presume that the colonists had a "template" for the beak. (*ibidem*, p. 59)

Of course, Marco Polo shouldn't have described the rhinoceros as unicorns, just as Australian colonists shouldn't have seen a mole in the platypus, but their interpretations made sense, and therefore had meaning, according to their *own* encyclopaedia. *Mutatis mutandis*, comparative lawyers may tend to deal with foreign *normative worlds* by repeating their *own* encyclopaedia, and then, may experience misperceptions. These problems of (re-)cognition and (mis-)interpretation in legal scholarship have been highlighted by Janet E. Ainsworth, who remarked how legal paradigms constitute 'a preconceived conceptual framework that can cause misinterpretation . . . [since they] tend to make the scholar observe what the paradigm predicts, sometimes literally causing the scholar to see things that do not exist' (1996, p. 30).[7] But, '[n]o matter how neutral and objective descriptive legal categories may appear, they are themselves creatures of a historically and culturally contingent social world, bearing the normative patina of the context from which they were derived' (*ibidem*, p. 31). And so, as a natural result, '[j]ust as fish always in the sea have no consciousness of being wet, scholars always immersed in the ocean of their own normative order may well be unaware that this order permeates the very conceptual tools that they use in attempting to understand the other' (*ibidem*).

Dealing with Islamic law, legal comparatists may behave exactly like 'fish always in the sea' by seeing a unicorn *in the place of* a rhino or a mole *in the place of* a platypus; by applying Western categories in defining what 'law' and 'religion' are, they may ground their research on the *wrong place*.

In this regard, let's look once again at Schacht's description, mentioned in the Introduction, of '[t]he sacred Law of Islam [a]s . . . the totality of Allah's commands that regulate the life of every Muslim in all its aspects; it comprises on an equal footing ordinances regarding worship and ritual, as well as political and (in a narrow sense) legal rules' (1964, p. 1). In this definition, law and religion overlap so much that any secular connotation of the average Muslim seems to disappear. Schacht's *place* for Islamic law cancels the secular in favour of the religious; consequently, in his opinion, 'it must . . . be kept in mind that the (properly speaking) legal subject-matter forms part of a system of religious and ethical rules' (*ibidem*).

In doing so, a point must be remarked: he does not contest at all the binary code of modernity; rather, by negating its applicability to Islam, this paradigm is re-affirmed as an exclusive quality of the West (see later, section 2.2). As a drawback, in front of this 'water mole,' the social reality does not exist anymore; rather, Schacht's Islamic law witnesses 'a continued *decadence* since the time of the caliphs of Medina . . . and it takes the *corruption* of contemporary conditions for granted,' due to the 'contrast between theory and practice' (*ibidem*, p. 199; italics added).[8] Lacking in any secular connotation and deprived of substantial social application, Schacht himself – in something of a paradox, with the title of his *Introduction to Islamic Law* – must admit that, within his representation of law and religion in Islam, '[i]t might therefore seem as if it were not correct to speak of an Islamic law at all, as if the concept of law did not exist in Islam . . . [if not as] part of a system of religious duties, blended with non-legal elements' (*ibidem*, pp. 200–201). That water mole may have been, in the end, a platypus. . . .

Unsurprisingly, due to his persistent legacy in Western academia, Schacht's feeling of misplacement still seems to endure today in legal scholarship, with Buskens and Dupret (2015), for instance, claiming that law did not belong originally to Islam but was 'invented' (by transplant) during the colonial move. If there are margins of truth in this assertion (see later, section 2.4.5 as well as 4.3.1), a more accurate discussion of the point certainly requires carrying the One Ring of non-identity *beyond* the Western Temple that we visited in Chapter 1. In particular, we need to expel the daemons of *our* law-religion (section 1.1) to advance the *absence* (Bhaskar: section 1.3.1) of religion (section 2.3) and law (section 2.4) in Islam as the proper *place* to discuss the nature of Muslim normativity. It is in this sense that the position of the sacred and the profane in what we mean by 'religion' must be preliminarily discussed.

2.2. Profanations: religious vs secular in the Temple of Western modernity

Any *translatio* necessarily starts from one side of the bridge, the language-source with the encyclopaedia of meanings that belongs to the translator; and it is this encyclopaedia that tells us a lot about the interpreter, prior to what-is-interpreted in the language-target. The encyclopaedia underlying Schacht's representation has been already linked in the Introduction to an Orientalistic approach that has been visually depicted in relation to Gérôme's *Almeh* (Figure 0.1). Since different law-religion languages *co-exist* in the bridge of *non-identity*, to move towards the other side of the bridge, we must depart from this image and *translate* Schacht's 'sacred Law' into the *wor(l)ding* of Islam.

More radically, to *carry* our daemons out from the Temple of Western modernity, a 'profanation' of its boundaries must be provoked. It is, in fact, 'in praise of profanation' (to quote the title of a famous essay by Giorgio Agamben, 2007) that we can find interpretive hints for our *translatio* of the essential categories of the 'sacred' and the 'profane' in different cultures.

The sacred conceptually exists in a dialectic with the profane, and when we place these words in the Western world, a visual space dominates their interpretation; a visual rationality that is grounded on division and separation as described by McLuhan (see section 1.3.3), and confirmed in El Greco's representation of *Christ Cleansing the Temple* (Figure 1.1). More specifically, in this visual rationality, the profane does not deny, but rather, re-affirms the sacred by denoting a direction, a position: *pro-fanus* stands for *pro-*, 'before,' hence, 'in front of' + *fanum*, 'the temple,' 'the sacred place.' We are precisely 'in the vicinity of,' 'beside' (hence related to, while separated from) the sacred. A separation between the sacred and the profane defines, for example, what was 'religious' in ancient Rome.

> The Roman jurists knew perfectly well what it meant to "profane." Sacred or religious were the things that in some ways belonged to the gods. As such, they were removed from the free use and commerce of men; they could be neither sold nor held in lien, neither given for usufruct nor burdened by servitude. . . . And if "to consecrate" (*sacrare*) was the term that indicated the removal of things from the sphere of human law, "to profane" meant, conversely, to return them to the free use of men.
>
> (Agamben, 2007, p. 73)

Hence, the *religio* of the Romans defined 'not what unites men and gods but what ensures they remain distinct' (*ibidem*, p. 75; on the point see also later section 2.3). There is here a conceptual distinction between the religious and the secular that the West grounds on a world of visual separation and that was later perpetuated by Christianity, as we have seen in the scene of *Christ Cleansing the Temple*. 'Religion can be defined as that which removes things, places, animals, or people from common use and transfers them to a separate sphere. Not only is there no religion without separation, but every separation also contains or preserves within itself a genuinely religious core' (Agamben, 2007, p. 74). In the end, the very roots of the Western thinking of religion, and hence, of 'religious law,' in opposition to 'secular law,' but also of the notion of law as a *corpus*, as well as of the construction of its social, political, and economic culture, stem from this paradigm.[9]

In the attempt to unveil the Western paradigm of religion, a critical school has recently emerged, with seminal works by Talal Asad (specifically on Christianity and Islam, 1993, 2003)[10] and Timothy Fitzgerald (2000, 2007). According to this critical approach, just as the category of religion represents an image of Western modernity that cannot be conceived independently from its secular counterpart, so the concept of non-Western religions (deprived of their *own* secularities) has been invented in various colonial contexts (in this sense Fitzgerald, 2007) as a tool of Western colonial domination. In her well-known contribution to the subject, Tomoko Masuzawa (2005) claims that, by inventing the category of 'world religions,' the West has been able to preserve its universality in a fictitious language of pluralism. Its pluralistic discourse, according to Masuzawa, is reduced to a 'discourse of othering' (*ibidem*, p. 14), where the secular of modernity remains exclusive to the Western identity (p. 20).[11] More radically, Fitzgerald argues that the concept of religion should be entirely abandoned in social research, since 'there is no coherent non-theological basis for the study of religion as a separate academic discipline' (2000, p. 3); and '[r]eligion cannot reasonably be taken to be a valid analytical category since it does not pick out any distinctive cross-cultural aspect of human life' (p. 4).

However, this radical critique may lead the interpreter, I believe, to surrender in front of Babel. Cutting off one side of the bridge by removing the language-source may make it impossible to deal with religion and law by 'moving the concepts from a place to another' – i.e. by means of translation. Nevertheless, Fitzgerald is right when he argues that religion should be studied as 'an ideological category, an aspect of modern western ideology, with a specific location in history, including the nineteenth-century period of European colonization' (*ibidem*). In fact, what is ideological is not religion itself (whatever its meaning may be) but the Western representation of religion as 'the basis of a modern form of theology' (a 'liberal ecumenical theology,' according to Fitzgerald, 2000, p. 5), developed in a world of meaning where '[r]eligion was one pole of the religion-secular dichotomy' (*ibidem*).

Thus, to proceed further via the bridge of translation, we need to depart from religion as a monovalent category and recognise how, paraphrasing the opening quotation of this chapter, 'religion' exists only in the form of specific 'religions.' In this regard, to move towards the other side of the bridge, a relevant hint can be found, I think, in the previously quoted passage by Eco, by recognising that '[o]ften, when faced with an unknown phenomenon, we react by approximation' (Eco, 1999, p. 57). The verb 'to approximate (to) something' derives from the Latin *ad-* ('to') + *proximare* ('to come near'), hence, 'to bring or put close' through 'that scrap of content, already present in our encyclopaedia, which for better or worse seems to account for the new fact' (*ibidem*).

To come closer to Islam, the Temple of Western modernity must be abandoned as the *place* for a valuable comparative investigation; within its conceptual boundaries, in fact, non-Western cultures are reduced to *sub-places* attached to the West and its hegemonic power. As we have seen in the Introduction, Edward Said specifically highlights how the imaginative geography of the West has represented the East as if it were 'enclosed' beyond some *sacred* borders, so as to keep it *external* from the Temple of modernity. 'The Orient then seems to be, not an unlimited extension beyond the familiar European world, but rather a closed field, a theatrical stage affixed to Europe' (Said, 1978, p. 63). To desecrate the conceptual boundaries of this fictitious language of pluralism (Masuzawa, 2005, previously quoted), the Orientalistic 'discourse of othering' must be abandoned and replaced with a 'discourse of non-identity.'

2.3. An absence of religion? Translating the non-identity of *dīn* as Islamic *bios*

How should we *think* of religion beyond modernity, then, in a space where its underlying (Western) ideology is *absent*? This question puts back in our discussion the central message of Bhaskar's *Dialectic* (1993; see section 1.3.1). 'At the core of *Dialectic* is the concept of absence. [...] Bhaskar sets great store by the need to think of absence. Very early in *Dialectic*, he writes that "by the time we are through, I would like the reader to see the positive as a tiny, but important, ripple on a surface of a sea of negativity" (DPF: 5)' (Norrie, 2009, p. 23).

Comparative lawyers acting as 'fish always in the sea' with 'no consciousness of being wet' (Ainsworth, 1996, see foregoing) should replace the ocean of sense that they *posit* by applying their *own* legal paradigms with Bhaskar's invitation to immerse *our*-selves in a 'sea of negativity.' In this reversed approach, it is the recognition of the primacy of *absence* that becomes crucial for an emancipation from the *positum* of *our* being (on this point specifically, see later, section 2.5). This moves from 'real *non-identity* (its first moment – 1M)' to the second edge (2E) of *negativity* (or *negation*) with an 'emphasis on the spatio-temporal character, the becoming, of being' (Norrie, 2009, p. 22), both in the third level (3L) of *totality* and the fourth dimension (4D) of *transformative praxis* (or *agency*), with a corresponding passage 'from thinking about the entities or products of social life to thinking about the *process* of their production, from "product" to "process", from being to becoming' (*ibidem*).

The primacy of *non-identity*, the One Ring of our journey, implies a process of thinking of Islam as *absence* of (Western) religion. Moving from the 'sea of negativity' by way of approximation in interpreting the phrase 'sacred Law of Islam,' we can note again how, for ancient Roman jurists, *sacrum* was a legal attribute describing what belongs to the gods (*sacrum est . . . quidquid est, quod deorum habetur*, writes the jurist Gaius Trebatius Testa, 1st century BC), and for this reason, removed from the free use of men (see Agamben, previously quoted). For the Romans, something was *sacer* not 'by nature' (the *physis* of the Greeks) but through procedures of customary and normative order (*nomos*) recognised within the human community;[12] hence, the *sacrificium* rendered something sacred not by natural law but by means of a human order. On a related stage, the *religiosum* referred to the scrupulous observance of rituals (towards gods, the dead, or ancestors); *homo religiosus* was the contrary of *homo negligens*, the one who is careless, unconcerned about rituals. Therefore, religion was not really meant to link men to gods, as an etymology from *religare*, 'to bind (again),' may imply – although this interpretation became later prevalent in Christian circles. It was the scrupulous observance, the *re-legere*, 'reading again' through 'careful consideration,'[13] of the *separation* between the sacred, property of gods, and the profane, property of men.[14]

> *[R]elegere* . . . indicates the stance of scrupulousness and attention that must be adopted in relations with the gods, the uneasy hesitation . . . before

forms – and formulae – that must be observed in order to respect the separation between the sacred and the profane. *Religio* is not what unites men and gods but what ensures they remain distinct. It is not disbelief and indifference towards the divine, therefore, that stand in opposition to religion, but "negligence," that is, a behavior that is free and "distracted" (that is to say, released from the *religio* of norms).

(Agamben, 2007, pp. 74–75)

While the current term 'religion' can translate the *religio* of the Romans as later embraced by Christianity by combining both the idea of *religare* and *relegere*, the concept becomes much more elusive in the Muslim world. Here, different terms can render its meaning: from Islam itself in the sense of 'submission of man to God' (the idea of *religare*) to *Šarīʿah*, the Right Path, the Way-to-be-followed; from *madhhab* (the Way-of-going along *Šarīʿah*, the 'legal school,' the 'doctrine' as observance of the tradition – here, the idea of *relegere* becomes prevalent) to *dīn*, which is commonly used to mean 'the religion of Islam' in Western scholarship. But, as Louis Gardet observes, *dīn* itself has in fact three distinct meanings: '(1) judgement, retribution; (2) custom, usage; (3) religion. The first refers to the Hebraeo-Aramaic root, the second to the Arabic root *dāna*, *dayn* (debt, money owning), the third to the Pehlevi *dēn* (revelation, religion)' (Gardet, 2012).

The movement 'from world to world' that belongs to the practice of translation reveals here all the difficulties in the background of 'saying almost the same thing' (Eco, 2003). The Arabic word *dīn* does not *say* exactly something related to *relegere* (a meaning that belongs more to *madhhab*, 'legal doctrine'), nor to *religare* (to bind bilaterally). Rather, what unites men to God in Islam is a unilateral judgement by which the human being is assessed; hence, the idea of retribution both as a 'direction,' *Šarīʿah*, and 'decision,' *ḥukm*, for human action (see the following, section 2.4.4). It is a relation of obligation, of debt (*dayn*), that implies the submission of the believer (*muslim* as the 'one who is submitted') in the revelation (the Pehlevi *dēn*) of Islam; not by chance, the Day of the Last Judgment is named *yawm ad-dīn*. *Dīn* gathers elements of 'obligation, direction, submission, retribution' (Gardet, 2012) related to a divine judgment of human actions which spans, in a general sense, both religion in terms of 'faith' towards a divine retribution and of 'creed' in a submission, Islam, which provides direction, *Šarīʿah*.

This translation [*dīn* as 'religion'] is not in doubt. But the concept signified by *dīn* does not match exactly the usual concept of religion. . . . *Religio* first evokes what connects the man to God [in the sense of *religare*]; and *dīn*, the obligations that God imposes to His "rational creature" (*aṣḥab al-ʿuqūl* . . .). Now, the first of these obligations is to submit and surrender to Him. Being the etymological sense of *islām* the surrender (to God), the well-known Qur'ānic verse acquires its full sense:

> "This day I have perfected your religion (*dīn*) and completed My favour upon you, and I have approved for you Islam as religion (*dīn*)" [Q. 5: 3].
> (Gardet, *ibidem*)

The approximated translation of *dīn* into religion, in the light of the previous passages, leads us to consider (1) what kind of relationship subsists in Islam between the religious and the secular, and (2) in what sense God's revelation has perfected men and women's *dīn*.

As far as the first point is concerned, the Muslim world has always known the formula *dīn wa-dunyā*, which may suggest the existence of an original Islamic distinction of the religious/secular. Gardet (2012) renders the couple as a synthesis between spiritual and temporal life, where religion takes primacy over the secular in the world. In this regard, we should note how, in the Qur'ān, the notion of *dunyā* (in the sense of 'earthly concerns') is coupled with *ākhirah*, 'the Hereafter:' 'And ordain for us the good in this world [*al-dunyā*] and in the Hereafter [*al-ākhirah*]' (Q. 7:156); 'You [my Lord] are my Protector in this world [*al-dunyā*] and the Hereafter [*al-ākhirah*]' (Q. 12:101). In both couples (*dīn wa-dunyā*, *dunyā wa-ākhirah*), there is no opposition between the two terms; the temporal world is not distinct from spirituality, and the 'ordered life' that connotes Islamic *dīn* spans both the eternal *ākhirah* and the temporal *dunyā*. On this matter, Gardet quotes the French orientalist Henry Laoust with regard to the doctrine by Ibn Taymiyya: 'Religion (*dīn*) is intimately connected [as a tool of good government] to the temporal (*dunyā*).' Consequently, the couple *dīn wa-dunyā* should be disregarded as equivalent to the dichotomy religious/secular that characterises the separation sacred/profane in Western *religio*. Rather, *dīn wa-dunyā* expresses an idea of unity, the two sides of the same coin: an ordered life that covers both the eternal and the temporal and that has been perfected for Muslim believers by the revelation of Islam (Q. 5:3).

Within this background, to grasp the full sense of the perfection of *dīn* in Islam, we should move away, I believe, from the Roman idea of *religio* (and the derived concept of 'Christian religion' as fully grounded on rationales of visual separation) to what ancient Greek philosophers described as *bíos* – i.e. 'the way of living of a single person or a human group.' *Bíos* referred to 'the formulas, the modalities of living' and in this meaning mirrors the 'ordered life' that characterises, in a general sense, the notion of *dīn*, the way of living a good life from a Muslim perspective. But, compared to the Greek world, where *bíos* was paired with *zoé*,[15] in Islam, the correlated concept becomes *dunyā*; namely, the 'temporal,' with its earthly concerns. It is by means of *dīn*, the perfected way of living an 'Islamic *bíos*,' that the human being, whose secular existence occurs necessarily in this world, *dunyā*, can pursue salvation in the eternity of the other world, *al-ākhirah*. In this sense, the religion of Islam qualifies the proper Muslim lifestyle (*dīn*) as (the right) way of living (*bíos*) for the person – while Arabic sources use the different word *milla* to describe the social community in terms of 'religious community.' Hence, we find the couple *dīn wa-milla* in Ibn Ḥanbal and al-Baqillānī (Gardet, 2012), as distinguished from *madhhab*, the religio-normative 'doctrine' to follow, and from the more general term *ummah*, which refers to 'community' as a collective nation of people (hence, the community par excellence, that of Muslim people: *ummah al-Islām*).

There are numerous verses in the Qur'ān that relate to the religion of Islam as ordered life (*dīn*) (see previously quoted, Q. 5:3). Regarding God's 'teaching of *dīn*,' Muslim scholars traditionally refer to the pivotal *ḥadīth* of Gabriel,[16] which gathers within the correct Islamic lifestyle (*dīn*): 'a) the contents of faith (*īmān*), b) the practice of *islām* (lit. the "surrender" to God), and c) *iḥsān* or internalisation of the faith ("to worship God as you are seeing Him")' (Gardet, 2012). On the authority of 'Umar, the *ḥadīth* says

> One day we were sitting in the company of Allah's Apostle . . . when there appeared before us a man dressed in pure white clothes, his hair extraordinarily black. . . . At last, he sat with the Apostle. He knelt before him, placed his palms on his thighs, and said: "Muhammad, inform me about *al-Islām*." The Messenger of Allah said: "*Al-Islām* implies that you testify that there is no god but Allah and that Muhammad is the Messenger of Allah, and you establish prayer, pay *zakāt*, observe the fast of *Ramaḍān*, and perform pilgrimage if you are solvent enough." The inquirer said: "You have told the truth". It amazed us that he would put the question and then he would himself verify the truth. The inquirer said: "Inform me about *īmān*." The Prophet replied: "That you affirm your faith in Allah, in His angels, in His Books, in His Apostles, in the Day of Judgment, and you affirm your faith in the Divine Decree about good and evil." The inquirer said: "You have told the truth." The inquirer again said: "Inform me about *al-iḥsān*." The Prophet said: "That you worship Allah as if you are seeing Him, for though you don't see Him, He, verily, sees you". . . . Then the inquirer went on his way but I stayed with the Prophet for a long while. He then, said to me: " 'Umar, do you know who this inquirer was?". . . . "He was Gabriel. He came to you [to] teach you your religion [*'atākum yu'allimukum dīnakum*]."
>
> (Moad, 2007, pp. 136–137)[17]

In the light of this *ḥadīth*, Edward Omar Moad proposes a comparison between Islamic and Western religious ethics following Frederick Carney's categorisation (1983) in 'the hypothesis that the ethic consists of an obligation, a virtue and a value component' (Moad, 2007, p. 135). Accordingly, he describes the religion of Islam as composed of the three fundamental elements mentioned in the *ḥadīth*, where the categories of *islām*, *īmān*, and *iḥsān* are respectively juxtaposed with the concepts of 'obligation,' 'value,' and 'virtue' (on the intersection between religion and ethics in Islam a classic source remains Izutsu, 1966). Moad also suggests that *Šarī'ah* (lit. 'a way to water') should not be translated as 'Islamic law' but in relation both to the obligation component (the normative dimension) and the entire structure of the Islamic ethic.

> A *Sharīʿah* shows you what you *ought to do* ("walk this way") to access the source of *that which you need* (water) in order to bring about the desired *state* (satiety and purity). In the concrete imagery invoked in the original meaning of the term "sharīʿah," then, we find represented an obligation component: the path, the traveling of which is *what ought to be done*. We also find a value component: the water, an object *the value and importance* of which is that in virtue of which the proposition that the path *ought to be taken* is *valid*. Lastly, we find a virtue component: the state of satiety and purity that the water promises for a thirsty traveler, representing a *human change* toward being *the kind of person* the being of which is *ideal*.
>
> (Moad, 2007, pp. 140–141; italics in the original text)

Within the space of the revelation of Islam, where *Šarīʿah* becomes the core of Islamic *bíos* and *fiqh* its normative understanding, a distinction was upheld in Muslim jurisprudence between the ritual 'acts of worship' (*fiqh al-ʿibādāt* – e.g. the formalities of prayer or the rites of pilgrimage) and the non-ritual 'worldly transactions' (*fiqh al-muʿāmalāt* – of which the contract, *ʿaqd*, is a paradigmatic example).

But does this imply any religious/secular separation in Islam that may reflect a sacred/profane distinction as in Western tradition? In fact, in the domain of *dīn*, any human temporal action can assume the value of worshipping God in a movement of *religere* that *brings together* this world (*dunyā*) and the hereafter (*al-ākhirah*) when the obligation of surrendering to God is related to the virtue of Muslim living. This observance (*relegere*) characterises both the ritual and the non-ritual nature that belong respectively to *ʿibādāt* and *muʿāmalāt*. Hence, *absenting* profanation, both *ʿibādāt* and *muʿāmalāt* are sacred: '[r]itual and secular concerns coexist in Islamic law . . . [and] the law may deem a prayer invalid or a sale reprehensible [. . . just as] it distinguishes carefully between the ritual (non-secular) and the non-ritual (secular)' (Abd-Allah, 2008, pp. 240–241). As we will see better in Chapter 3 (section 3.4.3), it is the intention (*niyya*) of the believer to devote the action to God that makes it an act of worship (*ʿibādah*), in the same way that human intellect (*ʿaql*) qualifies the validity of the action in the context of *muʿāmalāt* (for a critical discussion see section 3.6). Hence,

> Islamic law . . . distinguishes carefully between the ritual (non-secular) and the non-ritual (secular). Ritual acts require a good intention [*niyya*]. . . . Non-ritual acts need only conform to the formal provisions of the law, although any valid non-ritual acts can be transformed into an act of worship in the sight of God if it is performed with a religious intention. Thus, a commercial enterprise undertaken with the aim of alleviating poverty

> for God's sake would be elevated to an act of immense religious merit. . . . An important maxim states that "the foundational principle [of the law] is to have rationales (*al-aṣl al-taʿlīl*)". Ritual matters are an exception to this rule because of their intrinsic connection to the spiritual realm.
>
> (Abd-Allah, 2008, p. 241)

2.4. The revelation of Islam: the Wor(l)d and its understanding

2.4.1. Translating Šarīʿah *in human life: the normative science of* fiqh

The time has come to investigate how *Šarīʿah* is translated in the world by the human understanding of God's revelation and the central role to this aim of *fiqh* as a normative science. This is quite a different issue from what we have just examined in dealing with the translation of *religio* into *bíos*, moving from the Western Temple of modernity to the Muslim way of life. As we approach the other side of the bridge, the space of Islam has now to be further disclosed by considering how the revelation is rendered in terms of Islamic *nomos*. In particular, how is law conceived within the Muslim world as part of Islamic *dīn*?

With reference to the *ḥadīth* of Gabriel, we have just seen how *dīn* comprises the contents of faith, *īmān*, the practice of *islām* and *iḥsān*, the internalisation of the faith. None of these three components exactly matches the idea of 'law' in a Western perspective, while combining aspects of obligation, value, and virtue. If 'Western scholarship . . . has rarely presented Islamic law in such a way as to demonstrate its values rather than the values of the observer' (Calder, 1996, p. 979), it is by considering the translation of God's *Word* into the human *world* as the quintessential purpose of the science (*ʿilm*) of *fiqh* that our investigation can come closer to the *ʿaqd* as the vehicle of Islamic *nomos* (Chapter 3).

In a recent overview of the topic, Anver M. Emon (2016) writes that '[*f*]*iqh* is a curious term of art, let alone genre of literature, in Islamic legal history,' whose meaning is usually rendered, as it is in the entry by Ignaz Goldziher and Joseph Schacht (2012) in the *Encyclopaedia of Islam*, as 'understanding, knowledge, intelligence;' it is 'the technical term for jurisprudence, the science of religious law in Islam. It is, like the *iurisprudentia* of the Romans, *rerum divinarum atque humanarum notitia* and in its widest sense covers all aspects of religious, political and civil life' (*ibidem*). Emon recalls here the Roman idea of *iurisprudentia*, rendering *fiqh* as a kind of 'jurisprudence' (a translation which is widespread in academic literature) that is specifically devoted to the religious law of Islam (what Schacht defined as 'sacred Law').

However, the reference to 'jurisprudence' and '*iurisprudentia*' raises difficulties regarding the translation of *fiqh* when this is related to a principle of non-identity. On the one hand, if the English meaning of jurisprudence (covering legal theory and philosophy in common law systems) may cover the realm of *uṣūl al-fiqh* (the 'roots,' 'principles' of understanding – i.e. *fiqh* legal methodology), it excludes the field of *furūʿ al-fiqh* (Islamic substantive law in the form of 'branches' of knowledge) as the main subject of investigation for *fiqh* scholars. Moreover, the extract from the *Corpus Iuris Civilis* to which Emon refers (both in *Institutes* 1.1.1 and *Digest* 1.1.10.2, '*iuris prudentia est divinarum atque humarum rerum notitia, iusti atque iniusti scientia*:' 'jurisprudence is the knowledge of things divine and human, the science of the just and injust') does not refer at all to *religio* (the word itself is not mentioned in the passage). The original text deals with *ius* as normative science, and *prudentia*, 'care,' 'attention,' 'prudence' in terms of 'practical wisdom' (see also later, section 2.4.3). If one can agree that *prudentia* is the virtue par excellence of the scholars of *fiqh* (the *fuqahā'*, sing. *faqīh*), how does their wisdom translate the divine *Word* in the human *world*? What is the role of religion in the normative process?

In a space whose boundaries are not conceived of in form of visual separation but of an acoustic continuity that *brings together* this world (*dunyā*) and the hereafter (*al-ākhirah*) as 'simultaneously related with centers everywhere and boundaries nowhere' (McLuhan, 1989, p. 71; see section 1.3.3), the *sacrum* intrinsically belongs to the *real* as God's creation. The peculiar nature of this space has been meaningfully described by Clifford Geertz as being

> in its essence imperative, a structure not of objects but of wills. The moral and the ontological change places, at least from our [Western] point of view. It is the moral, where we see the "ought," which is a thing of descriptions, the ontological, for us the home of the "is," which is one of demands. . . . The "real" here is deeply moralized, active, demanding real, not a neutral, metaphysical "being," merely sitting there awaiting observation and reflection; a real of prophets not philosophers.
>
> (Geertz, 1983, pp. 187–188)

In this 'real of prophets not philosophers' the translation of the divine *Word* into the *world* occurs by echoing the divine revelation into human reality in the form of a practical wisdom, where the Pathway of *Šarī'ah* offers the 'roots of knowledge,' *uṣūl al-fiqh*, the sources of the *pre*-scribed Law, as much as it nourishes the 'branches of knowledge,' *furū' al-fiqh*, which, in turn, *de*-scribe the law for human actions. As God is the only *Wor(l)d*-giver (Lawgiver and all-Omnipotent Creator), the meaning of *fiqh* cannot be solved by maintaining the rationales of Western law-religion, nor can it replicate a *distance* between the profane and the sacred (as implicitly assumed in Schacht's definition of the 'sacred Law of Islam'); rather, it must be *replaced* by an *instance* of the sacred into the real as a distinctive manifestation of Islamic *bios* (see later section 2.4.4). It is by linking 'fact' and 'law' that *fiqh* rationales can be disclosed in terms of a 'conceptual replica of social life, not necessarily aspiring to be either complete or practical, but balanced between revelation, tradition and reality, all three of which feed the discussion and exemplify the concepts' (Calder, 1996, p. 981). In this law-religion space '[t]he literature of *uṣūl* identifies the divinely revealed sources of the law (Qur'ān and *Sunnah*), auxiliary sources (like consensus – *ijmā'*) and the hermeneutic disciplines which permit the complex intellectual cross-reference between revelation, tradition and reality which is exemplified in a work of *furū'* (*ibidem*).

2.4.2. The **dictum** *of the revelation as* **pre-***scribed Law and the* **uṣūl al-fiqh**

The revelation of God as the only *Wor(l)d*-giver represents the core of *fiqh* normativity. God's Word is engraved in the world and makes it sacred in Muslim life (*bíos*) as God's immediate creation. Accordingly, any person's right (*ḥaqq*) derives from God's Word, which is the way through which Truth has been communicated to mankind and, in this sense, it is the (Real) World that precedes the world experienced by human beings. The ontological inscription of God's Word into the world can be *seen* engraved in the walls of any mosque (Figure 2.1). Above all, its deontological presence is persistently *heard* in the recitation of the Qur'ān by Muslim believers (see section 2.4.5).

The act of recitation brings our discourse back to the comparison between God's Word in Islam and Christianity (see section 2.1), given that the textual character of the Qur'ān, as highlighted by Brinkley Messick is 'quite different from that of the Bible, or at least the Gospels, which are considered humanly authored and which constitute a "book" in a sense closer to the

Figure 2.1 The Word engraved in the world (Kufic inscription of Qur'ānic verses in the Mosque-Madrassa Sultan Hassan, Cairo; author's photograph, 2009)

contemporary Western meaning' (Messick, 1993, p. 22). By contrast, the Qur'ān,

> [r]eceived orally by a Prophet who, according to doctrine, could neither read nor write, . . . is a recitation-text. The Prophet was instructed by the Archangel Gabriel to "recite," and the Quran, an extented "recitation," was received by him and then orally reconveyed in this way to his companions. As the Quran circulated in the world, recitations were repeated and memorized, the text was preserved in human hearts, and, in the event, a discursive style was set in place. The Quran's written form, the physical text located "between the two covers," would always be backgrounded in relation to its emphasised recitational identity. A century ago, Snouck Hurgronje urged Western scholars "to give up the erroneous translations of Quran by 'reading,' and [the root verb] *qara'a* by 'to read' " [in favour of the idea of 'recitation': *qirā'ah*].
>
> (Messick, 1993, p. 22)

The very nature of the Qur'ān as 'recitation' (and not as 'book' or 'reading') is, probably, *the* crucial aspect that must be considered to deal appropriately with the *acoustic* space of Islam (sections 1.3.3 and 2.4.5). To further elaborate this point, a preliminary disclosure is required with regard to the *Wor(l) d* of Islam in relation to what Ian Netton defines as the 'Qur'ānic Creator Paradigm,' whose God '(1) creates *ex nihilo*; (2) acts definitely in historical time; (3) guides His people in such time; and (4) can in some way be known indirectly by His creation' (Netton, 1989, p. 22).

In Islam, the surrender of the believer (*muslim*) to God is complementary to God's omnipotence. Allāh is the Lord (*rabb*), the original Owner of all that He creates, and the believer is his/her *'abd* ('slave,' 'servant,' 'agent'),[18] with the root *'-B-D* carrying connotations of both worship and service that reappear in the notion of *'ibāda* (pl. *'ibādāt*), 'act of worship.' The absolute freedom of God's will (*irādah*) is the direct manifestation of His omnipotence (Hourani, 1985; Gimaret, 1990; Burrell, 2008, pp. 144–145). 'What He wills, is and what He does not will, is not,' writes Al-Ghazālī (d. 505/1111), in his doctrinal *kalām* work *al-Iqtiṣād fi'l-I'tiqād* (quoted by Ormsby, 1984, p. 192). This extends to the least, seemingly insignificant, occurrence: 'not even the casual glance of a spectator nor the stray thought in the mind come to be outside the sphere of His will' (*ibidem*). Will is also expressed by the term *mashī'ah*, 'volition,' and so it is that the word *shay'*, 'thing,' deriving from the same root, is sometimes glossed as 'what has been willed [by God] to exist' (*ibidem*). 'To Him is due the primal origin of the heavens and earth. When He decreeth a matter, He saith only "Be," and it is' (Q. 2:117).[19] God's command ('Be! and it is,' *kun fa-yakūn*) rules any event in time. In every instant, coherently with an atomic theory of time, God is creating the world anew: '[f]rom the "Be!" of a person's creation to the time of death, human existence falls under the decree of God: Allāh is the Lord of each instant; what He has determined happens' (Böwering, 1997, p. 58).

Accordingly, within the Islamic universe of sense, each instant is an act of God's *instance* (a case for the believer to submit to His will). This is a core point to understanding the very nature of the Qur'ān as a 'text' whose recitation happens in a reality where *time ceases* [to flow] and *space vanishes.*[20] God creates by locating each event as single occurrences that are co-existent with *no* distance (hence, *no* space) between the divine Word and the world; correspondingly, the presence of human action in time determines an instance of moral action for the believer (a 'request' of adherence to *dīn* by submitting to God's order in the '*no* time' of the instant). Muslim jurisprudents understood time in moral terms, in their attempt to balance submission to the divine commands and practical choice in temporal life (Farahat, 2022). Within this moral conception, as God's revelation interrupted the (ontological and deontological) silence of the desert by establishing an acoustic space of salvation, so the recitation of the Qur'ān by the believer verbally re-affirms this acoustic space. This is the space that provides the Right Path for the traveller; it is the Way (*Šarīʿah*, lit. 'the road leading to water': Q. 45:18) that replaces the *no-where* of the desert (an absent visual space made of 'distance') with the *now-here* of running water (a present acoustic space made of 'instance' in human action). By surrendering to God, the human being becomes the recipient (*maḥall*) of the Way *pre*-scribed by Law (what has been already established in the divine *Wor(l)d* of the Qur'ān).

Given this background, the understanding (*fiqh*) of the Path (*Šarīʿah*) becomes the specific knowledge of divine and human things which relate to *dīn*, the Islamic way of living which is witnessed by the recitation of the Word. The knowledge (*fiqh*) of the *dictum* of the revelation provides guidance for salvation through the 'roots, principles of understanding' (*uṣūl al-fiqh*) (Zysow, 2013). To make human beings responsible for their actions, God has given the Qur'ān, 'what is recited,' and sent the Prophet as a reminder of the Message. If *Šarīʿah* is eternal and ever-lasting as *pre*-scribed Law, the worldly performance of the rule by the believer implies its move (its translation) from the transcendental to the empirical, where the human understanding (*fiqh*) of the rule (*ḥukm*) *de*-scribes the revelation. *ʾIlm al-fiqh*, lit. 'science of comprehension,' is the discipline aimed at understanding God's Guidance, *Šarīʿah*, by deriving from the *uṣūl al-fiqh*, the 'roots,' 'principles' of understanding (i.e. the divinely provided sources of Law: Qur'ān and *Sunnah*, the Prophet's way of life as transmitted through His *aḥādīth*; plus auxiliary sources, like consensus, *ijmāʿ*, and analogy, *qiyās*) the 'branches' (*furūʿ*) of rules for a proper Muslim life (religion as *dīn*, *bíos*). Thus, in this sense, the meaning of *Šarīʿah* equals that of *dīn*: 'for the Muslim the whole religion itself is in a very real sense a synonym of God's guidance: Islam is "being rightly guided"' (Netton, 1989, pp. 24–25).

Alongside the nature of the Qur'ān as recitation that has been mentioned previously, another fundamental element, often neglected in legal scholarship, confirms the acoustic nature of 'being rightly guided' in Islam. In fact, with regard to the *Sunnah*, the authority of reports about what the Prophet had said or done depends in Muslim *fiqh* 'on the existence of an unbroken and unimpeachable series of reputable and reliable word-of-mouth transmitters' (Messick, 1993, p. 24) of the contents of the *aḥādīth*. This 'uninterrupted chain (*isnād*) of trustworthy persons' (Schacht, 1964, p. 34) discloses 'a kind of textuality in which writing, or the text in written form, was considered secondary and supplementary' (Messick, 1993, p. 24). 'The privileging of the recited word over the written text and an associated concern with the specific connections of oral-aural transmission' (*ibidem*) further differentiate the Islamic and the Western legal traditions in a framework of ***non-identity***.

Moreover, just as the Word becomes direction (*Šarīʿah*) and ordered life (*bíos*) by means of the discovery of God's commands (*aḥkām*) and its chain (*isnād*) of transmission, the revelation (*logos*) of Islam does not only say but, in fact, performs God's Mercy: it leads man to salvation. In Islamic normativity, the distant ideal of a divine Law separated from human affairs (Western legal tradition) is replaced by an 'instance of action' of the rule (*ḥukm*) into the right (*ḥaqq*) that belongs to the reality of God's creation (see section 2.4.4).

2.4.3. **Furūʿ al-fiqh** ***as*** **de-*****scribed law in a*** **iurisdictio** ***of verdicts***

'Sharīʿah may be defined as the totality of guidance that Allāh s.w.t. has revealed to the Prophet Muḥammad pertaining the dogma of Islam, its moral values, and practical legal rules' (Kamali, 1998, p. 42). '*Fiqh* . . . is defined as the knowledge of the practical rules [*aḥkām*] of Sharīʿah which are deduced from their detailed evidence in the sources [i.e. from the *uṣūl*]' (*ibidem*, p. 43).[21] Pursuing our approximation to the city of the *ʿaqd* by locating its place in the space of Islam, two additional comments can be added to the previous paragraphs on the relation between *Šarīʿah* and *fiqh* jurisprudence.

(1) As noted previously, the meaning of *fiqh* (the 'science of religious law in Islam:' Emon, 2016) is much broader than that of English jurisprudence to which may correspond – roughly – the domain of *uṣūl al-fiqh*, the 'roots,' 'principles,' 'methodology of understanding.' In fact, the core of *fiqh* relates to the knowledge of practical rules, the 'branches' (*furūʿ*) of understanding derived from *Šarīʿah* sources. It is in this respect that Reinhart can remark how 'Islamic law is both practical and theoretical, concerned with human action in the world, and (strictly speaking) religious' (1983, p. 186). At the same time, the original Roman notion of ***iurisprudentia*** (***humanarum atque divinarum notitia***, 'the knowledge of things divine and human') may better illuminate the 'care, attention for legal things' (***prudentia iuris***) which inherently belongs to the practice of Muslim jurisprudence. Dealing with the translation of the Roman idea of *iurisprudentia* a significant point is made by Neil MacCormick when he notes that

> *prudentia* is the normal Latin translation of the Greek *phronesis*, perhaps best rendered in English as "practical wisdom". This is the same as the English "prudence" . . . in the sense of the "reasonable man" . . . who has regard for the common good as well as particular goods in his actings. . . . [In this context] "[l]aw" is at best an imperfect rendering of *ius*, for there is as much of *lex* as of *ius* in "law". *Recht*, *droit*, *diritto* work better as translations, precisely in being ambiguous between the English "right" in various of its senses and the English "law" (MacCormick, 2001, pp. 80–81).

Indeed, the German *islamische Recht*, the French *droit musulman*, as well as the Italian *diritto musulmano*, and the Spanish *derecho musulmán* work better than the English 'Islamic law' in translating *fiqh* jurisprudence as a distinctive science between the law (the 'rule,' *ḥukm*, given by God) and the right (*ḥaqq*, again, provided by God). Referring to the passage of the *Corpus Iuris Civilis* that we mentioned before, MacCormick advances a more precise translation in the sense of a 'practical wisdom in matters of right . . . [through the] awareness of God's and men's affairs, knowledge of justice and injustice' (2001, p. 81).

How far can this definition also be applied to *fiqh*?

For Norman Calder, as we have seen previously, Islamic law constitutes 'a hermeneutic discipline which explores and interprets revelation through tradition' (1996, p. 980). Calder underlines the radical difference of this discipline from the practice of law in a Western sense, and he is right in arguing that, in the Muslim juristic discourse, the search for practical rules is 'certainly present, but strangely hard, sometimes, to find' (*ibidem*, p. 979). At the same time, the commitment of Muslim jurists to discovering God's will within the domain of *furūʿ al-fiqh* has never been purely theoretical and speculative (something that explains its distance from the science of speculative theology, *kalām*). Rather, *fiqh*, in connecting the divine and the human, has always maintained the essence of a practical wisdom in the search for rules that echo the revelation of the Truth. In this regard, paraphrasing MacCormick's translation, a definition of *fiqh* can be advanced as a 'practical wisdom in legal questions whose rationale lies in echoing God's revelation into person's rights.' *Fiqh* interpretive effort does not remain within the boundaries of hermeneutics in the understanding of the revelation; on the contrary, the divine rule (*ḥukm*) is always *linked* to human acts, so as to put God's command *in action* into man's rights (*ḥuqūq*). In other terms, *fiqh* rules are located within the person's rights for the *ḥukm* to be performed; it is this performative aim that nurtures the *prudentia* of *fiqh* in dealing with the Word. Its practical wisdom operates by 'saying the Law' (in Latin, *ius dicere*) in *de*-scribing the rules revealed by God.

(2) It is precisely by focusing on the translation of the *pre*-scribed Law of *Šarīʿah* into the *de*-scribed law of *fiqh* that the rationale of Muslim jurisprudence consists in a *iurisdictio* that echoes God's revelation into man/woman's rights. This leads our discussion to investigate more closely how the *pre*-scribed Law (the transcendental rule, *ḥukm*) is echoed into the right (*ḥaqq*) through the empirical rule (again, *ḥukm*) discovered by Muslim jurists.

In this regard, al-Ghazālī (d. 505/1111) observes in his *Al-Mustaṣfā min 'Ilm al-Uṣūl* (*The Quintessence of Legal Theory*) that 'a rule (*ḥukm*) . . . denotes the dictum of the revelation when it is linked to the acts of those made responsible [*inna 'l-ḥukm 'indanā 'ibāra 'an khiṭāb al-šar' idhā ta'allaqa bi af'āl al-mukallafīn*]' (quoted by Moosa, 1998, p. 9). Subsequently, he defines *fiqh* as the 'knowledge of revealed judgments (*al-aḥkām al-šar'iyyah*) associated with the actions of legally capable subjects (*al-thābita li-af'āl il-mukallafīn*).' We can note from both the passages how the link between God's decree (*ḥukm*) and the action of the responsible human being (*mukallaf*) (the person legally capable, so under *taklīf*, 'legal charge or obligation to act') lies at the heart of Islamic law. It is between the dual nature of the rule, *ḥukm* (first transcendental, as *pre*-scribed Law, and then empirical, as *de*-scribed law) that the right, *ḥaqq*, can be related to the responsibility of the *mukallaf*. The *ḥaqq* makes 'real' the divine *Word* in the *world* (see also section 2.4.4); the revealed rule (*ḥukm*, pl. *aḥkām*) finds its 'real' meaning 'when it is linked to the acts of those made responsible.' This matches the moral nature of reality as God's creation, where human beings are constituted in their ethical existence as '*by way of word*' (Stelzer, 2008, p. 169). Within this peculiar *iurisprudentia*, Islamic law *de*-scribes human rights (*ḥuqūq*, pl of *ḥaqq*) in the *world* of social reality as direct manifestation of the Law *pre*-scribed by the revealed *Word*. More precisely, the practical wisdom of Muslim jurisprudence resides in 'echoing the divine revelation' by 'stating the law' (*ius-dicere* in Latin): a *iuris-dictio* that consists in making explicit, manifest the *Wor(l)d* of *Šarī'ah*, so that the discovery of the divine rule leads to the delivery of a verdict (from the Latin *vere-dictum*, 'to say the truth') for the particular case under consideration. This confirms a logic where, Allāh being the only Ruler, the transcendental *ḥukm* of the *Word*, the *pre*-scribed Law, precedes any right (*ḥaqq*), which is *de*-scribed in Islamic law.[22] At the same time, the verdict is never an isolated assessment by the singular jurist; on the contrary, it is part of a collective construction of *fiqh iurisdictio* in a long-lasting tradition of knowledge that belongs to the *madhāhib* (the schools of law as 'ways of going' along the Path of *Šarī'ah*: in the Sunnī universe, the Ḥanafī, Mālikī, Šāfi'ī, and Ḥanbalī schools: see later in Chapter 3). The intersection law-fact makes the understanding of the rule, bound, on the one hand, to the revealed proofs of the transcendental rule (*ḥukm*)[23] and, on the other hand, to the right (*ḥaqq*) as direct effect of the empirical dimension of the *ḥukm*. Accordingly, if in the making of Islamic law it is the delivery of a verdict by the single Muslim jurist that nurtures the process of discernment, the discovery of the rule finds its epistemological unity through its transmission in each legal school (*madhhab*), within 'a discipline that explores tradition, and uses tradition to discover (and limit) the meanings of the revelation' (Calder, 1996, p. 980). In its centripetal fugue towards the *Word* (Cattelan, 2016, p. 383), *fiqh* tradition relates the transcendental *ḥukm* to its empirical manifestation by the 'way of walking,' 'going' (as per the literal meaning of *madhhab*) along the Path (*Šarīʿah*). While 'Western legal theory locates the (specific, empirical) case within the (general, abstract) norm to deduce the judgment, the logic of *fiqh* sees law as an epistemological issue, *fiqh*-judgement being an atom of what constitutes *fiqh*-knowledge, deposited in the tradition (an echoing amplification, where the human *word* reflects the divine *Word*)' (*ibidem*, p. 384).

Within the process of law-making that characterises Muslim *iurisdictio* as *de*-scribed law, the relationship between the 'ideal' and the 'real' also changes in comparison to the Western legal tradition, as we will see in the next section (section 2.4.4). This is an aspect that will finally lead us to summarise the qualities of *fiqh* practical wisdom in terms of a 'law without *corpus*' (section 2.4.5).

2.4.4. *From the rule (*ḥukm*) to the right (*ḥaqq*): an instance of action in the wor(l)d*

Fiqh practical wisdom locates legal questions between the divine and the human by echoing God's Word in the believer's life; by stating the law (*ius-dicere*), it tells the Truth (*vere-dicere*) of the revelation's *dictum*. This *iurisdictio* (a 'tradition of thought and of education': Calder, 1996, p. 981) will be investigated with reference to the *ʿaqd* in Chapter 3. But, before moving in this direction, we still need to consider how the *dictum* of the revelation and *fiqh* tradition interact in Islamic legal reasoning. In other terms, how does the Muslim jurist move from the transcendental to the empirical rule (*ḥukm*) so as to identify what is right (*ḥaqq*) according to *Šarīʿah*?

As previously noted (section 2.4.2), in Islam, God is the Creator of all the universe and the human being is the receiving subject (*maḥall*) of God's creation; God attributes acts to man by acquisition (*kasb*, *iktisāb*), for which the believer becomes responsible. Between the dogmas of divine creation and human responsibility, Ebrahim Moosa notes that, just as *Šarīʿah* 'provides the interface between the eternal and the temporal,' '[t]he crucial intersection of the divine will into history occurs by means of the *ḥukm*' (1998, p. 5). Hence, in Muslim jurisprudence 'the term *ḥukm* is employed to describe two moves simultaneously: it involves an empirical judgement, as well as a transcendental judgement' (*ibidem*, p. 7). Most importantly,

> the authority of the empirical dimension is dependent on its relationship with the transcendental and metaphysical *ḥukm*. If we do show some awareness of these two dimensions, we will begin to understand the complexity of the human-divine interaction in the process of discovering "God's rule" in Islamic law. The *ḥukm* proper is a transcendental norm, of which the empirical *ḥukm* is but a temporal manifestation. It is in such

scenario that God is the real *ḥākim* (transcendent monothete or sovereign ruler) and the real *shāri'* (Supreme Legislator).

(*ibidem*)

On the one hand, the sacred Law, *pre*-scribed in the revelation, appears to the Muslim jurist as a 'decision (*ḥukm*) of the Ruler (*ḥākim*), whose essential object (*maḥkūm bihi*) is the qualification of human actions according to God's will and the determination of their effects, the rights and obligations of human beings; the decision is addressed to the person, who is subject to the rule (*maḥkūm lahu, 'alayhi*)' (Milliot and Blanc, 2001, p. 171; my translation). On the other hand, the *de*-scribed law, in stating the truth of *Šarī'ah*, qualifies the moral performance of the ethical being in the life (*bíos*) of any Muslim believer. It is in this precise sense that '[h]umans can therefore not be adequately understood in their ethical dimension as already constituted beings "before the Law" who are then asked to find out by which means they will reply. Or rather, they can be understood in this way only because the law as a particular manifestation of the divine Word constitutes them *by way of word*' (Stelzer, 2008, p. 169).

In the understanding of *Šarī'ah*, *fiqh* practical wisdom moves from the roots (*uṣūl*) towards the branches (*furū'*) of substantive law, whose rules are located in the real life of the individual Muslim believer – never in an abstract generalisation, as in Western legal tradition. Proofs of the revelation detached from the reality of the creation are like a voice without a medium of transmission; human reality without the revelation is like a moral desert deprived of salvation. The real provides the setting for God's Guidance (*Šarī'ah*) about how to sort, filter, and interpret the proofs of the revelation, turning them into operative norms of human conduct. With this purpose, Muslim jurisprudence refers to the notion of *sabab* (the 'empirical circumstance' to whose existence or appearance the rules of Law are linked). *Sabab*, as the underlying 'reason' for human action (directly dependant on its 'divine cause,' *'illa*, in the revelation), relates in Islamic theology to the innate accessibility of human reason (*'aql*) to moral knowledge, discerning through Qur'ānic indicators (*adillah*) the status (*ḥukm*) of the action revealed by *Šarī'ah*.[24]

It is in the move from the transcendental to the empirical *ḥukm* that the materialisation of God's Law implies its contextualisation within the specific social reality by the Muslim jurist in order to *de*-scribe man's right (*ḥaqq*) as human law. Thus, in this sense, 'a rule (*ḥukm*) . . . denotes the dictum of the revelation *when* it is linked to the acts of those made responsible' (al-Ghazālī, see section 2.4.3, italics added). The point is remarked in contemporary scholarship also by Mohammad Hashim Kamali: '*ḥukm* is defined as a communication from the Lawgiver concerning the conduct of the *mukallaf* (legally competent person) and consisting of a demand (something obligatory [*wājib*] or prohibited [*ḥarām*]), an option (*takhyīr*), or an enactment (*waḍ'*)' (1993, p. 347). The centrality of the rule in Muslim jurisprudence is confirmed by a normative ethics that derives from the concept of *ḥukm* the taxonomy of the 'quintuple qualification' (*al-aḥkām al-khamsa*, lit. 'the five states,' *aḥkām*, pl. of *ḥukm*). In the framework of the ethical status of the action created by God, Muslim jurisprudence *collocates* any human act into one of the five status already established by God: (1) obligatory, duty: *wājib*, *farḍ*; (2) recommended: *sunna*, *mandūb*, *mustaḥabb*; (3) neutral, indifferent: *mubāḥ*; (4) reprehensible, disapproved: *makrūh*; (5) forbidden: *ḥarām* (whose opposite is *ḥalāl*, not forbidden) (Schacht, 1964, p. 121; in relation to the contract, see later section 3.3.2).[25] Therefore, the task of the Muslim jurist is not to qualify the action (its status is already established by God); the effort, *ijtihād*, of the jurist is to find out how the 'right,' *ḥaqq*, belongs to the 'real,' again, *ḥaqq*.

So, while the divine rule establishes the status of the human act, the rights, *ḥuqūq*, are the means thanks to which God *realises* (in the sense of 'making real') the rule, *ḥukm*, as empirically known by human agents. The term *ḥaqq* stems from the Arabic root *Ḥ-Q-Q*, whose primitive meaning was 'to carve' (on wood, metal, or stone), and later, 'to be real, true, legal, right, correct;' notably, the idea of carving brings to mind the divine Word carved into reality (Figure 2.1). '[A]lthough the primary meaning of *ḥaqq* is "established fact" or "reality" (*al mawjūd al thābit*), in the field of law its dominant meaning is "truth" or "that which corresponds to facts". Both meanings are equally prominent' (Kamali, 1993, p. 342).

> The primitive sense of *ḥaqq* is "established fact" (*al-thābit ḥaqīqat^{an}*), from which "reality", and the sense: "that corresponds to the facts". . . . "*Ḥaqq* . . . is one of the names of God . . . and it appears several times in the Qur'ān with this meaning. . . . But the usage of *ḥaqq* in the Qur'ān, in the Islamic traditions . . . and in the Arabic literature in general is not limited to the divine name; it can designate all the "reality", every "fact", all the "truth". . . . Another meaning of *ḥaqq* (pl. *ḥuquq*), deriving directly from the first sense, is "demand" or "right", as legal obligation . . . this usage of the term is already utterly developed in the Qur'ān. . . . To sum up, the meanings of the root *Ḥ-Q-Q*, from that of the "carved" statute, valid and permanent, have extended to the ethical concepts of legal and real and right and true, and developed till including the divine and spiritual reality.
>
> (MacDonald and Calverley, 1975)

It is by merging the *ḥukm* and the *ḥaqq* that *fiqh* practical wisdom *translates* the divine into the human. The legal question, which holds in itself a demand for action, determines a statement of the right (an *iuris-dictio*) by means of a verdict (*vere-dictum*) that echoes the *dictum* of the divine *Word* into the human *wor(l)d*. This interpretation of the couple *ḥukm-ḥaqq* confirms Clifford Geertz's translation of *ḥaqq* as 'right' and *ḥukm* as 'law, rule,' 'from a root relating to delivering a verdict, passing a sentence, inflicting a penalty, imposing a restraint, or issuing an order' within 'a vision of reality as being in its essence imperative, a structure not of objects but of wills' (1983, p. 187).

An article by Andrey Smirnov (1996), dealing with the cosmological background of Muslim jurisprudence, can help to further elaborate on the distinctive connotations of *fiqh* in comparison to Western jurisprudence.[26] Smirnov's analysis moves from the conception of truth in Islam, underlining how Truth, as the core of Muslim jurisprudence, 'though of supreme (divine) origin, is not at all unearthly . . . [as] it is *presented* to us' (Smirnov, 1996, p. 338; italics in the original text). 'The truth, established and secured by its certainty, makes no distinction between "momentary" and "eternal". The truth is valid not because it has ascended above the nonlasting; the truth is valid because it stands firmly *established* amid the flow of things nonlasting' (*ibidem*) as *pre*-scribed Law. There is no 'ideal' in such truth detached from the 'real,' as in the Western tradition of legal thought; the deontological is not remote from the ontological. On the contrary, coherently with the 'atomic theory of time developed in classical Islamic thought' (*ibidem*, p. 339; see also Böwering, 1997), the truth of Islam 'preserves its identity in any of the possible temporal transformations. To be true does not mean to be un-associated with time; to be true means to stay one and the same in the flow of time' (*ibidem*, p. 340). Far away from the *distance* between the ideal and the real of the Western philosophical tradition (with the logical implication that the ideal becomes a *utopia*, a *no-where*),[27] the truth of Islam is real 'not because it envelops time (and the temporal) but because it *precedes* . . . any given moment of time (and any given temporal thing)' (*ibidem*). Accordingly, its *pre*-scribed Law implies for the believer an *instance* of action (*ḥukm* as a 'demand'): something that is present to us *now-here*.

In brief, the *distance* of the (general) law from the (particular) fact which belongs to Western legal tradition is replaced by an *instance* of the (*pre*-scribed) Law, the *Word* into the *world* of human actions. Muslim jurisprudence echoes the former into the latter in a *iurisdictio* that does not aim at any 'representation' (with an inherent distance that separates the present from the absent: see Introduction) but, rather, at a '*re*-presentation' of God's Truth – in the sense of 'presenting it again (here-and-now)' in the flow of time, as in an echo of the revelation (section 2.4.5).

> When true in this way, the truth by no means has to be a general case for all the particulars that would fall under it and thus presuppose its authority. . . . [In Islam] the law is not an abstract order (of things or ideas) that claims the validity of truth and has a general character . . . the law is a line drawn and fixed, a set of exact requirements, an exemplar. Such is the law as presented by the *shari'a* and the *sunna* – a line of behavior, an everlasting established specimen. . . . The main feature of these laws, as formulated by medieval [Muslim] thinkers, appears to be their non-abstract character.
>
> (Smirnov, 1996, pp. 340–341)

Empirical rules (*aḥkām*) coexist one next to the other not because particulars of a general but because derived from the same transcendental rule (*ḥukm*). In

Islamic normativity, it is the *ḥukm* as 'rule in the instant/in the instance' that makes the right (*ḥaqq*) 'real' (again, *ḥaqq*). While God creates by locating each event as single occurrences co-existent in space, human agency in time determines an *instance* of action (a 'request' of adherence to *dīn* by submitting to God's *ḥukm*; on the issue of the nature of moral action in relation to time, see Farahat, 2022) to which the justice of the *ḥaqq* intrinsically belongs.

Three corollaries can be drawn from the previous remarks, with additional thoughts about the *non-identity* of *fiqh* in comparison with Western law-religion.

First, a fundamental coherence subsists within *fiqh* 'incoherence' when the Western pair of the general/particular is removed.[28] In Muslim jurisprudence, 'legal unity' does not stand in an 'ideal,' but in the 'preceding fixity' that makes it possible to move from the *uṣūl* to the *furūʿ*. In the link between the secured truth and its interpretation, the 'branch' concept does not imply a necessity of non-contradiction with other 'branches' for an empirical rule to be valid.[29] As a result, differences and contradictions belong to the very core of Islamic legal theory, grounded on the diversity of doctrines (*ikhtilāf*). 'A tree, whose network of branches and twigs stems from the same trunk and roots; a sea, formed by the merging waters of different rivers; a variety of threads woven into a single garment; even the interlaced holes of a fishing net: these are some the metaphors used by Muslim authors' (Coulson, 1964, p. 86) to explain this phenomenon. 'The various schools of law [*madhāhib*], in which such diversity of doctrine was crystallised, are seen as different but inseparable aspects of the same unity' (*ibidem*).

The second corollary recalls the etymology of *ḥaqq* as 'right,' 'just,' 'real,' and 'true.' The definition of *fiqh* proposed earlier as a 'practical wisdom in legal questions whose rationale lies in echoing God's revelation into person's rights' assumes further clarity when the *ḥaqq* is conceived as 'expressing the unity of the concepts of *truth*, *right* and *obligation*' (Smirnov, 1996, p. 344) in

> both the reality of a thing's existence and the validity of its cognition. The true, the due, the really existent, and the really recognized serve as the foundation for each other and are mutually transformable: each presupposes the rest and brings with itself a part of the sense of others . . . [so that to provide the *ḥaqq* in Islam] is not only and not just an act of moral righteousness; it is first and foremost done to secure the ontological *stability* of the thing in question, that is to say, its being truly established in the flow of change.
>
> (*ibidem*, pp. 344–345)

Thirdly, all this can also shed further light on Calder's definition of *fiqh* as 'a conceptual replica of social life' (1996, p. 981), from which our journey started. The nature of *fiqh* is not that of an ideal body of legal unity but of a ramified echo; a polyphony, where contradictions enjoy mutual legitimacy, since they are validly derived from the preceding unity of the divine Word

(Cattelan, 2016). The Western *distance* ideal-real is replaced in Islamic law-religion by an *instance* of action that *presents again* the *Word* in the *world*. 'Justice is not to be reached as an *ideal* outcome of specific and exceptional efforts. Justice is a function of the ontological organization of the thing' (Smirnov, 1996, p. 346) – a function that belongs, in the end, to a 'real of prophet not philosophers' (Geertz, 1983, p. 188).

2.4.5. Echoing the revelation in an acoustic space: a sacred law without corpus

Fiqh has been defined in the previous pages in terms of a practical wisdom echoing God's revelation within person's rights. Our discussion has focused on the *ḥukm* as the *dictum* of the revelation when it is linked to the acts of those made responsible. Subsequently, it is by attributing the 'right,' 'just,' 'true,' 'real' (*ḥaqq*) to persons that the science of *fiqh* fulfils its function as a normative discipline in the reality of social life. In this sense, Muslim normativity has never been purely speculative or theoretical; rather, by moving from the 'roots' to the 'branches' of God's Will, it appears 'factual' by anchoring rules to a 'real of prophets not philosophers' (Geertz). It is for this specific reason that, adhering to the specificity and casuistry of real life, *fiqh* becomes 'a conceptual replica of social life' (Calder) which is deprived of any abstract idealism; in brief, the sacred Law, the Wor(l)d, is present *now* and *here* in each *instant* of Muslim life (*bíos*).

At this point, recalling the metaphor of the desert to which I referred in Chapter 1 (see section 1.3.3) may help to reach some conclusive remarks. In Islam, as Louis Milliot has pointed out,

> [t]he Sharīʿa is the Path, the way to be followed, daily concern of the inhabitant of the desert, here symbol of the believer's anxiety. The same idea can be found in the term Sunna, the way followed by the Prophet, that is to say, Imitation of God's Envoy; and in the term madhhab that we imperfectly translate as "rite" or "school" and that is, in reality, the "direction" to take, indicated by the Masters. As far as fiqh is concerned, it is the discernment – understanding, explanation and interpretation – of the Sharī'a, the revealed Law.
>
> (1952, p. 670; my translation)

The *Šarīʿah* is the Route that provides salvation to the traveller lost in the desert; a place where *no visual* references are available. It is in the moral vacuum symbolised by this ethical desert (a state of ignorance, *jāhiliyya*, of the 'real' good, where man is fated to ruin: see Izutsu, 1966) that God's Mercy intervenes by interrupting the silence and locating the believer in the *acoustic space* of the *Word*. The revelation provides the Right Path for the traveller in search for salvation; it is the Way, *Šarīʿah*, that replaces the *no-where* of the desert (the absence of a visual space made of 'distance') with the *now-here* of present running water (which then calls for an 'instance' of action). Thus, the *Šarī'ah*, the Way to the water, qualifies the actions of a Muslim life as Islamic *bíos* (*dīn*), outside of which there is no possible salvation. As God's omnipotence makes any instant complete in itself, *fiqh* locates human responsibility in the precise life-situation of Muslim reality as understanding, explanation, and interpretation of *Šarī'ah*. It translates God's *pre*-scription into the real, true, and just of man/woman's right (*ḥaqq*), making the believer responsible for his/her actions by a process of *de*-scription of the revelation, within an *iuridictio* that states the truth, *vere-dictum*, of the Message (section 2.4.3). By conceiving the right as rule-in-the-real, 'if on the one hand the *pre*-scription (*ḥukm*) of the Law is discovered through the revealed juridical proofs (*uṣūl*), on the other the jurist has to justify the right (*ḥaqq*) through a verdict *de*-scribing the fact in the *furū'*, for the . . . law to be validly stated (*found*) for the given situation' (Cattelan, 2016, p. 368). In the process of justification of the rule-in-the-real as linked to the right, the contingency of the empirical rule is co-determined by the everlasting certainty of the transcendental rule '[u]nder a criterion on probability . . . [where] a plurality of norms co-exist as possible interpretations of God's will, leading to the ramification of rules in the *furū'*' (*ibidem*, p. 375). This explains why, as remarked by Wael Hallaq, 'stating the law' as a system of general and abstract norms, according to the Western model of codification (Chapter 4, Section 4.3), has *no* space in the Islamic legal tradition.

> Shari'a's law was not an abstraction, nor did it apply equally to "all," for individuals were not seen as indistinguishable members of a generic species, standing in perfect parity before a blind lady of justice. Each individual and circumstance was deemed unique, requiring *ijtihad* that was context-specific. . . . [T]he *law* was an ijtihadic process, a continuously renewed exercise of interpretating. It was an effort at mustering principles as located in specific life-situations, requiring the legists to do what was right at a particular moment of human existence . . . to resolve a situation in due consideration of the unique facts involved therein. As a fully realizable and realized worldly experience, Islamic law was not fully revealed unto society until the principles meshed with social reality and until the interaction of countless social, moral, material and other types of human relations involved in a particular case was made to come full circle. . . . To know what Islamic law was, therefore, is to know how actual Muslim societies of the past *lived* it.
>
> (Hallaq, 2009, pp. 166–167)

Calder's description of Islamic law as 'a conceptual replica of social life' matches Hallaq's view, which also 'explains why Islamic law never accepted the notion of blind justice, for it allowed the rich and the powerful to stand on a par with the poor and the weak' (*ibidem*, p. 166); correspondingly, as we noted in the Introduction, the Western allegory of Lady *Iustitia* is absent in the Islamic legal tradition. At the same time, this sheds light over the particularistic approach of the *furūʿ*, with a casuistry which 'is part of doctrine, not an exterior element that explains it' (Johansen, 1995, p. 156). In the same way in which this casuistry looks like an improper legal *corpus* from a Western perspective (the 'body' of the *Arab Girl*, metaphor of the Orientalistic bias of Western comparatists: Figure 0.1), a sense of confusion may be felt by the Western traveller with regard to the admissibility by Muslim jurists of disagreement (*ikhtilāf*) and contradictions as constitutive elements of their elaboration. In fact, the *divergence* of verdicts (the *de*-scribed law of *furūʿ*), as we have seen, does not undermine at all (rather, it nourishes in 'branches') their shared *convergence* to the Truth (the *pre*-scribed Law of *uṣūl*). It is in this conceptual framework that *fiqh* practical wisdom echoes God's revelation: as the echo can be *heard* differently from different amplifying surfaces, so, by *listening* carefully, all Islamic law derives from a unique original source, the *Word* of the revelation. Echoing

> God's will while amplifying it, a "centripetal fugue", a "polyphony compressed" . . . describes the history of *fiqh* . . . if *fiqh*-judgement in the fact/law interplay implies a ramified casuistry, a polyphony (*furūʿ*) of legal opinions, it is the tradition of *fiqh*-literature that guarantees its *epistemic unity*, the centripetal nature of *fiqh*-knowledge in the narrative function . . . resulting from the record of verdicts. . . . [Hence] the tradition defines the constant continuity, the echoing, of the explanatory function of *fiqh* in "actualizing" (by amplification) God's message in the everyday life of the Muslim community and by answering practical problems that emerge from social differentiation.
>
> (Cattelan, 2016, p. 383)

Therefore, in Islam, not only is *fiqh* 'a conceptual replica of social life' (Calder), but its practical wisdom describes human nature as agency of the divine *Word*, where individuals as ethical beings can be 'understood only because the law as a particular manifestation of the divine Word constitutes them *by way of word*' (Stelzer, 2008, p. 169). Correspondingly, the guidance offered by *fiqh* scholars is also the channel through which, in the ramification of *furūʿ*,

> the mundane, earth-hugging realities, including new factual developments, were formally noticed by and reflected upon by qualified scholarly minds, leading to analogical extensions of the body of legal knowledge. In a dialectical manner, locally generated questions were related to locally interpreted jurisprudence. Muftis [i.e., *fiqh* scholars] were the creative mediators of the ideal and the real of the shariʿa.
>
> (Messick, 1993, p. 151)

Within the nature of *fiqh* as *iurisprudentia by way of word*, McLuhan's paradigm of the acoustic space (section 1.3.3) can finally illuminate **(a)** why contradictions do not affect the *epistemic unity* of *fiqh*-tradition; and **(b)** why this tradition (outside the visual space of Western law) has never enjoyed the quality of a *corpus iuris.*

(a) In section 1.3.2, we noticed how normative pluralism belongs to 'the mutually constitutive relationship between Islam and Muslims: . . . how Islam makes Muslims as Muslims make Islam' (Ahmed, 2016, p. 543). The unity of pluralities in Islamic law precisely characterises 'a human and historical phenomenon . . . constituted, not merely by immense variety and diversity, but by the prodigious presence of outright contradiction' (*ibidem*, p. 542). Casuistry and contradictions do not represent a limit; rather, they are an inherent part of a juristic rationality that necessarily grows 'not by elimination of difference but by inclusion of difference,' in a 'logic of difference and contradiction [that is] . . . coherent with and internal to Islam' (*ibidem*). The valid co-existence of contradictions in a ramified knowledge (*furūʿ*) matches the pair contingency-certainty, within an epistemic unity grounded on a plural *iurisdictio* that *de*-scribes the *pre*-scribed Law by verdicts. It is the *dictum* of the revelation (God as the only *Word*-giver) that implies the epistemological unity (certainty) of *fiqh*, just as the different waves of sounds coming from the same source define an echo in human space; (human) *contra-dicere* does not alter the unity of the (divine) *dictum*. The coherence of *fiqh*-knowledge belongs to an *acoustic cognitive space* that, as noted by McLuhan, grows without separations and boundaries (precisely as a route that cannot be traced with margins in the desert). As the *Word* provides orientation to the stranded traveller in the desert, so it shapes an acoustic space, a *Wor(l)d* of salvation, the Path of *Šarīʿah*, whose 'right' human intellect is asked to discern. The co-existence of concordant and discordant rules, in the end, constitutes the distinctive nature of an acoustic *iurisdictio* that intrinsically belongs to the contingency of Islamic law as the outcome of the elaboration of Muslim jurisprudence.

(b) In section 1.3.3, this book has already remarked how *ius-dicere*, 'to say the law,' may well substitute the allegory of the *corpus iuris* of the Western legal tradition to describe the law of Islam. Both the nature of the Qur'ān as 'recitation' as well as the oral-aural chain (*isnād*) of transmission of the *aḥādīth* in the *Sunnah* (section 2.4.2) converge in this allegorical shift. In this framework, not only is it true that ' "a valid and sensible corpus of laws" was not what Muslim jurists had in mind' (Calder, 1996, p. 979) but *sic et simpliciter* a *corpus iuris* could not exist within the rationales of *fiqh*-tradition. Since the Islamic pair law-religion belongs to an acoustic rather than visual space, the *non-identity* of *fiqh* is grounded on echoing the revelation within a legal rationality that has nothing to do with the scopic regimes of Western modernity (Jay, 1988). If '[t]he rational man in our Western culture is a visual man' (McLuhan and Fiore, 1967, p. 45) and the 'visual space is uniform, continuous, and connected' (*ibidem*), in the desert (a space with no centre and no margin), the believer is asked only to rely on the Word of the Revelation. The individual is asked to (choose to) *hear* (the only option for salvation) and then to *listen to* (hence, to discern carefully) the Word in a potentially indefinite echo through the transmission of the tradition. It is this echoing, with no boundaries and no centre, its own discontinuity, replication, and non-linearity (McLuhan), that defines a unity made of differences and contradictions (Ahmed), where the rationale of *fiqh* is no longer grounded in framing a visual body of law (as in the *Corpus Iuris Civilis*) but in echoing the Word of the Law. Human intellect does not choose how to frame the law; it locates the Law in the status that is already established by God. Significantly, the geometrical visual space depending on the eye of the beholder (hence, on his/her *choice* of 'looking at' as an act of will) is replaced in this way by the 'ear of the believer,' who 'listens to' the revelation as an act of intellect, thanks to the innate accessibility of human reason (*'aql*) to moral knowledge. Correspondingly, the utopia (*no-where*) of the ideal law (Lady *Iustitia*) of Western tradition is substituted by the *now-here* of God's creation in the non-ideal, non-abstract, non-speculative nature of *fiqh* as conceptual replica of social life. An *instance* (rather than a distance) of action nourishes Islamic law, whose right (*ḥaqq*) is true and just to the extent to which it corresponds to a rule(*ḥukm*)-in-the-real. Above all, moving from the 'eye of the beholder' to the 'ear of the listener' implies a radical change in what law is in the context of *fiqh*: a *surrender* of the centrality of man's freedom in favour of the *dictum* of the revelation – an element that, as we will see in Chapter 3, has fundamental implications for the nature of the Islamic contract.

In summary, far removed from Western law-religion, *fiqh* normativity arises from a practical wisdom regarding legal questions whose rationale is not to affirm the centrality of the human being. Rather, *fiqh* entails a *surrender* (Islam) to God, an *absence* of human centrality, where, by echoing the revelation in the reality of social life, no *corpus iuris* can delimit the sacred Law of Muslim *bíos*.

2.5. The bridge of Babel: from the negation of *fiqh* (2E) to the comparison of the *'aqd*

By dealing with the issue of translating the revelation of Islam, this chapter has considered how the construction of its space must move from the non-identity of law-religion.

As the concept of *absence* lies at the core of Bhaskar's *Dialectic* (1993), so the deep sense of the myth of Babel is grounded in the absence of a universal language for all human beings. Law itself exists only in the form of specific laws, as religion exists only in the form of specific religions. Far from any assumption of monovalence, it is from a paradigm of non-identity that 'the positive [for us, the *presence* of Western law-religion as hermeneutical background] [can appear] as a tiny . . . ripple on the surface of a sea of negativity'

(Bhaskar, 1993, p. 5; see section 2.3 in this chapter). From the absence of Western law-religion a move for emancipation from the Occident can be fostered in a Middle-Earth of comparative research, while the Tower of Babel still stands at the very centre of the city of the *ʿaqd* as allegorical destination of our journey. This emancipation relates to the primacy of non-identity (the first moment, 1M, of Bhaskar's dialectic), which liberates the interpreter from

> an overall vision of the ways in which human being in western societies is marked by a sense of what is lacking – or, of course, absent. At its heart, Bhaskar's dialectic . . . involves a vision of a world in which dominant social and economic power suppresses human possibilities, and the resulting lack is then repressed in its philosophy. *Dialectic* is at once a reflection on the philosophical effects of such power relations and a pointer to how things could begin to be different. Absence is a concept that denotes both a geo-historical and a philosophical problem.
>
> (Norrie, 2009, pp. 22–23)

In the Introduction to this book, Orientalism was presented as a signifying practice related to a dominant vision of a world: the improper body of the *Arab Girl*, the decadent setting of its urban space, and the corrupted destiny of her *corpus* (metaphor of Islamic law – *rectius*, of its Orientalistic representation) stemming from the *positum* of Western *presence*.

Challenging this *positum*, this chapter has concentrated on the *absence* of Western religion (replaced by *dīn* as Islamic *bíos*: section 2.3) and law (substituted by the *iurisdictio* of *fiqh*: section 2.4) in the Muslim world. It is through the *negation* (2E in Bhaskar's dialectic) of Islamic law-religion and its non-identity with the West (a 'real' *absence* opening a 'sea of meaning' of which the Western positive is a tiny ripple on the surface) that *fiqh* normative pluralism can be thought of as an echo of the *Word* into the *world* in the translation of the revelation. But how does the non-identity of *fiqh-dīn* as *absence* of Western law-religion affect legal comparison? Indeed,

> jurists adopt different methods to elaborate what they call "law," and approach differently the question of what is "lawful." It is not unusual for the Western orientalists, as well as jurists engaged in comparative studies, to mention the "total absence" of developed theory in *fiqh*. This statement overlooks the fact that this theory, as it was developed by Western law, simply could not exist in *fiqh*. What so often appears to the Western mind as an involvement in concrete and minor details was only a painstaking elaboration of quite another type of legal theory.
>
> (Smirnov, 1996, p. 343)

The total absence of a Western theory of law explains how its rationales make *no sense* for the tradition of *fiqh*. What may look contradictory to Western eyes becomes coherent in Islam as the fundamental rationale for a collective *iurisdictio* echoing the revelation. It is, in fact, the logical primacy of *absence* (the One Ring of non-identity) that can lead us to the second edge (2E) of *negativity* (*fiqh-dīn* as negating Western law-religion). '[T]he hiatus, the margin, the void, the hidden, the empty, the anterior, the exterior, the excluded, the omitted, the forgotten and the feared' (Bhaskar, 1993, p. 238) *translate* the intelligibility of an *absence* of Western visual coherence, completeness, and non-contradiction (the ideal *corpus iuris*) into the pair *fiqh-dīn*, whose jurisprudence relies upon incompleteness, contradictions, plurality, and inclusion of differences; in summary, upon the *non-corpus* of an acoustic space. Thus, the incoherence of *fiqh iurisprudentia* acquires its *own* coherence, as '[i]deas of absence, negation and negativity, when viewed in this light, are much more present in our practical and philosophical views of thinking than we might otherwise think' (Norrie, 2009, p. 24). The *inclusion* of the *non-being* of Islam replaces its *exclusion* by Western Orientalism by recognising *negativity* as

> the motive of all dialectics. . . . It is the single most important category, more general than negation because it [includes] the absent without a present or positive; it connotes more directly the negating process whereas negation suggests merely the outcome or result. Negativity embraces the *dual* sense of the (evaluatively neutral) *absence* and the (pejorative) *ill*, united in dialectical critical realist explanatory critique, the aim of which is precisely to *absent ills*.
>
> (Bhaskar, 1993, p. 238)

This *absenting* the *ills* of Orientalism provides the background for the *negativity* of the *'aqd* – to wit, for the 'total absence of Western contract law' in the Islamic legal tradition. Indeed, it is from the etymology of 'absence' – which 'derives from the Latin "to be" (*esse*) and "away from" (*ab*) – "away from being" or "being away from"' (Norrie, 2009, p. 24) – that the 'real non-being' of the '*aqd* can be disclosed by means of *translation*. Above all, absence allows for a process of *duality* (embedded in negativity) from which the practice of comparison can be nurtured: precisely what we will do in Chapter 3 regarding the *'aqd*.

If the original 1M unifies non-identity and alterity, the 2E of negativity can enhance the causality of co-determined co-constitution in the process of comparison (with the 'being' and the 'non-being' put in their *becoming*). Comparison itself, when located in human history, translates the *totality* of the *'aqd* as third level (3L; here, Chapter 3) of analysis into the *transformative praxis* of the contract as fourth dimension (4D; Chapter 4) of dialectical engagement. Negativity in terms of a process rather than a product also allows the 'shaped possibility of becoming' (Bhaskar, 1993, p. 142), where '[t]he past shapes the present and therefore shapes, without determining, possible futures' (Norrie, 2009, p. 34), while it interconnects levels of ontology, epistemology, and moral praxis (*ibidem*, pp. 27–28). Put 'another way around, the pursuit of a world with an enhanced sense of freedom requires praxis, understanding and the bringing about of change' (*ibidem*, p. 28).[30] By moving from Western contract law to the *'aqd* in Muslim *fiqh*, the process of negativity can be related to the becoming of human praxis precisely by means of the comparison of alternative legal traditions, in the search for an enhanced freedom of the Orient from the Occident (see Conclusions).

Hence, comparing the Western and Islamic traditions from a dialectical perspective allows us to study the *'aqd* in a mutual non-identity. When *negation/negativity* (2E) is applied to Islam in relation to the West, it generates a dialectics of 'process, transition, frontier and node [no longer just a 'stage' for an 'imaginative geography' that replicates the Occident: see Introduction], but also generally of opposition including reversal' (Bhaskar, 1993, p. 392; quoted in Norrie, 2009, p. 29). More specifically, 2E (*fiqh*) negativity in the form of a legal tradition in comparison with the West does three things: first, it 'emphasises the tri-unity of causality, space and time in tensed rhythmic spatialising process;' second, it thematises 'the presence of the past;' and third, it asserts the importance of its 'existentially constitutive process' (*ibidem*).

> "[T]here is a sense in which we, and entities generally, may be said to contain possible futures within us, and these may be vital to our being" (DPF: 143). But these possible futures "are so qua product-in-process, that is as possibilities existentially constituted by their geo-histories" (ibid.). Therefore, there is a sense "in which the most interesting case of the present as a future is mediated by, or even *dependent* upon the presence of the past" (ibid.). More generally, the future is always prefigurated in human action, always present to us, since intentional agency is necessarily oriented to the future, which is "the intentional object of every act" (DPF: 144).
>
> (Norrie, 2009, p. 34)

Accordingly, the *negativity* of 'non-being has ontological *priority* over being' (Bhaskar, 1993, p. 39), since 'one cannot grasp the nature of any entity without seeing what it is not, as well as what it is' (Norrie, 2009, p. 35). Looking at the Orient from the Occident, the *negation/negativity* of the Islamic legal tradition takes priority over the Western one. *Absence* comes prior to *presence*; the Occident of Western contract law cannot be understood without the Orient of the *'aqd*, and vice-versa, as they are mutually entailed. More precisely, the transformative negation (a real absenting as *process*) relies on a 'constellation of possibilities' in Bhaskar's account of *totality* as a third level (3L) of dialectic – where absence and presence interact (in this book, Islamic and Western contract law in their comparative investigation).

> By this, Bhaskar means a sense of being as the totalised whole of being and non-being in their constellational relation. The priority of absence stems from the fact that in a dynamic world, there is always more to come than what presently exists, and, given that what is presently absent shapes

> what is to come, this gives it priority. What is present to us may look compelling, but its presence as well as its future is powerfully shaped by what it lacks. Absence always exercises its hidden power through shaping what is, and making it move on, become what it is not. It is observed in absenting process (becoming), but also in existing product (being), and this conditions, shapes and determines how absenting occurs. This gives us the dialectical realist formula of the absenting of absence and gives absence its asymmetric priority over presence.
>
> (Norrie, 2009, p. 38)

By adhering to Bhaskar's dialectics, Chapter 3 will outline the *ʿaqd* in its multiple pluralities (Ahmed) – a ***totality*** not to be 'observed,' but rather, to be 'listened to' (the acoustic space of Islam: McLuhan) in a dialectical relation with the Western *corpus* of contract law. The dual totality of Western and Islamic contract law will co-exist in the Middle-Earth of the law-religion comparison, as if they were *The Two Towers* of *The Lord of the Rings*, Barad-dûr and Orthanc. They appear as two distinct normative discourses with their own respective *nomos*, whose singular existence can make sense only in a dialectical relation. To 'hear' the unity-of-diversities that defines 'how Islam makes Muslims as Muslims make Islam' (Ahmed, 2016, p. 543), Chapter 3 will engage with *fiqh* normative pluralism in the construction of the *ʿaqd*, in order to examine later, in Chapter 4, its *transformative praxis* in the Muslim world (the fourth dimension, 4D, of Bhaskar's dialectic).

Of course, to explore the place of the *ʿaqd* in the space of Islam, we will 'need a map, one that registers the many features of the landscape: contours, boundaries, and conceptual marshy areas' (Reynolds, 2016, p. 3). More precisely, we are going to craft the place of the *ʿaqd* (section 3.1) to map its ***absent*** body through the 'voices' of the Islamic legal tradition as transmitted in the *madhāhib*, the schools of *fiqh* jurisprudence. In this regard, if the blessing of Babel relates to the fact that '[t]ranslation builds bridges between languages' (Duncan, Harrison *et al.*, 2019, p. 7), enabling people to understand each other, our entering the city of the *ʿaqd* may be rendered by a significant image of Walter Benjamin's regarding the construction of a vessel.

> Fragments of a vessel that are to be glued together must match one another in the smallest details, although they need not be like one another. In the same way a translation, instead of imitating the sense of the original, must lovingly and in detail incorporate the original's way of meaning, thus making both the original and the translation recognizable as fragments of a greater language, just as fragments are part of a vessel.
>
> (Benjamin, 1996, p. 260)

From the myth of Oedipus and the Sphinx (Introduction) to the biblical story of the Tower of Babel, acting as dragomans whose ship has been shaped in the format of the One Ring, as already announced at the end of Chapter 1, our destination will no longer be a place but a new way of listening to the *'aqd* in the echo of the revelation.[31]

Notes

1 *Bāḇel* in Hebrew stands for the Akkadian *Babilu* and the Greek Babylon, the cosmopolitan capital of the ancient Sumer people (the Bible refers to the 'land of Shinar,' Genesis 11:2), imagined by the contemporary as ruled by a confusion of languages. Not by chance, the Hebrew name *Bāḇel* was close to the word *bālal*, which meant 'to confuse, confound.'

2 This is the well-known thesis by Joseph Schacht (please refer to Chapter 1), based on the assumption that '[a]t the very time that Islamic law came into existence, its perpetual problem, that of the contrast between theory and practice, was already posed' (1964, p. 209). Consequently, the 'secular law' of Islam coincided for him with the 'customary commercial law which developed, beside the ideal law of strict theory, in the Islamic countries in the Middle Ages' (*ibidem*, p. 210). The *ḥiyal* ('legal stratagems') become, in Schacht's view, the core evidence of the contrast theory/practice; for a critique of this interpretation, see section 4.2.3.

3 I wish to thank my friend, Dr Maria Luisa Langella, for mentioning to me the role of dragomans in Orient-Occident relations and the origin of the word 'dragoman' from *tarjama*.

4 The word 'paradigm' (from the Greek *paradeikunai*, 'show side by side') entails an idea of understanding that reflects the visual rationality of the West: section 1.3.3.

5 He went on to give even more detail:

> It has one horn in the middle of the forehead very thick and large and black. . . . It is very ugly beast to see and unclean. And they are not so as we here say and describe, who say that it lets itself be caught in the lap by a virgin girl: but I tell you that it is quite the contrary of that which we believe that it was (Polo, *The Description of the World* . . .).
>
> (quoted by Eco, 1999, pp. 57–58)

6

> On the average about fifty centimeters long and roughly two kilos in weight, its flat body is covered with a dark-brown coat; it has no neck and a tail like a beaver's; it has a duck's beak, bluish on top and pink or variegated beneath; it has no outer ears, and the four feet have five webbed toes, but with claws; it stays underwater (and eats there) enough to be considered a fish or an amphibian. The female lays eggs but 'breast-feeds' her young, even though no nipples can be seen (the male's testicles cannot be seen either, as they are internal).
>
> (Eco, 1999, p. 58)

7 One should note, again, how the use of terms like 'paradigm' (here, endnote 4), 'framework,' 'observe,' 'to see' confirms the scopic regime of modernity (Jay, 1988) of Western visual rationality (section 1.3.3) and affects *our* way of thinking of the 'law' and the 'real' – a point to which we will return in dealing with the nature of *fiqh* (see later section 2.4).

8 Schacht's conception itself largely draws on Max Weber's definition of *fiqh* as a sacred law, a legal system characterised by the lack of practical outcomes, with 'the predilection for the construction of a purely theoretical casuistry' (Weber, 1922, p. 458).

9 Referring to a fragment by Walter Benjamin, 'Kapitalismus als Religion' (1921; unpublished in Benjamin's lifetime), Agamben notes that also

> capitalism, in pushing to the extreme a tendency already present in Christianity, generalizes in every domain the structure of separation that defines religion.

> Where sacrifice once marked the passage from the profane to the sacred and from the sacred to the profane, there is now a single, multiform, ceaseless process of separation that assails every thing, every place, every human activity in order to divide it from itself. . . . [C]apitalist religion realizes the pure form of separation . . . an absolute profanation.
>
> (Agamben, 2007, p. 81)

10 Asad (1993) discusses the genealogy of religion as an anthropological category using as his starting point (at pp. 29–30) Geertz's definition of religion as

> (1) a system of symbols which act to (2) establish powerful, pervasive, and long-lasting moods and motivations in men by (3) formulating conceptions of a general order of existence and (4) clothing these conceptions with such an aura of factuality that (5) the moods and motivations seem uniquely realistic.
>
> (Geertz, 1973, p. 90)

In *Formations of the Secular* (2003), Asad investigates 'the connection between "the secular" as an epistemic category and "secularism" as a political doctrine' (p. 1) in the rise of modernity in Christianity; the political evolution of the nation-state; its impact in the construction of Muslims as a religious minority in Europe; as well as the colonial background of secularism or its universal humanism (see p. 22) to contextualise the 'secular' in Islam.

11

> The modern discourse on religion and religions was from the very beginning – that is to say, inherently, if also ironically – a discourse of secularization; at the same time, it was clearly a discourse of othering. My suspicion, naturally, is that some deep symmetry and affinity obtain between these two wings of the religion discourse; that they cojointly enable this discourse to do the vital work of churning the stuff of Europe's ever-expanding epistemic domain, and of forging from the ferment an enormous apparition: the essential identity of the West.
>
> (Masuzawa, 2005, p. 20)

12 Following Gaius Trebatius Testa, a thing was sacred because of its '*belonging* to the gods,' *quidquid deorum habetur*, and not because of its '*being* of the gods,' *quidquid deorum est.*

13 Still today, the etymology of religion is under debate. Agamben's position traces back to Cicero, while the etymology from *re*-('again') *ligare* ('to bind') goes back to St. Augustine, who followed the interpretation by Lactantius in his *Institutiones Divinae.*

14 I would like to thank Dr Doralice Fabiano for clarifying to me the distinction between *sacrum* and *religiosus* in the anthropology of ancient Rome.

15 I.e. the life 'in the nature of things' that belongs to the universality of living entities (animals, men and also gods).

16 Narrated by 'Umar ibn al-Khaṭṭāb, the second Caliph, as reported by *Saḥiḥ Muslim* and *al-Bukhārī* and inserted in the famous compilation of an-Nawawī's *Forty Ḥadīths.*

17 I refer here to the translation of the *ḥadīth* as reported by Moad (2007, pp. 136–137), with some minimal variations regarding the transliteration of Arabic words.

18

> The Arabic terms most commonly used in Islamic literature to characterize the Creator-creature relationship are *rabb* and '*abd*, 'Lord' and 'slave'. The word 'Lord' connotes not only sovereignty but also proprietorship. The Creator is the original owner of all that he creates; he possesses full property rights over his creatures. For this reason, 'slave' best conveys the true meaning of '*abd*, notwithstanding the currently widespread preference for rendering less jarring

> to modern ears. A slave is one owned by another, and that is exactly what man is before God. God's slaves in fact have no original rights whatsoever, no rights apart from those granted by God, who alone possesses original rights.
>
> (Weiss, 2006, p. 24)

19 Similar texts in Q. 3:47, 59; 6:73; 16:40; 36:82; 40:68. There are eight names for God, among the canonical 99, which direct our attention to Allah as the source of all that is: *al-Badī'* (Absolute Cause), *al-Bāri'* (Producer), *al-Khāliq* (Creator), *al-Mubdi'* (Beginner), *al-Muqtadir* (All-Determiner), *al-Muṣawwir* (Fashioner), *al-Qādir* (All-Powerful), and *al-Qahhār* (Dominator), each with various connotations of creating (Burrell, 2008, p. 141).

20 This is precisely the way in which McLuhan describes the acoustic space: a world of 'simultaneous happening,' where '"[t]ime" has ceased, "space" has vanished' (McLuhan and Fiore, 1967, p. 63; see also section 1.3.3).

21 A similar definition is given by Johansen: '*[f]iqh* is a system of rules and methods whose authors consider it to be the normative interpretation of the revelation, the application of its principles and commands to the field of human acts' (1999, p. 1).

22 On the point of the discovery of the transcendental Law in *fiqh*, Bernard Weiss remarks how

> a fundamental principle of Islamic jurisprudence that the law properly so called – that is to say, the Sharīʿah – exists independently of all human deliberation, whether legislative or judicial. . . . The law, is, for the Muslim jurist, 'out there' before human beings even exist . . . for the real 'locus' of the law is within God, and God is beyond time and space. Islamic theology, which provides the philosophical underpinnings for Islamic jurisprudence, subsumes the law under the divine attribute of speech.
>
> (Weiss, 1990, p. 53)

For this reason, the Law is 'something to be discovered, not created or developed, by human agents' (*ibidem*, p. 61).

23 With regard to the probative value of the revelation,

> [f]rom the perspective of the Muslim jurist, legal theory can be regarded as a 'science of proofs,' leading to standards that regulate human actions. These standards derive primarily from a discovery, through a defined set of sources and techniques, of the *aḥkām*, the qualification of actions or, more specifically, God's determination of the moral value of individual acts.
>
> (Wakin, 1990, p. 33)

24 Notably, the notions of *ʿilla* and *sabab* (as theological concepts) will reappear in Chapter 4 (specifically, section 4.3.2) in examining how the encounter of *fiqh* with Western law has radically transformed their meaning in the process of codification in Muslim countries.

25

> Ethics occurs in Islamic theology first and foremost as a matter of the assessment or the evaluation of acts . . . this differs from Western philosophical thought where the ethical occurs first of all in regard to the constitution of an act. Accordingly, in Islamic moral thought 'ethical' refers to a knowledge which allows us to locate a particular act on a predefined scale of categories, while 'ethics' denotes the science which defines the means for such a localisation.
>
> (Stelzer, 2008, p. 165)

26 In introducing his article, Smirnov refers explicitly to the need for the social researcher to care about the incidence that 'cognitive procedures elaborated by this or that tradition' can have on the apprehension of the 'fundamentals' of justice

(1996, p. 337). Not only does this advice recall Ainsworth's metaphor of the 'fish always in the sea' (section 2.1) but also the reflections that have been advanced here, in the Introduction, regarding the role of representations as signifying practices.

27 The term 'utopia' was coined by Thomas More in 1516 from the Greek *ū*, 'no', *tópos*, 'place.'

28 In this precise sense, Shahab Ahmed (as we have seen in section 1.3.2) correctly praises divergence and contradiction as fundamental expressions of Islamic legal rationality.

29

> Within the framework . . . we find it absolutely natural and logically valid . . . that the judge is allowed to choose the most 'suitable' norm for the given case from a number of contradictory norms of one *madhhab* or between different *madhhabs*. Islamic thought grows diverse and contradictory 'branches' simultaneously from the same 'root,' and their incompatibility does not interfere with their overall unity and is not regarded as a drawback or as something abnormal.
> (Smirnov, 1996, pp. 342–343)

30 If *absence* constitutes the ground of *non-identity*, 'meaning irreducible, real difference in the world and our categories' (Norrie, 2009, p. 28) (of 'law,' and thus, consequently, of 'contract law,' in this book), it is 'the move to 2E that most directly implicates absence, for that move is constituted by introducing negativity into critical realism' (*ibid.*).

31 Please refer to Chapter 1, endnote 19.

References

Abd-Allah, U.F. (2008) Theological dimensions of Islamic law. In: Winter, T. (ed.) *The Cambridge Companion to Classical Islamic Theology*. Cambridge: Cambridge University Press, pp. 237–257.

Agamben, G. (2007) *Profanations* (trans. by Fort, J. (2005) from the original Italian version *Profanazioni*. Roma: Nottetempo). New York: Zone Books.

Ahmed, S. (2016) *What Is Islam? The Importance of Being Islamic*. Princeton and Oxford: Oxford University Press.

Ainsworth, J.E. (1996) Categories and culture: on the rectification of names in comparative law. *Cornell Law Review*. 82, pp. 19–42.

Asad, T. (1993) *Genealogies of Religion: Discipline and Reasons of Power in Christianity and Islam*. Baltimore and London: The Johns Hopkins University Press.

Asad, T. (2003) *Formations of the Secular: Christianity, Islam, Modernity*. Stanford: Stanford University Press.

Benjamin, W. (1921, 1985) Kapitalismus als religion. In: Tiedemann, R., and Schweppenhäuser, H. (eds.) *Gesammelte Schriften*, Vol. VI. Suhrkamp: Frankfurt, pp. 100–103.

Benjamin, W. (1996) The task of the translator. In: Bullock, M., and Jennings, M.W. (eds.) *Selected Writings, Vol. 1, 1913–1926*. Cambridge, MA and London: The Belknap Press of Harvard University Press, pp. 253–263.

Bhaskar, R. (1993) *Dialectic: The Pulse of Freedom*. London: Verso.

Böwering, G. (1997) The concept of time in Islam. *Proceedings of the American Philosophical Society*. 141(1), pp. 55–66.

Burrell, D.B. (2008) Creation. In: Winter, T. (ed.), *The Cambridge Companion to Classical Islamic Theology*. Cambridge: Cambridge University Press, pp. 141–160.

Buskens, L., and Dupret, B. (2015) The invention of Islamic law: a history of Western studies of Islamic normativity and their spread in the orient. In: Pouillon, F., and Vatin, J.-C. (eds.) *After Orientalism: Critical Perspectives on Western Agency and Eastern Re-Appropriations*. Leiden and Boston: Brill, pp. 31–47.

Calder, N. (1996) Law. In: Nasr, S.H., and Leaman, O. (eds.) *History of Islamic Philosophy*. London and New York: Routledge, pp. 979–998.

Carney, F. (1983) Some aspects of Islamic ethics. *Journal of Religion*. 63(2), pp. 159–174.

Cattelan, V. (2016) *Alice's adventures*, abductive reasoning and the logic of Islamic law. *International Journal for the Semiotics of Law*. 29(2), pp. 359–388.

Coulson, N.J. (1964) *A History of Islamic Law*. Islamic Survey Number 2. Edinburgh: Edinburgh University Press.

Duncan, D., Harrison, S. *et al.* (2019) *Babel: Adventures in Translation*. Oxford: Bodleain Library.

Eco, U. (1999) *Kant and the Platypus: Essays on Language and Cognition* (trans. by McEwen, A. (1997) from the original Italian version *Kant e l'Ornitorinco*. Milano: Bompiani R.C.S. Libri). London: Secker & Warburg.

Eco, U. (2003) *Dire Quasi la Stessa Cosa: Esperienze di Traduzione*. Milano: Bompiani.

Emon, A.M. (2016) Fiqh. In: Emon, A.M., and Ahmed, R. (eds.) *The Oxford Handbook of Islamic Law*. Available at: www.oxfordhandbooks.com. Accessed 1 August 2019.

Farahat, O. (2022) Time and moral choice in Islamic jurisprudence. *Canadian Journal of Law & Jurisprudence*. 35(1), pp. 141–167.

Fitzgerald, T. (2000) *The Ideology of Religious Studies*. New York and Oxford: Oxford University Press.

Fitzgerald, T. (ed.) (2007) *Religion and the Secular: Historical and Colonial Formations*. London: Equinox Publishing.

Gardet, L. (2012) Dīn. In: Bearman, P., Bianquis, T. *et al.* (eds.) *Encyclopaedia of Islam*, 2nd ed. Leiden: Brill. Accessed 8 February 2019.

Geertz, C. (1973) *The Interpretation of Cultures*. New York: Basic Books.

Geertz, C. (1983) Local knowledge: fact and law in comparative perspective. In: Geertz, C. (ed.) *Local Knowledge: Further Essays in Interpretive Anthropology*. New York: Basic Books, pp. 167–234.

Gimaret, D. (1990) *La Doctrine d'Al-Ash'arī*. Patrimonie Islam. Paris: Les Éditions du Cerf.

Goldziher, I., and Schacht, J. (2012) Fiqh. In: Bearman, P., Bianquis, T. *et al.* (eds.) *Encyclopaedia of Islam*, 2nd ed. Leiden: Brill. Accessed 1 August 2017.

Hallaq, W.B. (2009) *An Introduction to Islamic Law*. Cambridge: Cambridge University Press.

Hourani, G.F. (1985) *Reason and Tradition in Islamic Ethics*. Cambridge: Cambridge University Press.

Izutsu, T. (1966) *Ethico-Religious Concepts in the Qur'ān*. Montreal: McGill University Institute of Islamic Studies.

Jay, M. (1988) Scopic regimes of modernity. In: Foster, H. (ed.) *Vision and Visuality*. Dia Art Foundation – Discussions in Contemporary Culture Number 2. Seattle: Bay Press, pp. 3–23.

Johansen, B. (1995) Casuistry: between legal concepts and legal praxis. *Islamic Law and Society*. 2(2), pp. 135–156.

Johansen, B. (1999) *Contingency in a Sacred Law: Legal and Ethical Norms in the Muslim Fiqh*. Studies in Islamic Law and Society, Vol. 7. Leiden, Boston and Köln: Brill.

Kamali, M.H. (1993) Fundamental rights of the individual: an analysis of *ḥaqq* (right) in Islamic law. *The Americal Journal of Islamic Social Sciences*. 10(3), pp. 340–366.
Kamali, M.H. (1998) Sharīʿah as understood by the classical jurists. *IILM Law Journal*. 6, pp. 39–88.
MacCormick, N. (2001) De Iurisprudentia. In: Cairns, J.W., and Robinson, O.F. (eds.) *Critical Studies in Ancient Law, Comparative Law and Legal History*. Oxford and Portland: Hart Publishing, pp. 79–81.
MacDonald, D.B., and Calverley, E.E. (1975) Ḥaqq. In: Bearman, P., Bianquis, T. *et al.* (eds.) *Encyclopédie de l'Islam*, Tome III. Leiden: Brill.
Masuzawa, T. (2005) *The Invention of World Religions: Or, How European Universalism Was Preserved in the Language of Pluralism*. Chicago: The University of Chicago Press.
McLuhan, M. (1989) Visual and acoustic space (from McLuhan, M., and Powers, B.R., *The Global Village*. New York: Oxford University Press). Reprinted in Cox, C., and Warner, D. (eds.) (2004) *Audio Culture: Readings in Modern Music*. New York and London: Continuum, pp. 67–72.
McLuhan, M., and Fiore, Q. (1967) *The Medium Is the Massage: An Inventory of Effects*. New York: Bantam Books; London: Penguin Books.
Messick, B. (1993) *The Calligraphic State: Textual Domination and History in a Muslim Society*. Berkeley, Los Angeles and London: University of California Press.
Milliot, L. (1952) L'idée de la loi dans l'Islam. *Revue Internationale de Droit Comparé*. 4(4), pp. 669–682.
Milliot, L., and Blanc, F.-P. (2001) *Introduction à l'Étude du Droit Musulman*, 2nd ed. Paris: Éditions Dalloz.
Moad, E.O. (2007) A path to the oasis: *sharīʿah* and reason in Islamic moral epistemology. *International Journal for Philosophy of Religion*. 62(3), pp. 135–148.
Moosa, E. (1998) Allegory of the rule (*ḥukm*): law as simulacrum in Islam? *History of Religions*. 38(1), pp. 1–24.
Netton, I.R. (1989) *Allah Transcendent: Studies in the Structure and Semiotics of Islamic Philosophy, Theology and Cosmology*. London: Routledge.
Norrie, A. (2009) *Dialectic and Difference: Dialectical Critical Realism and the Grounds of Justice*. London: Routledge.
Ormsby, E.L. (1984) *Theodicy in Islamic Thought: The Dispute over al-Ghazālī's "Best of All Possible Worlds"*. Princeton: Princeton University Press.
Reinhart, A.K. (1983) Islamic law as Islamic ethics. *The Journal of Religious Ethics*. 11(2), pp. 186–203.
Reynolds, M. (2016) *Translation: A Very Short Introduction*. Oxford: Oxford University Press.
Reynolds, M. (2019) Translating the divine. In: Duncan, D., Harrison, S. *et al.* (eds.) *Babel: Adventures in Translation*. Oxford: Bodleain Library, pp. 58–77.
Said, E. (1978) *Orientalism*. London and Henley: Routledge & Kegan Paul.
Sartori, G. (1975) The tower of Babel. In: Sartori, G., Riggs, F.W., and Teune, H. (eds.) *Tower of Babel: On the Definition and Analysis of Concepts in the Social Sciences*. Occasional Papers of the International Studies Association Number 6. Pittsburgh: ISA, pp. 7–37.
Schacht, J. (1964) *An Introduction to Islamic Law*. Oxford: Oxford University Press.
Smirnov, A. (1996) Understanding justice in an Islamic context: some points of contrast with Western theories. *Philosophy East & West*. 46(3), pp. 337–350.

Stelzer, S.A.J. (2008) Ethics. In: Winter, T. (ed.) *The Cambridge Companion to Classical Islamic Theology*. Cambridge: Cambridge University Press, pp. 161–179.
Wakin, J. (1990) Interpretation of the divine command in the jurisprudence of Muwaffaq al-Dīn Ibn Qudāmah. In: Heer, N. (ed.) *Islamic Law and Jurisprudence: Studies in Honor of Farhat J. Ziadeh*. Seattle and London: University of Washington Press, pp. 33–52.
Weber, M. (1922) *Wirtschaft und Gesellschaft* (*Economy and Society*). Tübingen: Mohr.
Weiss, B.G. (1990) Exotericism and objectivity in Islamic jurisprudence. In: Heer, N. (ed.) *Islamic Law and Jurisprudence: Studies in Honor of Farhat J. Ziadeh*. Seattle and London: University of Washington Press, pp. 53–71.
Weiss, B.G. (2006) *The Spirit of Islamic Law*, paperback ed.; 1st ed. 1998. Athens, GA and London: The University of Georgia Press.
Zysow, A. (2013) *The Economy of Certainty: An Introduction to the Typology of Islamic Legal Theory*. Resources in Arabic and Islamic Studies Number 2. Atlanta, GA: Lockwood Press.

3 Comparing legal traditions

Contract law and Muslim *fiqh*

Crossing the bridge of Babel from West to East in the attempt to translate the non-identity of law-religion, we have postulated the dialectical coexistence of *presence* and *absence*, with the latter taking primacy over the former (Bhaskar, 1993, p. 5). This coexistence constitutes the background for the comparison between Western and Islamic contract law to which this chapter is dedicated. Here, it is not by (re-)affirming the Western juristic discourse (which reduces *fiqh* to an improper *corpus*) but by *absenting* its presence in Muslim jurisprudence that the *totality* (third level, 3L, in Bhaskar's dialectic) of the Islamic contract can be disclosed: a totality where *absence* and *presence* necessarily interact.

At this point, we can finally enter *our* Babel, the city of the *'aqd*.

The *Almeh*, after our preliminary meeting in the Introduction, has patiently waited for our visit to start. Much of the previous chapter has been devoted to explaining the meaning of *listening* to the revelation of Islam as echoed in Muslim jurisprudence – whose outcome consists in 'a conceptual replica of social life, [. . . that is] balanced between revelation, tradition and reality' (Calder, 1996, p. 981). It is now time to explore the second dimension of this echo: the *'aqd* as a vehicle of the Islamic legal tradition, where the *nomos* of the revelation is amplified by the unity-of-diversities that belongs to *fiqh* plural *iurisdictio* (section 2.4.3).

3.1. The *'aqd* as a craft of place in the space of Islam

To further position the *'aqd* within the *nomos* of Islam by *absenting* Western law-religion, some valuable input can be found in Clifford Geertz's idea of interpretive anthropology.

> Like sailing, gardening, politics, and poetry, law and ethnography are crafts of place: they work by the light of local knowledge. . . . [T]hey are alike absorbed with the artisan task of seeing broad principles in parochial facts . . . [by means of] a to-know-a-city-is-to-know-its-streets approach to things (Geertz, 1983, p. 167). . . . [But if] [t]he legal representation of fact is normative from the start; . . . [t]he problem it raises is how that

DOI: 10.4324/9781315145761-4

> representation is itself to be represented (*ibidem*, p. 174). . . . It is here, then, that anthropology . . . enters the study of law (*ibidem*, p. 181) [. . . as it . . .] welds the processes of self-knowledge, self-perception, self-understanding to those of other-knowledge, other-perception, other-understanding; that identifies, or very nearly, sorting out who we are and sorting whom we are among (*ibidem*, pp. 181–182). . . . [If] "law," here, there, or anywhere, is part of a distinctive manner of imagining the real . . . then the whole fact/law problem appears in an altered light. The dialectic . . . turns out to be between . . . a language, however vague and unintegral, of general coherence and one, however opportunistic and unmethodical, of specific consequence. It is about such "languages" (that is to say, symbol systems) and such a dialectic that I want now to try to say something at once empirical enough to be credible and analytical enough to be interesting (*ibidem*, pp. 184–185).

Geertz locates the study of law and anthropology between the *self* and the *other*, just as this book (following Bhaskar's principle of non-identity) assumes the coexistence of *absence* and *presence*. Other similarities between this book and Geertz's approach are noteworthy: from the interpretive nature of representations to the conception of languages as symbolic systems, vehicles of meaning, and the metaphor of 'knowing-a-city' that has been adopted to investigate the *ʿaqd* in a journey of discovery. Following Geertz, the Islamic contract itself can be depicted as a 'craft of place' that works 'by the light of local knowledge': that of *fiqh* tradition.

To insert the *ʿaqd* in its *own* world, the space of Islam, the codification of the contract according to Western standards, must be *absented*. No *corpus iuris* belongs to the *ʿaqd*; nor can a general theory or a systematic outline of the subject be found in the tradition of *fiqh*. Nabil Saleh is clear on the point: '[u]ntil the 19th century no definition of a contract as such is to be found in the treatises of Islamic law' (Saleh, 1990, p. 101). Indeed, 'visual maps' of the *ʿaqd*, in the form of ordered *corpora*, have been crafted only in the last century by Western-educated scholars that have represented (and so culturally codified) the *ʿaqd* either according to the language of civil law (for instance: Chehata, 1969; Linant de Bellefonds, 1965) or common law (Rayner, 1991). The *Almeh* 'has got dressed' in Western legal clothes, in order to become 'more proper' in the style of foreign *corpora iuris*. Before that, the process of (political) colonisation and later (legal) codification transplanted Western legal culture into Muslim countries as well, defining new coordinates for Islamic contract law (see later, Chapter 4). It was at that time that the *corpus* of the *ʿaqd* was invented (Buskens and Dupret, 2015) under the Western dogmas of the *Codified Norm*, within a textual polity that radically departed from that of medieval Islam (section 4.3.1). Both these processes (modern scholarship and legal codification) have given rise to new conceptual maps for Islamic contract law and moved the *ʿaqd* away from the *nomos* of Muslim jurisprudence; the 'urbanity' of the city has been reshaped by renaming its streets according to Western toponymies (i.e., the categories of civil and common laws).

However, if any representation 'depends on a difference between what presents and what is presented' (Eagleton, 1991, p. 213), these new coordinates have *dis-orientated* the explorer by suggesting itineraries of civil or common law that were, in fact, *absent* in the original tradition of *fiqh*. Itineraries that, by making the *'aqd* more intelligible to Western scholars by means of the application of their languages, have, in the end, *dis-located* the *'aqd* outside the Orient (reducing it to another stage of the Occident, 'a closed field, a theatrical stage affixed to Europe:' Said, 1978, p. 63).

If contract law is a 'craft of place' that works 'by the light of local knowledge,' how can we *re-orient* the understanding of the *'aqd* in its *own* place – that of *fiqh* jurisprudence? With this aim in mind, Bhaskar's dialectics of non-identity can work as a hermeneutical compass to 'craft a place' *other-than* that of Western law-religion. In fact, if common/civil lawyers know-the-city of the contract according to streets that belong to their *own* traditions, a different 'map' must be crafted for a stage *other-than* the Western one; in particular, the visual space of Western rationality must be replaced with the acoustic space of Islam.

3.2. A map of the city? *The Two Towers* and the plural itineraries of the *madhāhib*

Only by assuming the non-identity which exists between the tradition of *fiqh* and the *corpus* of Western contract law can the *totality* of the *'aqd* in its multiple pluralities (Ahmed) be 'observed,' or rather, 'listened to,' as an echo of the revelation of Islam. Keeping the allegory of Tolkien's trilogy that this book has already followed, the Western and Islamic legal traditions can then be imagined as *The Two Towers* of *The Lord of the Rings*. The Babel of the *'aqd* in the East, with Sauron's Barad-dûr at the centre of Mordor; and the tower of Orthanc for Western contract law in Saruman's citadel of Isengrad, in the West of Middle-Earth.

This duality underlines the inescapable intersection between Western law and Muslim *fiqh* when dealing with the *'aqd* from a comparative perspective, where *presence* and *absence* are mutually dependent. To 'hear' the unity of diversities that defined 'how Islam makes Muslims as Muslims make Islam' (Ahmed, 2016, p. 543), one must refer to *fiqh* normative pluralism as well as being aware of one's *own* bias embedded in Western legal categories. The importance of *translating* ('moving from a place to another') *ourselves* from the West of Orthanc to the East of Barad-dûr raises the urgency of identifying a proper map with which we can safely proceed into the city.

Indeed, every map (with its North and South, West, and East, coordinates, sections, and sub-sections) is a work of craft and it is itself a craft of place; it also tells a story about both its makers, interpreters, and readers. Maps 'tell us about the places they depict and the people that make and use them' (Bodleian Library, 2019):[1] 'maps are neither transparent objects of scientific communication, nor baleful tools of ideology, but proposals about the world that help people to understand who they are by describing *where* they are' (*ibidem*; italics in the original text). Texts of law are themselves maps[2] – instruments that 'help people to understand who they are' by setting their normative world, their *nomos*; they narrate *who* people are through the normativity to which they subscribe. Law and narrative, as we have seen in the Introduction, are always combined in any normative *nomos* (Cover, 1983, p. 5).

The style of the paragraphs and sub-paragraphs of a textbook of civil contract law, for instance, tells us a lot about a tradition that looks at the contract in the form of a systematic *corpus iuris* 'mapped' according to a normative history derived from Roman *ius*, with the contract conceived of as a sub-category of the law of obligations. While sharing the same space as law-religion within the tower of Orthanc, the common lawyer will advance another map to the contract, referring to categories (such as that of 'consideration') that are unknown to his civilian counterpart. More radically, neither of these maps will 'narrate' Muslim scholars, who think of the *ʿaqd* not as a valid and sensible corpus of laws but as the direct outcome of the divine revelation (section 2.4.5): a Word that has been echoed in the legitimacy of diverse rules; a plurality of itineraries (with the coexistence of differences, variations, if not contradictions) shaped by Muslim jurists in their own 'way of walking' through the city of the *ʿaqd*. Not by chance, *madhhab*, the Arabic term used to designate a 'juristic school,' literally refers to a 'way of going/travelling' along the Path of the *Šarīʿah*. Scholars *de*-scribe God's will by exercising a collective *iurisdictio* underpinned by their loyalty to the *madhhab* (pl. *madhāhib*) to which they belong:[3] in the Sunnī universe, the Ḥanafī, Mālikī, Šāfiʿī, and Ḥanbalī juristic schools.

By adhering to the acoustic space of Islam and its rationales of multiplicity, diversities, and contradictions (see Chapter 2), the *corpora iuris* of civil and common contract laws are replaced by a space whose *logos*, echoed in the literature of *fiqh*, can be 'listened to' through the Islamic contract. Walking through the streets of the city of the *ʿaqd*, 'sounds' of contractual rules overlap one over each other; in this unity of diversities, the Islamic contract finds its *own* place in the literature of Muslim *fiqh*; its *own* map within the Islamic legal tradition. To represent these overlapping pluralities this chapter, after a preliminary contextualisation of the nature of *ʿaqd* within Islamic *dīn* (section 3.3), in the following pages, will deal first with the psychological formation of the contract (section 3.4), and later, with its construction – i.e. its concrete occurrence (section 3.5) according to the different interpretations of the *madhāhib*. Moving from the inner to the outer dimension of contractual dealings, the research will touch aspects of *fiqh* literature whose rationales, as we will see, reflect the *logos* of Islam into the *nomos* of the contract, witnessing a conceptual unity that is maintained beyond (and fosters) the discordances of the schools' positions. In this way, by referring to the divergent opinions of the four Sunnī classical schools (namely Ḥanafī, Mālikī, Šāfiʿī, Ḥanbalī, as mentioned previously), the 'local knowledge' of *fiqh* tradition will be depicted according to diverse 'itineraries' by means of which the believer can 'walk' along the Path of *Šarī'ah* in the city of the *'aqd*. Itineraries that the Western traveller can conceive as spaces of 'choral transmission' that are peculiar to each juristic school.

To help the reader in their visit, the list that follows indicates the names of the most significant Muslim scholars (*fuqahā'*, pl. of *faqīh*), to which the next pages will refer for each school:

- for the Ḥanafī school: Abū Ḥanīfa (d. 150/767), the epitome of the *madhhab*; Abū Yūsuf (d. 182/798), his direct disciple; al-Šaybānī (d. 189/804), the second direct disciple of Abū Ḥanīfa, author of the earliest Ḥanafī legal handbook, the *Aṣl*;[4] al-Ṭaḥāwī (d. 321/933), author of the *Mukhtaṣar*; al-Qudūrī (d. 428/1037), Bagdadien jurist, author of the brief but precious opuscule *Mukhtaṣar* and the famous *Matn*; al-Bazdawī (d. 482/1089), author of a *Uṣūl* treaty; al-Sarakhsī (d. 490/1097), author of a significant thirty-volume-work, the *Mabsūṭ*; al-Samarqandī (d. 539/1144), author of the *Gift to Jurists* (*Tuḥfat 'l-Fuqahā'*); al-Kāsānī (d. 587/1191), whose monumental treatise *Badā'i' 'l-Ṣanā'i'* (quoted in the present work simply as *Badā'i'*) constitutes one of the pinnacles of Ḥanafī thought in contract law; al-Qādīkhān (d. 592/1196); al-Marghīnānī (d. 593/1197), a contemporary of al-Kāsānī and author of the *Hidāya*, intended as a commentary to al-Qudūrī's *Mukhtaṣar*; Ibn Māza (d. 616/1219–20); Ibn Nujayim (d. 970/1563), an Egyptian scholar, author of *al-Baḥr 'l-Rā'iql*;
- for the Mālikī school: Mālik Ibn Anas (d. 179/795), founder of the school and editor of the *Muwaṭṭa*, authoritative collection of *aḥādīth*; al-Saḥnūn (d. 240/855), whose *Mudawwana al-Kubrā* (his version of the teachings by the master Mālik, as transmitted by Ibn al-Qāsim, d. 191/806) constitutes, next to the *Mukhtaṣar* by al-Khalīl ibn Isḥāq, the core of the *madhhab*; Ibn Rušd al-Jadd (d. 520/1126); Ibn Rušd (d. 595/1198, better known in West as Averroës), a great philosopher but also judge, legal scholar, and author of the famous *Bidāyat al-Mujtahid wa Nihāyat al-Muqtasid*; Šihāb al-Dīn al-Qārāfī (d. 684/1285), an eminent jurist of Berber origins and influential legal theoretician (i.e. expert of the field of *uṣūl al-fiqh*) of the 13th century; al-Khalīl ibn Isḥāq (d. 767/1365), whose *Mukhtaṣar* is still today the principal textbook of the Mālikī school; al-Ḥaṭṭāb (d. 954/1547), author of the *Mawāhib al-Jalīl*, usually mentioned as *Commentary* of Khalīl, with reference to the *Mukhtaṣar* by al-Khalīl b. Isḥāq;
- for the Šāfi'ī school: al-Šāfi'ī (d. 204/820), founder of the *madhhab* and author of the fundamental *Kitāb al-Umm*; al-Muzanī (d. 264/877–8); al-Suyūṭī (d. 911/1505), an Egyptian writer and juristic expert;
- for the Ḥanbalī school: Ibn Ḥanbal (d. 241/855), the epitome of the school; Ibn Qudāma (d. 620/1223), author of the *Mughnī*, the most important source of the Ḥanbalī school, with extensive commentary of the *Mukhtaṣar* by al-Khiraqī (d. 334/945); the neo-Ḥanbalī doctrine finds its best expression in the legal thought of Ibn Taymiyya (d. 728/1328), whose fundamental work is the collection *Majmū'a Fatāwā*; Ibn Qayyim al-Jawziyya

(d. 751/1350), a disciple of Ibn Taymiyya and author of the famous *Iʿlām al-Muwaqiʿin*.

It is by adhering to the alternative itineraries in the choral transmission of classical *madhāhib* – each offering, in the end, its *own* map to the city, in their non-identity with Western contract law – that this book will try to clarify the meaning of the *ʿaqd* as manifestation of Islamic *dīn* and Muslim *bíos* (Chapter 2).

3.3. *ʿAqd* and Islamic *dīn*

If any voluntary act by which the agent binds himself can be called *ʿaqd* (so that the meaning of *ʿaqd*, pl. *ʿuqūd*, can be generally translated as 'binding act,' from the Arabic root *ʿ-Q-D*, 'to tie'), in *fiqh* literature, the term is often used in the narrower sense of a bilateral/synallagmatic relation (such as sale, lease . . .) within the realm of *muʿāwaḍāt* (civil/commercial transactions).[5] This chapter will concentrate on this narrower meaning.

Before visiting the city of the *ʿaqd*, using the multiple itineraries of the *madhāhib*, a preliminary remark by Chafik Chehata is worth mentioning. 'The contractual phenomenon is a universal one. It is found at all latitudes and throughout history. The core question is: how has the law translated and integrated this phenomenon within its framework? Moreover: according to which rationales has the law, which presupposes a philosophy, admitted the contract as one of its "values"?' (Chehata, 1968a, p. 129; my translation).

While the contract constitutes a universal phenomenon – a 'fact' for any human society – the core issue in comparative studies is to understand how each legal system has translated this fact, giving it 'legal value;' a meaning, through which the contract becomes itself vehicle of the *nomos* of that society. For instance, in common law, the 'value' of the contract is that of a promise or a set of promises which 'the law will enforce if consideration is provided' (as in the classic definition by Pollock, 1911, p. 1). 'Consideration' (i.e., something 'of (economic) value:' a price, a benefit, a property to exchange) is needed to render the promises binding, so that the rationale of the contract in common law is that of a bargain, performed or to be performed; in brief, an idea of contract-bargain. In contrast, in the civil law tradition, the contract is 'an agreement thanks to which one or more parties bind themselves towards one or more others, to give, to do, or not to do something' (Art. 1101 French Civil Code; my translation). The French *contrat* is a source of obligations provided that the support of a valid *cause* is given. In civil law, the 'value' of the *contrat* is not that of a bargain; rather, the social fact of 'giving, doing, or not doing something' is intended as the manifestation of human freedom in a model of contract-consent, where the autonomy of the person (in French *autonomie de la volonté*, roughly 'self capacity to create binding rules for the parties') is underpinned by the 'reason,' the 'rationale' (in Latin, *causa*) of the contract.[6] Wim Decock (2013) gives a significant account of the Christian theological background behind the contract of civil law as developed in the European thought of the 16th and 17th century; it was at that time that the concept of 'freedom of contract' (which would be paired to the *autonomie de la volonté* only much later, in the 20th century: Ranouil, 1980) became part of a moral universe grounded on the individuals' power to undertake contractual obligations by virtue of mutual consent.[7]

If the tower of Orthanc may be split in two, as the contract is different in common and civil law,[8] the Babel of the *ʿaqd*, with its Barad-dûr tower, cannot be understood unless located within the space of Islamic *dīn*, which provides its conceptual unity within the revelation of Islam. In fact, if the believer acts *by way of word* (see Chapter 2) by performing the divine rule (*ḥukm*) in connection to parties' rights (*ḥuqūq*), the 'value' of the *ʿaqd* is necessarily inserted within the space of a created agency whose effects are already established by Law (*ḥukm al-ʿaqd*). Accordingly, within Islamic *dīn*, the *ʿaqd* becomes a distinctive means of performance of God's revelation, where its religious dimension (the contract as an act of devotion) overlaps with the secular one (the contract as a means of exchange of properties); for the reformulation of the categories of 'religious' and 'secular' according to the notion of Islamic *bíos*, see section 2.3 of this book. In other words, differently from the contract-bargain and the contract-consent of common and civil law traditions, Muslim *fiqh* embodies in the *ʿaqd* an idea of contract-performance (of God's will), which represents a distinctive element of the Islamic legal tradition (see section 3.6 of this chapter).

*3.3.1. The rule (*ḥukm al-*ʿaqd), its subject, and its object: from legal capacity (*ahliyya*) and personality (*dhimma*) to the duty (*wujūb*) of the* mukallaf

Assuming God as the only Ruler, the value of the *ʿaqd* moves from a legal philosophy that *translates* the 'fact' of the contract into Muslim life, *bíos*, in the religion of Islam (section 2.3). In this frame, the notion of *ḥukm al-ʿaqd* (that is to say, the 'effect(s) of the contract' established by Law and linked to corresponding rights, *ḥuqūq al-ʿaqd*: see section 2.4.4) is discussed by Muslim classical scholars in relation to how the believer becomes responsible not only towards the counterparty but also towards God by performing the *ʿaqd*.

Hence, from the concept of *ḥukm*, Muslim jurisprudence derives the notions of '[ruled] subject' (*maḥkūm lahu*) and 'matter' (*maḥkūm bihi*) of the contractual rule (*ḥukm al-ʿaqd*): respectively, the contractual party that is 'subject to the rule' and the contractual 'matter which is ruled.' The believer is 'subject to the rule' when she/he enjoys legal subjectivity or capacity (*ahliyya*) (Zahraa, 1995). This comprises both the faculty of acquiring rights and duties (*ahliyyat al-wujūb*, 'capacity of being obliged,' but also enjoying rights, as specified by classical scholars through the expression *al-wujūb lahu wa-ʿalayh*) and the faculty of exercising/accomplishing them (*ahliyyat al-adāʾ*, 'capacity of execution,' 'capacity to contract,' to dispose and validly fulfilling what the subject is obliged to do). Both may be variously limited according to permanent or temporary restrictions.[9] Legal capacity begins with birth and reaches its highest degree for the free Muslim who is of sound mind (*ʿāqil*) and of age (*bāligh*), and therefore, fully responsible and under the *taklīf*, 'charge,' of obeying God; 'the *mukallaf* has the capacity to contract and to dispose (*taṣarruf*), [and] he is bound to fulfil the religious duties, . . . being capable of deliberate intent' (Schacht, 1964, p. 124).

As it is related to the theological foundations of *fiqh*, the topic of *ahliyya* finds its natural collocation in the treatises of *uṣūl al-fiqh*. In the Ḥanafī school, al-Bazdawī (d. 482/1089) explains that 'legal capacity . . . lies on the existence of the "personality" (*dhimma*) given to man through his birth: this personality is "apt to the duty" (*ṣālihatun li-l-wujūb*), according to . . . all the jurists, thanks to the (original) pact between God and the man' (quoted in Brunschvig, 1976b, p. 42) (see Q. 7:171 and 17:14). In addition, 'the necessary and sufficient condition . . . to be apt to the duty is to be apt . . . to the nature of the duty: *man kāna ahlan li-ḥukmi l-wujūbi bi-wajhin, kāna huwa ahlan li-l-wujūbi, wa-man lā fa-lā*' (*ibidem*). The notion of *ḥukm al-wujūb* represents the key-element of al-Bazdawī's approach as one of the three constitutive elements of legal/religious duty (*wujūb*):

1. the *maḥall*, the 'basis,' 'plate,' 'location' of the duty, in a theology where God is the creator of human acts, of which man is merely the receiving subject (*maḥall*) as performer of God's will. The general substratum for all the duties is the legal 'personality,' the *dhimma* of the person;
2. the *sabab* (pl. *asbāb*), the empirical circumstance (effect of the divine cause, *ʿilla*: see section 2.4.4) for the occurrence of the duty. The pair *sabab/ʿilla* depicts the divine will which sustains all creation: the *sabab* is, according to al-Bazdawī, 'what defines the route that leads to the thing' (*ʿibāratun ʿammā huwa ṭarīqun ila š-šay'*) (Brunschvig, 1976b, p. 43);
3. in addition to the *maḥall* and *sabab*, duty doesn't exist if there is no 'aptness' to its very nature (*ḥukm al-wujūb*). Here, the term *ḥukm*, previously translated as 'judgement,' 'rule,' 'decree,' 'effect of the rule,' also indicates the 'nature' of the duty itself, whose essential character is established by God in His judgement (again, *ḥukm*).

3.3.2. Religious qualifications (al-aḥkām al-khamsa) *and the legal validity of the* šarʿī *act, its constitutive* (arkān) *and conditional* (šurūṭ) *elements*

The cause of the action (*sabab*) brings about the rise of a 'legal,' or rather, 'guided' (*šarʿī*) duty of performance, both for physical (*fiʿl al-jawāriḥ*) and mental actions (*fiʿl al-qalb*). Physical acts include physical movements or omissions and oral/written/gestural expressions. Mental acts, if not revealed in words or actions, escape from worldly judgement; nevertheless, the individual remains responsible towards God (Milliot, 1953, p. 199).

The intersection between law and religion in Muslim jurisprudence (according to the formula of Islamic *bíos*) clearly emerges in the double qualification that is applied to human actions; whereas 'the five qualifications' (*al-aḥkām al-khamsa*) are concerned with the ethical status of the action, what 'corresponds to the Law' (*mašrūʿ*) in terms of legal validity is assessed according to a 'secular' ('temporal', 'worldly') stance where normativity takes primacy. The two systems of qualification are concurrent and do not override one another; as noted by Schacht, this is not contradictory, since 'the two predicates refer . . . to separate aspects of the [same] situation' (1964, p. 122) – what Western scholars would describe, respectively, as 'internal' and 'external' *forum*. As previously noted in section 2.3, they represent the two sides of the same coin in a space where 'religious' and 'secular' are not separated.

Dealing with the concept of *ḥukm*, the normative ethics of the 'quintuple qualification' (*al-aḥkām al-khamsa*) has already been mentioned in section 2.4.4, in relation to the following taxonomy: (1) obligatory (*wājib*, *farḍ*); (2) recommended (*sunna*, *mandūb*, *mustaḥabb*); (3) neutral, indifferent (*mubāḥ*); (4) reprehensible, disapproved (*makrūh*); (5) and forbidden (*ḥarām*, as opposed to *ḥalāl*, permitted). If a valid act from a legal perspective (*forum externum*) usually enjoys an ethical connotation (*forum internum*), the concurrent application of the two scales of qualifications to the same set of facts can occasionally lead to discordant results, with the action being legally valid (*ṣaḥīḥ*, see later), but forbidden (*ḥarām*). 'For instance, a sale concluded at the time of the call to the Friday prayer is *makrūh* . . .; it is legally effective but its conclusion at that particular time is forbidden' (Schacht, 1964, p. 122). Another relevant example relates to the field of 'legal devices' (*ḥiyal*) which can be considered valid by Muslim scholars when they conform to the letter of the Law, regardless of the underlying motive (on the topic, see section 4.2.3).

Focusing on the dimension of legal validity, any *šarʿī* act produces legal effects when it enjoys the contemporary presence of its constitutive/essential (*rukn*, pl. *arkān*) and conditional elements (*šarṭ*, pl. *šurūṭ*).

On the one hand, the *arkān* refer to the existence, the 'root' (*aṣl*), of the action. Together with the specific *arkān* of each *šarʿī* act, essential elements of any action (Milliot, 1953, p. 203) are 1) the divine injunction (*taklīf*) towards the *mukallaf*; 2) the legal capacity (*ahliyya*) of the ruled subject; 3) the 'place'/'location' (*maḥall*) of the juristic relation. For a 'disposition by fact' (*al-taṣarrufāt al-fiʿliyya*) (e.g. the cultivation of a piece of land; the appropriation of something), the 'place' is the relation cause-effect from which the legal effects derive; for a juristic act *stricto sensu*, 'disposition by words' (*al-taṣarrufāt al-qawliyya*), the *maḥall* becomes the subject matter (*al-maʿqūd alayh*) on which the mutual consent (*tarāḍī*) is expressed (Rayner, 1991, p. 131).

On the other hand, the *šurūṭ* affect the validity of the action, its compliance with the extrinsic circumstances (*waṣf*) required by *Šarīʿah*, and may refer, for instance, to the capacity of the subject (e.g. the honour of the witness); the subject matter (e.g. the equality of the counter-values: prohibition of *ribā*); personal consent (*riḍā*); and so on.

Providing that the *arkān* and/or the *šurūṭ* are fulfilled or not, a *šarʿī* act can be

1. *ṣaḥīḥ*, correct, sound, 'valid,' if both its *arkān* and its *šurūṭ* fulfil the Law. As noted previously, a *ṣaḥīḥ* act may be *makrūh* if 'its *aṣl* and *waṣf* correspond with the law, but something forbidden is connected with it' (Schacht, 1964, p. 121). Moreover, a *ṣaḥīḥ* act can enjoy different grades of effectiveness:
   a. fully binding (*nāfidh*, 'operative,' *lāzim*, 'binding,' or *wājib*, 'obligatory,' 'due'), if its enforceability doesn't depend on confirmation, and cannot be unilaterally cancelled;
   b. *ghayr lāzim*, 'not binding' or 'suspended,' when it can be unilaterally cancelled, even if valid *ab initio* (as for the contract affected by option, *khiyār*, according to the Ḥanafīs: on the topic of *khiyār* see section 3.4.4 of this chapter);
   c. Ḥanafīs and Mālikīs recognise a third category of valid acts, the acts that are *mawqūf*, whose validity depends on the ratification by a third person (e.g., the guardian of a minor); the act is consequently 'suspended' and its effects postponed, but, as opposed to the *ghayr lāzim* act, without the external ratification it will be considered inexistent *ab initio* (Linant de Bellefonds, 1965, pp. 87–101);
2. *fāsid*, defective, voidable, 'broken,' if its *arkān*, but not the *šurūṭ*, are fulfilled (*al-fasād*, defectiveness, invalidity but not inexistence) (Linant de Bellefonds, 1977);
3. *bāṭil*, null, void, inexistent, but also 'false,' if it lacks any *rukn* (*al-buṭlān*, inexistence).

The distinction between *fāsid* and *bāṭil* is theorised only by the Ḥanafīs and not recognised by the other schools (Mālikīs, Šāfiʿīs, Ḥanbalīs).

3.3.3. *At the borders of the city: the act of disposal* (taṣarruf) *in relation to contractual rights* (ḥuqūq al-*ʿaqd)*

As clarified in the previous section, in commercial relations which are concluded through a disposition by words (*al-taṣarrufāt al-qawliyya*), the 'place' (*maḥall*) of the contract consists in the subject matter (*al-maʿqūd alayh*) on which the mutual consent (*tarāḍī*) of the parties is expressed.

The distinctive value of the *ʿaqd* in Islamic *dīn* can be further disclosed here in relation to the new setting of *ḥuqūq* ('rights') to which the contract gives rise. As we have seen in Chapter 2, the concept of *ḥaqq* (stemming from the Arabic root *Ḥ-Q-Q*) involves the ideas of 'reality,' 'truth,' 'justice,' where it is God's piety that guarantees the just allocation of rights for the contracting parties. In this conception of justice, the contractual rights of an individual are never in competition with those of others; since they both represent a manifestation of God's will, they are not separate portions of human justice but 'shares' of the unique, divine, justice (*ʿadl*). Hence, the 'right' in Islam does not belong to a single person but defines (both) the right and the obligation, in the unity of the two elements (Smirnov, 1996, p. 345).

> Alluding to the archetype of the scale, one may say that Western thinking is concerned with the pans of the scales and their contents, while for classical Islamic thought the stress lies on the central balancing pivot. . . . In the second case it is the fact of balancing the opposites that is important, this balance being reached by means of the centring and mediating pivot; the theoretical task is to find out how the two might be linked to form a balanced unity and what the conditions are for such a linkage.
> (*ibidem*, pp. 346–347)

This emphasis on linkage and reciprocity regarding the *ḥaqq* is confirmed by Rosen:

> this richly nuanced concept is commonly translated as "right" or "duty", but its implications are far more diverse and subtle than those translations alone convey. Basically, *ḥaqq* is the distribution of rights and duties, the interconnected set of obligations and associations by which man and God, and man and man, are linked to one another. Indeed, it is precisely the distribution of obligations which constitutes the fundamental reality of human existence, which is why *ḥaqq* also means 'reality' and 'truth.'
> (Rosen, 2000, pp. 156–157)

The distinctively 'Islamic value' of the *ʿaqd* as an act of disposal (*taṣarruf*), thus, is inherently grounded in the nature of contractual rights (*ḥuqūq al-ʿaqd*) as manifestation of God's reality, justice, and truth in the unity of 'man and God, and man and man,' where the action of the believer represents the performance of God's will. It is within this specific philosophy of Muslim jurisprudence that the following pages will try to *translate* the meaning of the *ʿaqd* to the Western explorer, both as part of the divine creation and as a human enterprise.

With this aim, while still at the borders of the city, we can add some details to the general definition of the *ʿaqd* that we have already introduced. In Muslim jurisprudence, as we have seen, the Arabic word for contract, *ʿaqd* (pl. *ʿuqūd*), derives from the root *ʿ-Q-D* (whose corresponding verb *ʿaqada* means 'to tie' or 'to bind') and describes not only bilateral contracts but is 'loosely employed to describe all manifestations of the will which tie their author to the obligations arising therefrom' (Rayner, 1991, pp. 87–88).

> The most common use of the word however is to denote synallagmatic transactions . . . which are concluded by an offer (*ījāb*) and an acceptance

> (*qabūl*). The term *ʿaqd* is also used by the jurists to denote dispositions of property by will (*mortis causa*) which are concluded by the offer of one party only, such as gift (*hiba*), guarantee (*ḍaman*), *waqf* bequests, the remission of debts and the . . . liberation of slaves. Mere juristic acts such as marriage (*nikāh*) and divorce (*ṭalaq*) . . . also fall under the heading of *ʿuqūd*.
>
> (*ibidem*, p. 88)

Yvon Linant de Bellefonds summarises the point by noting that 'the word *ʿaqd* has a very large connotation [in classical *fiqh*] . . . which embraces any kind of commitment, either the contract or the unilateral obligation;' 'every manifestation of will that ties its author and binds him is an *ʿaqd*' (1965, p. 62; my translation). For Chafik Chehata, 'the *ʿaqd* . . . is the juristic act, both as contract or a as simple unilateral declaration, such as the testament' (1960). Interestingly, the term *ʿaqd* appears in the Qur'ān only in two passages (Q. 2:235 and Q. 2:237), both with reference to the contract of marriage (*nikāḥ*) (as noted by Chehata, 1970b, p. 124).

Given these general borders, the chapter will explore the city by focusing on the role of human will and rationality in performing the action (section 3.4) and, later, on the empirical elements involved in the formation of the contract (section 3.5). This investigation of the *ʿaqd* in comparison with civil/common law categories will finally lead to conclusive reflections over the *totality* (third level, 3L, in Bhaskar's dialectic) of the Islamic contract in *fiqh* normative pluralism, where the *non-identity* of law-religion will reformulate its rationales from an idea of bargain (common law) and consent (civil law) to the performance of God's will (section 3.6).

3.4. The role of human will and rationality in the psychological formation of the *ʿaqd*

By locating the *ʿaqd* in the space of Islamic *dīn*, its underlying values have been related to the condition of the believer who is 'subject to the rule' in the world created by God and performs contractual duties in a reality where 'man and God, and man and man, are linked to one another' (see foregoing, Rosen, 2000, p. 157). Two crucial questions immediately arise from this observation: if the human being is guided by God in his role of vice-regent (*khalīfah*) on earth, to what extent does he/she enjoy contractual freedom – in the sense of an autonomous determination of the terms and rules of the transaction? Moreover, how does this freedom relate to human intention (*niyya*) or rationality (*ʿaql*) in the formation of the *ʿaqd*?

On the relevance of the *niyya*, the manuals of Muslim jurisprudence quote repeatedly one of the most famous *aḥādīth* in the field of civil transactions; namely, 'actions are defined by intentions, and to every person what he intends (*innamā al-aʿmāl bil-niyyāt wa-innamā li-kull imriʾin mā nawā*)' (Powers, 2006, p. 1).[10] However, as we will see, although *niyya* is the most frequent word in the treatises for 'intention,' a plurality of other terms (*qaṣd*, *irāda*, and *rīḍa*) are used in the context of the psychological formation of the contract. In addition, the significance of the intention varies greatly from acts of worship (*'ibādāt*) to worldly transactions (*mu'āmalāt*) (as already noted in section 2.3). In this second category, it also assumes different levels of importance in the four Sunnī schools, for which the dictum 'actions are defined by intentions' (*innamā al-a'māl bil-niyyāt*) 'serves as a prism directing Muslim legal thought in a wide array of directions, reflecting a rich understanding of intentions, actions, and the human agents who produce – and are produced by – them' (Powers, 2006, p. 5) Indeed, the role of intention and rationality in the formation of the contract is one of the most widely debated topics in the tradition of *fiqh*, giving rise to that normative pluralism made up of differences and divergences which is peculiar to the acoustic space of Islam.

At the same time, the topic raises fundamental, comparative issues with the Western legal tradition. Maintaining a dialectical approach towards the totality (3L) of the *'aqd*, the following pages will investigate these issues by moving from the doctrines of *cause* (civil law) and consideration (common law) in relation to the Islamic concepts of *'illa* and *sabab* (section 3.4.1) to the idea of contractual freedom in Western law and Muslim *fiqh* (section 3.4.2). Later, the book will focus on the various psychological elements analysed by Muslim scholars: will (*irāda*), intention (*niyya*), *animus contrahendi* (*qaṣd*), choice (*khiyār*), and individual consent (*riḍā*) (section 3.4.3); here, a radical divergence will be highlighted between a tendency to 'objectivism' (for Šāfi'īs and Ḥanafīs) and 'subjectivism' (for Mālikīs and Ḥanbalīs). To conclude, a final section will be dedicated to the impact on the contract of the vices of the consent (duress, *ikrāh*, fraud, *tadlīs*, and error, *ghalaṭ*) and their relation to the doctrine of *al-khiyār* (section 3.4.4).

3.4.1. **Autonomie de la volonté** *and the 'reason' underlying the contract: 'illa and* **sabab** *in comparison with the civilian* **cause** *and the consideration of common law*

As previously remarked (section 3.3), all legal traditions translate 'facts' into 'legal facts' by means of their *own* underlying 'values.'

In the civil law tradition, the doctrine of the *autonomie de la volonté* lies at the very heart of contract-consent. Originating in the context of private international law at the end of the 19th century, this doctrine soon gained access to the national legal systems of continental Europe as the core of 'juridical individualism,' designating 'the power that the will enjoys of giving itself its own laws' (Ranouil, 1980, p. 9; my translation). Its underlying assumptions were the promotion of the trust in a 'sovereign [human] will, creator of law' (*ibidem*, p. 15); the faith in the autonomy of each human being as an independent entity; the utter conviction that the human will, source and measure of any individual rights, is the 'organ *creating* law.' In the field of contractual relations, the *autonomie de la volonté* underpins the core nature of the contract in civil law as an agreement which is source of obligations: the convergence of two or more human free wills in the mutual consent being the 'origin,' the 'source' of any valid right and obligation (for the historical origin of contractual freedom in modern Europe from the 16th century, see Decock, 2013). The sovereign will of the parties finds its underlying 'reason' in a valid *cause* (*causa* in Latin), which incorporates a legitimate purpose for the law to enforce the contract. Accordingly, the *cause* still represents, today, an essential element of the *contrat* in the French Civil Code, Art. 1131: '*L'obligation sans cause, ou sur une fausse cause, ou sur une cause illicite, ne peut avoir aucun effet*' ('the obligation without cause, or with a false cause, or with an illicit cause, cannot have any effect'). In contrast, the doctrine of the *cause* as underlying reason for the contract is unknown in the tradition of common law, where the enforceability of promises depends on the provision of consideration. The basic idea behind the concept of consideration is that both parties to a contract must bring something to the bargain, either conferring an advantage on the other party or incurring some detriment or inconvenience towards oneself. In this sense, a deep conceptual distance separates the civilian *causa* from the consideration of common law. Whereas civil law founds the enforceability of the contract on the concurrence of wills (contract-consent), common law focuses on the exchange of something for something; this contract-bargain implies a negotiation between two or more parties that leads to a consensual transfer of something of value (consideration).

Moving now to the city of the *'aqd*, can we find in the works of Muslim jurists anything comparable to the civilian *cause* or to the consideration of common law? I think not.

Since God is the beholder of any right (*ḥaqq*), His will has complete supremacy on the agency of the Muslim believer; hence, no autonomous centre of power can compete in the 'creation' of norms (civil law), nor is the exchange itself (common law) sufficient for the enforceability of promises, beyond God's authoritative intent. From the juristic perspective of Islamic law, the *'aqd* is part of God's creation, which is 'acquired' and 'performed' (*kasb*) by the human being (hence, the notion of a contract-performance). In brief, Muslim scholars never developed a doctrine of consideration or *cause*.[11]

What can be found in Muslim jurisprudence, rather, are two concepts that have already been mentioned in Chapter 2: *'illa* ('preliminary cause') and *sabab* (pl. *asbāb*), the 'immediate cause' created by God at the very moment of the action (Brunschvig, 1976a, p. 191). But their 'value' is radically distant from (and not comparable to) the idea of *cause* of civil law (apart from a literal translation, that can mislead the interpreter). *'Illa* and *sabab* belong to the domain of *uṣūl al-fiqh*, where they are applied, respectively,

- to admit analogy (*qiyās*) in describing the connections among a qualification (*ḥukm*) and a novel set of entitlements (*ḥuqūq*) in equivalent circumstances: *'illa* constitutes 'the relevant similarity which justifies the transference of the judgement from the precedent to the new case' (Hallaq, 1985–86, p. 86);

- while *sabab* indicates the 'efficient cause' that determines the action: *asbāb aš-šarā'i'* are 'the objects or the circumstances to whose existence or appearance the legal institutions, the duties created or sanctioned by the Law, are linked' (Brunschvig, 1976b, p. 44).

If no direct relationship can be found between the notions of *'illa* and *sabab* as the 'reason' of the action with the civilian *cause* (nor with the consideration of common law), further insights into the 'values' of Muslim *fiqh* can be obtained thanks to a comparison of the notion of *'illa* with the Western concept of *ratio legis*. Van Ess warns the Western traveller that

> [t]he equation [*'illa* = *ratio legis*] has the disadvantage of insinuating the idea that the *'illa* might help to discover the reason God had in mind when promulgating the law. . . . [T]he *'illa* only generates the qualification by the fact that the legislator (i.e. God) uses it for this (*mūjib lil-ḥukm bi-ja'l aš-šāri'*) . . . God's will is no longer bound to a rational structure standing of itself, and the internal reason for his decisions and commands is thereby removed from the comprehension of man; he acts voluntarily, without a specific *ratio legis*.
>
> (Van Ess, 1970, p. 36, note 74)

As far as the idea of *sabab* is concerned, an alteration of its original meaning was brought about by its re-interpretation as 'objective cause' in the Ḥanafi-inspired (but deeply affected by the French model of codification) Ottoman Civil Code, the Majalla, in Arts. 97 and 1248, and in other codifications of Muslim countries of the 20th century (see later, Chapter 4).[12]

> Art. 97. No one is to acquire the property of another without a legal cause (*lā yajūz li aḥad an ya'khudha māl aḥad bilā sabab šar'ī*).
>
> Art. 1248. The legal causes of possession (*asbāb al-tamalluk*) are three in number. First, the transfer of property from one owner to another: this is so in sale (*al-bay'*) and donation (*al-hiba*). Second, a person might be a successor kin of another: this is the case of inheritance (*al-irth*). Third, one might acquire a permissible object which has no owner . . . such as in collecting rain-water or hunting.
>
> (quoted in Arabi, 1997, p. 203, note 8)

In remarking the distance between Muslim *fiqh* and the Western legal tradition, Chafik Chehata states that 'a theory of the cause [in the civil law sense] doesn't exist at all' (Chehata, 1969, p. 67; my translation); rather, it is replaced by a theory of equivalence in the performance of the *'aqd* (*ibidem*). On the point, the position by Chehata can be fully supported by referring to the Ḥanafī scholar al-Kāsānī (d. 587/1191):

> Equality . . . is the aim of the contracting parties (*al-musāwāt . . . maṭlūb al-ʿāqidayn*). . . . The entirety of the sold object is to be considered equivalent to the entirety of the price (*kull al-mabīʿ yuʿtabar muqābalan bi-kull al-thaman*), and the entirety of the price equivalent to the entirety of the sold object. Any increment (*ziyāda*), whether in price or in the object which has no corresponding equivalent, would be an additional value without compensation . . . and this is the meaning of usury (*ribā*).
> (Abū Bakr al-Kāsānī, *Badāʾiʿ al-Ṣanāʾiʿ fī Tartīb al-Šarāʾiʿ*, Vol. 4, 201; Vol. 5, 285; quoted in Arabi, 1997, p. 208)

Following Chehata, we may say that the cause and the consideration of Western legal languages are *replaced* in Islamic law by the 'equality of the counter-values,' a principle that will shed further light on the prohibition of *ribā* (see later, section 3.5.4). In fact, as clarified by Saleh, there is no theory of 'inducing motive' as valid *causa* in Muslim *fiqh*, in the sense of 'the sum of all external and internal motives which induce a party to conclude a legal act as well as the aim which is intended to be achieved through the legal act' (Saleh, 1992b, p. 116): 'the word cause (*sabab*), understood as inducing motive, is seldom found in the classical law treatises. What is found instead is *niyya* or *qaṣd*, that is, the intention of the contracting parties in bilateral contracts and of the one party in unilateral undertakings' (*ibidem*, p. 121). These concepts will be further investigated in section 3.4.3.

3.4.2. Freedom of contract, nominate contracts, and attached stipulations

Closely related to the matter of the *autonomie de la volonté* is the existence (or not) of a doctrine of contractual freedom in Islamic contract law (the former more related to the source, the creation of contract rules; the latter, to the contents of parties' rights). On the topic of contractual freedom, *fiqh* shows a variety of discordant positions. On the matter Yanagihashi notes that

> [i]t is difficult to answer the question whether Islamic law admits contractual liberty. On the one hand, the Shāfiʿī jurist al-Muzanī (d. 264/877–8) quotes his master, al-Shāfiʿī (d. 204/820), as saying, "We have demonstrated that God has legalised sales except those that He prohibited through His Messenger ad those that are analogised to them". . . . In fact, there are many cases in which a customarily practiced contract that is not mentioned in orthodox legal manuals was validated. For example, the Ḥanafī jurist Ibn Māza (d. 616/1219–20) refers to a form of *waqf* practiced in the mountainous region near Nihāvand (in western Iran), in which seeds are lent to the poor, who are to sow them and return the same quantity of seed as they borrowed, earning for themselves the

> remaining produce. . . . When asked about the validity of a labour contract concluded between the owner of a mountain and a planter, by virtue of which the former charged the latter with the planting and the taking care of trees, in return for which the latter was to acquire one half of the mountain – the Mālikī jurist Ibn Rushd al-Jadd (d. 520/1126) issued a *fatwā* invalidating it because of ignorance, not because it failed to meet the requirements of any of the nominate contracts.
>
> (Yanagihashi, 2013)

The *madhāhib* show various degrees of favour towards the enforceability of contractual relations that fall outside the list of nominate contracts recognised by the tradition. While no general and systematic theory of the *ʿaqd* can be found in Muslim jurisprudence, the classical sources proceed by reference to a list of nominate contracts, whose prototype is the sale (*bayʿ*) as the model of any commutative exchange (Zahraa and Mahmor, 2001). The centrality of the contract of *bayʿ* explains why '[i]n most Islamic legal manuals, principles governing contracts in general are explained in detail primarily in the chapter on sales, while other nominate contracts are explained in separate chapters' (Yanagihashi, 2013; see also Rayner, 1991, p. 91).

> The system used by the jurists to categorize the nominate contracts was to determine whether, in any given contract, right passed in ownership or possession, and whether consideration passed or otherwise. The basic nominate contracts number four:
>
> (1) *Bayʿ* (sale): where right of ownership passes for consideration (*tamlīk al-ʿayn bi-ʿiwād*);
> (2) *Hiba* (gift): where right of ownership passes without consideration (*tamlīk al-ʿayn bilā ʿiwād*);
> (3) *Ijāra* (hire): where transfer of possession occurs for consideration;
> (4) *ʿĀriya* (loan): where transfer of possession occurs without consideration.
>
> Other nominate contracts include those of *Salam* (a contract for delivery with prepayment), *Muḍāraba* ([sleeping] partnership agreement; equity sharing between bank and client), *Sharika* (partnership), mortgage (*Rahn*), *Juʿāla*, *Wadīʿa* (deposit), *al-Muzāraʿa* . . . and *ʿUmra*.
>
> (Rayner, 1991, pp. 100–101)

In addition to this categorisation, in their ways of 'walking' (*dhahāb*, verbal noun) through the city of the *ʿaqd*, Muslim scholars provide guidelines about 'how far, if at all, . . . the parties [may] vary this rigid scheme [i.e., the strict defining of each contract in terms of its purpose and effect] by introducing agreed special terms as appendages to the particular nominate contracts they are purporting to conclude' (Coulson, 1984, p. 51). Hence, the extent to which *fiqh* admits freedom of contract may be deduced from the attitude of Muslim scholarship on the admission of new types of contracts or of variations/additions to named contracts.[13] In general, they appeared to maintain a narrow view on the admissibility of new contracts, except for the Ḥanbalīs.

> The early jurists were concerned that all contracts were free from suspicion of usury and uncertainty, characteristics which served to nullify any transaction. As a result of this, they decided that individuals should contract according to the rules of nominate contracts, and thus, not generally free to establish or create any new and possibly illegal stipulations. Nevertheless, the Ḥanbalī jurists constituted an exception, for they permitted freedom of contract under the doctrine of *ibāha*: non-restriction was, for the Ḥanbalīs, the general rule.
>
> (El-Hassan, 1985, p. 54)[14]

In this sense, the Ḥanbalīs claim that the 'only condition required . . . for the validity of any contract is the mutual consent of the contracting parties' (Rayner, 1991, p. 94), and support the 'reasonable presumption that all contracts are valid subject to their being expressly forbidden by rule of law, or they contain voidable stipulations, or contravene Islamic prohibitions (especially those of *Ribā*, *Maysir* and *Gharar*), or public policy or morals' (*ibidem*, p. 95). As a result, they validate any innominate contract, provided that it conforms with the principle of liberty to contract within the limits of divine law and the principle of sanctity of contracts (*pacta sunt servanda*) (Saleh, 1998).

Nevertheless, the Ḥanbalī position was strongly opposed by the other Sunnī schools (Ḥanafī, Mālikī, Šāfi'ī) following the *Sunna* of the Prophet: 'How can men stipulate conditions which are not in the book of Allah? All stipulations which are not in the book of Allah are invalid, be they a hundred in number. Allah's judgment alone is true and His stipulations alone are binding' (reported in El-Hassan, 1985, p. 57; see also Coulson, 1984, pp. 100–102). This resistance to contractual freedom, as we will note when discussing the topic of *ḥiyal* in Chapter 4, was mitigated in the interplay between theory and practice through the elaboration of legal stratagems as a means to orient the believer's performance of God's will in the world of commercial affairs.

Another field linked to 'the question of contractual liberty is that of the validity of clauses (*šurūṭ*, sing. *šarṭ*) that may alter the terms and conditions of a contract' (Yanagihashi, 2013). The admissibility of conditions, stipulations, clauses attached to a [nominate] contract (*šurūṭ al-muqtarina bi-l-ʿaqd*) represents further evidence of the rich normative pluralism embedded in Muslim *fiqh* (for the Ḥanafī school, see Chehata, 1969, pp. 104–109; for a comparative analysis of the schools, Linant de Bellefonds, 1965, pp. 224–242; Rayner, 1991, pp. 352–363). On this matter, the approach of the Sunnī schools to contractual freedom and the validity of attached stipulations can be summarized through Diagram 1, as follows.

Diagram 1 Theoretical approaches of the Sunnī schools to contractual freedom (author's elaboration)

In general, Šāfi'īs and Ḥanafīs appear more restrictive, whereas Ḥanbalīs and Mālikīs are more lenient with regard to the admissibility of attached clauses. In brief, for the Ḥanafīs and the Šāfi'īs, the attached stipulations are generally void, with the validity being the exception; for the Mālikīs and the Ḥanbalīs, by contrast, the *šurūṭ* are generally valid, with the invalidity being an exception. In particular, the Ḥanafīs show particular strictness on the *šurūṭ al-muqtarina bi-l-'aqd*, distinguishing four categories, as formulated in the works by al-Sarakhsī (d. 490/1097) and al-Kāsānī (d. 587/1191): (1) the conditions inherent in the nature of the contract (*šarṭ yaqtaḍīh al-'aqd*); (2) the conditions appropriate to the contract (*šarṭ mulā'im li'-l-'aqd*); (3) the customary conditions (*šarṭ muta'āraf*) – which the Ḥanafīs consider valid only on the ground of *istihsān* (equity); and (4) the invalid conditions (*šarṭ fāsid*) (Arabi, 1998, p. 29).

3.4.3. *Psychological components of the 'aqd: will (*irāda*), intention (*niyya*), animus contrahendi (*qaṣd*), choice (*khiyār*), and individual consent (*riḍā*)*

The literature of *fiqh* refers to a variety of psychological dimensions for the formation of the *'aqd*. This variety is relevant for our investigation for three reasons. First, it sheds supplementary light upon the interaction between human will and rationality in the formation of the Islamic contract. Second, it gives further evidence of the inherent normative pluralism that belongs to the Islamic legal tradition. Third, it will lead our discussion to deal more in depth with the nature of the agreement (*tarāḍī*, 'mutual assent' in the translation by Hamid, 1977) (section 3.5.2) as an essential element (*rukn*) of the *'aqd*.

Muslim jurisprudence employs different terms to refer to the internal dimension of the agreement; namely, will (*irāda*); intent/intention/motive (*niyya*); *animus contrahendi* (*qaṣd*); choice/option (*khiyār*); and (personal) consent or approval of the contract (*riḍā*).

Preliminary attention, in the context of *fiqh* as manifestation of Islamic *dīn*, must be addressed to the notion of human will and its precise role in the formation of the contract; interestingly, if, with regard to the Ḥanafīs, Chehata can affirm that 'the term *irāda*, utilised in modern times to signify will, cannot be found in Šaybānī' (Chehata, 1971, p. 164; my translation), more in general, the concept does not entail any similarity with the implications related to the *autonomie de la volonté* of the civil law tradition. *Irāda* in classical treatises simply indicates 'the faculty of taking the decision' (here, to enter the contract), *never* the human will as 'source' of contractual obligations. Moreover, if this faculty, linked to man's rationality, finds its expression in the *niyya* as motive of the action ('*il faut que cette volonté soit dirigée dans un sens déterminé, que l'auteur ait eu le dessein,* al-niyya, *d'accomplir tel acte en particulier*:' Linant de Bellefonds, 1965, p. 70), this should not lead the interpreter to assume that the intention of the parties defines the nature of the Islamic contract as an act of human autonomy. Rather, the presence of a valid *niyya* confirms the performance of the act as devoted towards God, making the action itself beneficial *both* between man and man, and man and God. Accordingly, the term is employed with a broad variation of conceptual nuances among the Sunnī schools in requiring a good intention (or not) for the validity of the contract (according to patterns of 'subjectivism' and 'objectivism' that respectively privilege the 'man to God' or the 'man to man' relation in the conception of the contract-performance as God's will: see as follows).

In fact, as we have already noticed in section 2.3, if the *niyya* constitutes an essential element for the action in the field of *ʿibādāt* (acts of worship), its relevance in the field of *muʿāmalāt* (human transactions) varies greatly among the *madhāhib*. The divide between *ʿibādāt* and *muʿāmalāt* in Muslim jurisprudence is underlined by Umar F. Abd-Allah (2008) by referring to the 'voluntarism' of the former in contrast to the 'rationalism' (the adherence of the intellect to the Law) underpinning the latter. Hence, as seen before, while an action can be legally valid just by complying with the Law (by 'way of intellect'), it requires proper intention (a 'way of will') to fully become an act of devotion and worship towards God.

> Ritual acts require a good intention, while non-ritual acts require no conscious intention at all [this is, indeed, a very contentious point among the *madhāhib*: see below]. Non-ritual acts need only conform to the formal provisions of the law, although any valid non-ritual act can be transformed into an act of worship in the sight of God if it is performed with a religious intention. Thus, a commercial enterprise undertaken with the aim of alleviating poverty for God's sake would be elevated to an act of immense religious merit.
>
> (Abd-Allah, 2008, p. 241)

The role of the *niyya* is further clarified by the influential Mālikī jurist Šihāb al-Dīn al-Qarāfī (d. 684/1285) in his *al-Umniyya fī Idrāk al-Niyya*.

> [Qarāfī] observes that legal commands are of two types: first, those for which the *simple performance* of the commanded act achieves the *benefit* of the act (the *muʿāmalāt*: e.g., payment of a debt, returning entrusted property, and forwarding support payments to a spouse or relative); second, those that *external performance* of which does not alone achieve

> the benefit for which God commanded the act (the *'ibādāt*: e.g. prayer, ritual purification, fasting, the rites of the *ḥajj*). *Intention*, for Qarāfī, constitutes the distinction: compliance with rules of the first type, regardless of the intention, benefits someone other than the actor immediately [in a 'man to man' relation] and may, if intended as an act of obedience or worship, also bring reward in the afterlife [hence, in a 'man to God' relation]. Compliance with rules of the second type brings benefit to the actor, primarily in the hereafter, and only if intention is present and proper. *Niyya* on this view is that which makes a given action one of obedience and worship, making possible divine reward. The *'ibādāt* have no other function, while the *mu'āmalāt* do.
>
> (Powers, 2006, p. 9; my italics)

As noted by Jackson, 'it is not al-Qarāfī's contention that acts of the first category [*mu'āmalāt*] are not religious acts. On the contrary, these should be performed with the intention of worshipping God and winning salvation in the Hereafter. His point, however, it that the rules of the first category are designed first and foremost for the benefit of man here and now. As such, whenever they are complied with, man benefits, even if God does not' (1996, pp. 201–202). The overlap between the conception of the contract as a 'man to man' and/or a 'man to God' relation in Islamic *dīn* as Muslim *bíos* (see again, on this point, section 2.3) can shed further light upon the divergences among the *madhāhib* in their interpretation of the need of a good *niyya* within the realm of *mu'āmalāt*. In fact, beyond the divide between *'ibādāt* (ritual) and *mu'āmalāt* (non-ritual) that is subscribed to by all the juristic schools, when dealing with human transactions (*mu'āmalāt*) *stricto sensu* (that is to say, as human actions *not directly* aimed at the benefit in the hereafter), the relevance given to the *niyya* varies enormously: from the 'objectivism' of Šāfi'īs and Ḥanafīs (with a 'secular' prevalence of the outer declaration over the inner intention), the attitude shifts towards 'subjectivism' in the Mālikī and Ḥanbalī schools (bearing a more implicit 'religious' connotation for the validity of the contract).

- *Šāfi'īs and Ḥanafīs: objectivism*

The marginalisation of the subjective intent in commercial transactions when the intent is not made manifest in the terms of the contract constitutes the rule for Šāfi'īs and Ḥanafīs.

The Šāfi'īs always give precedence to the 'declared will over the internal will. For the Šāfi'īs to found legal relations . . . on such a secret psychological phenomenon as the internal will means creating in the economic and social life arbitrariness and therefore injustice' (Linant de Bellefonds, 1965, p. 125; my translation). 'Al-Shafi'i himself left no doubt about his view on that issue in a famous section of *al-Umm*. . . . Contracts are lawful in view of their apparent validity. The unlawful intention of the parties is reprehensible (*makruh*), but does not cancel their act, unless expressed in the act' (Saleh, 1992b, p. 123). Hence, whereas an illicit intent made express in the contract invalidates the transaction, an implicit and undisclosed *niyya*, though religiously reprehensible (*makrūh*), has no legal consequence on its validity.[15]

As far as the Ḥanafī school is concerned, their attitude is very similar to that of the Šāfi'īs, with a general prevalence of the declared will over the internal will. Thus, the famous Ḥanafī saying *al 'ibra bi-l-ma'ānī lā bi-l-alfāẓ wa-l-mabānī* ('[in contractual stipulations] what has to be considered is the meaning [and] not the words or phrases') must be interpreted not in the sense of the prevalence of the inner intention over the external declaration but of the need to give the words their common, usual sense, as established by customs, and not their literal or etymological meaning. In fact, Qāḍī Khan, in his commentary (*Šarṭ*) to *Djāmi 'as Saghir* by Al-Šaybānī, specifies that '[w]hat must be considered in the fulfilment of the orders of God is the intention, but, in the worldly dimension, it's the words and the sentences' (quoted by Linant de Bellefonds, 1958a, p. 512). From the perspective of the Ḥanafīs, according to Chehata, the motive (*niyya*, which he defines as 'the thought underlining the declaration:' 1971, p. 173 and p. 208, note 2) represents a marginal element in the formation of the contract. In his *Al-Ašbāh wal-Naẓā'ir* ('The Resemblances and the Correspondences'), the Ḥanafī scholar Ibn Nujaym (d. 970/1563) quotes the *uṣūl* author Al-Taftazānī (8th century H.) ('the *niyya* is the intention – *qaṣd* –, in the act, of obeying and approaching God,' *Al-Talwīḥ*) and the judge Al-Bayḍānī ('the *niyya* is the will directed towards the act – aiming at pleasing God and obeying his rules') (reported by Chehata, 1971, p. 207; my translation). In these texts, the relevance of the *niyya* is reduced to the 'will directed towards performing a religious duty' (Schacht, 1964, p. 116); that is to say, an essential element for the acts of worship (*'ibādāt*: man to God relations).

By contrast, the concept of *niyya* has a marginal role in worldly transactions (*mu'āmalāt*: man to man relations). For the Ḥanafīs, it remains simply the internal purpose of the act, which must be investigated only in case of ambiguous declarations. In all other cases, the parties are held to their statements, and 'when the ultimate aim of the contracting party is not apparent either from the terms of the contract or from the prevalent usage of the object under contract, the Ḥanafīs (and Šāfi'īs) ignore ulterior motivation, which has no legal effect on the validity of the transaction' (Arabi, 1997, p. 215). In brief, the determining motive is marginalised by their doctrine when not 'materially' declared in the terms of the contract.[16] Specifically for the Ḥanafī school, the position is shared by al-Ṭaḥāwī (d. 321/933) and al-Kāsānī (d. 587/1191) and clearly exemplified by the usurious sale of *'īna* (*bay' al-'īna*). Al-Ṭaḥāwī: 'The vendor of grape juice may sell it with no fear – without making certain that the buyer will not make wine from it. For the juice of grapes is legally permissible (*ḥalāl*) and its sale is as permissible as that of any permissible object whose vendor is not supposed to inquire about what the buyer does with it' (*al-Mukhtaṣar*). Al-Kāsānī: 'For Abū Ḥanīfa the transport itself does not constitute disobedience (*ma'ṣīya*) [of the law], as the transport of wine for medicinal purpose is permissible. Hence the [mere] transport of wine does not necessarily cause the act of disobedience, which consists in its consumption' (*Badā'i'*) (both quotations can be found in Arabi, 1997, p. 215).

> The *'īna* sale has the following structure: one buys from another an item while postponing payment of the price; then the buyer sells back the same item to the vendor at a lower price than the first; he thus receives a sum of money which he will have to pay back later with an increment. The procedure is designed to circumvent the prohibition of usury, *ribā*, by Qur'ānic and Prophetic dicta. Yet, despite the illicit aim of the parties – their motive being usurious – the fact that the motive is not mentioned in the contract makes it of no consequence and the contract is valid for the two companions [of Abū Ḥanīfa, Abū Yūsuf and al-Šaybānī] and in the Shāfi'ī school.
>
> (Arabi, 1997, p. 216; see also later, Chapter 4)

Regarding the psychological formation of the contract the Ḥanafis collocate next to the *niyya* the concepts of *qaṣd*, *animus contrahendi* or 'intention to contract.'

While the *niyya* corresponds to the ultimate motive of the action – the purpose for which the act is performed – in the classical texts, the word *qaṣd* seems to have the narrower sense of the consciousness of the action of contracting – i.e. the awareness of being bound and the will in itself to be bound (*animus contrahendi*), considered separately from the purposive reason for the action. An example may help to distinguish the two notions. Two parents want to avoid the inheritance tax, which is applied for the transfer of the property of their house to their son, as heir; for this reason (*niyya*), they decide to sell the house to their son for a much inferior price to the real value of the estate. The rational intent to sell the house (considered in itself, without the reference to the aim of avoiding the application of inheritance tax) is the *qaṣd*.

Once again, it is important to note that this 'intention' (either as *niyya* or *qaṣd*) is *not* the 'will' as 'source of promises or obligations' known in the Western legal tradition. The *qaṣd* is simply the 'intention to make the act effective in law' (Chehata, 1971, p. 187; my translation) or, rather, the 'intention to declare in order to provoke an effect [established] in law [*ḥukm*]' (*ibidem*, p. 188), not the 'will, as creator of rights.' This radically differentiates Islamic law from the tradition of civil law and its idea of the *autonomie de la volonté*: '[t]he intention is not the will that creates the act as in our modern law. In Islamic law, it simply promotes the declaration following reflection. . . . And it is the declaration itself that brings about legal effects' (*ibidem*, pp. 168–169) in the performance of God's will. Hence, when the *'aql* is lacking (due to madness, interdiction, or the person being underage) or there is no *qaṣd* in provoking an effect at law (*ḥukm*) (words said under duress or fraud; in sleep; in jest, *jocandi causa*, *hazl*), the act does not exist (it is void, *bāṭil*) (see Chehata, 1971, pp. 247–249).

According to the Ḥanafī doctrine, the presence of *ʿaql* and *qaṣd* leads to the existence of a valid *khiyār* ('choice,' 'option' to contract), and then, to the 'personal, unilateral consent,' or 'approval,' *riḍā* (defined by Al-Taftazānī as 'the result of the *ikhtiyār*') of the contract. As far as the *riḍā* is concerned, the Ḥanafīs do not consider it as a prerequisite for the existence of the contract, but rather, for its validity. In other words, it does not appear to be an essential/constitutive element (*rukn*) of the contract, since even the vices of mistake or misrepresentation do not prevent its existence, though it may be open to rescission due to invalidity (violation of required condition, *šarṭ*) (Chehata, 1970b, pp. 129–130) (for more details about vitiating factors and the role of *ikhtiyār* see section 3.4.4 in this chapter). As Vogel notes, 'when the term "lack of consent" (*riḍā*) is used, it expresses only a finding that a contract, though existent, was formed in illegal circumstances' (Vogel, 2006, p. 32). The limited role of consent (*riḍā*) for the Ḥanafīs reflects their high level of objectivism in the evaluation of the declarations, where the expressed statements prevail over the inner will of the contracting parties. This objectivism is testament to an empirical conception of the contract as a concrete set of declarations (offer and acceptance) determining a new setting of properties. As this book will clarify later: '[t]he will of the declarant plays no role whatsoever in the contractual process. . . . The contract, as juristic act, is at first a concrete fact: the fact of the declaration. The objectivism of Islamic law [in the Šāfiʿī and Ḥanafī tradition] is pushed to its extreme limits' (Chehata, 1968b, p. 89; quoted in Vogel, 2006, p. 32) (see here, section 3.5.2).

• *Mālikīs and Ḥanbalīs: subjectivism*

While the Šāfiʿīs and the Ḥanafīs share an objective approach inclined to external declarations, the Ḥanbalīs and, to a certain degree, the Mālikīs are led by a subjective perspective, as they both claim the need to interpret and apply contracts according to the intents of the parties.

The Ḥanbalīs, moving from the internal morality of legal acts (somehow giving primacy to the 'man to God' over the 'man to man' relation within the realm of *muʿāmalāt*), make the inner intention override external declarations. Ibn Qayyim al-Jawziyya (d. 751/1350), a follower of Ibn Taymiyya (d. 728/1328), distinguishes three hypotheses:

1. inner will and declared will are concordant. No difficulty arises;
2. the invalid intention of the party is masked by the validity of the external words, but it is impossible to prove the real will, even though this may be presumed; in this case, the agent will be responsible towards God, but the declaration will produce its legal effects;
3. there is a divergence, and it is possible to determine the inner intention of the declarant; if this purpose is condemned by the *Šarīʿah*, then the contract will be invalid, despite the apparent regularity of the declarations (Linant de Bellefonds, 1958a, p. 512).

The Ḥanbalī concern for the moral dimension of the *ʿaqd* leads them to consider legally accountable those contracting parties who are aware of the illicit intentions of the other party, an element which, by contrast, is deemed irrelevant by the Šāfiʿīs and the Ḥanafis *if not made explicit* in the contract. Thus, with regard to the unlawful purpose, the Ḥanbalī Ibn Qudāma (d. 620/1223) states: 'if the unlawful motive is proven, it invalidates the sale, which is also void if the seller knows the (illicit) intention of the buyer, either from the words of the buyer or by presumption' (*Al Mughnī*, quoted by Linant de Bellefonds, 1958a, p. 517; my translation). He refers to the teachings of the master, Ibn Ḥanbal, in the following terms.

> Aḥmad [b. Ḥanbal] brought attention to this matter in a number of cases. In relation to the butcher and baker he said: if they know that what they sell serves the buyer to invite others to drink intoxicants, then they should not sell. Similarly, the maker of glasses should not sell them to one whom he knows is drinking intoxicants with them. He also forbade the selling of silk to men [desiring to wear it]. All these sales are null and void (*bāṭil*).
>
> (*Al Mughnī*, quoted in Arabi, 1997, p. 219)

Ibn Qudāma also elaborates on the doctrine of his master with reference to the sale of grape juice to a person whose intention is to make wine.

> The sale of grape juice to someone whom the vendor is aware is making wine from it is null and void (*bāṭil*) . . .; if one were to object by saying that the formal conditions of the sale are properly met, we would reply: yes, but there is something which prevents it from taking effect. The sale is prohibited and nullified if the vendor knows the intention of the buyer (*idhā ʿalima al-bāʾiʿ qaṣd al-mushtarī*) to make wine, whether from the buyer's declaration of from the specific signs indicating this.
>
> (*ibidem*, p. 219)

As far as the Mālikīs are concerned, David Santillana, in his *Istituzioni di Diritto Musulmano Malichita*, based on the *Muhtaṣar* by Khalīl Isḥāq (d. 767/1365) and the *Muwaṭṭaʾ* by Mālik Ibn Anas (d. 179/795), argues that, among the essential elements (*arkān*) of the contract, the *niyya* 'qualifies the act and it determines its nature; the external act . . . is only the body, whose intention or will, the internal element, is the soul' (Santillana, 1938, p. 22; my translation). Saleh reaches the same conclusion, commenting on the studies of Linant de Bellefonds of 1958 and 1965:

> [de Bellefonds] was puzzled by Maliki teachings on intention and its effects on the validity of the contracts. In an article dated 1958 the author reached the conclusion that Maliki jurists – but even more so the Hanafi ones – have a real repugnance towards rendering a legal act

> dependent upon such an uncertain element as the motive which inspired the contracting parties. The same author treated that very subject in a book published subsequently in 1965. Then a totally different conclusion was drawn, namely, that the Maliki school takes into consideration the remote reasons which made the vendor decide to sell, and, more generally, that the Maliki school takes into account, in numerous specific cases, the subjective motive which was in the mind of the obligor at the time the obligation came into existence. As a result the author acknowledged that inducing motive has an undeniable influence on the validity and interpretation of contracts or undertakings which give rise to obligations. The later position conveys a more faithful appraisal of the Maliki doctrine.
>
> (Saleh, 1992b, pp. 123–124)

To summarise the divergent positions of the Sunnī schools by considering the example of the sale of grape juice to the person who is going to produce wine (illicit motive), the Ḥanbalīs declare it invalid; the Šāfiʿīs and the Ḥanafīs classify it as valid, with no hesitation; in the Mālikī school, some divergences arise on the case, but the position in favour of the invalidity seems to prevail. The Mālikī al-Ḥaṭṭāb (d. 954/1547) states: 'The sale of grapes to someone who makes wine from it, and the sale of silk clothing to one who wears it, are not permissible' (*Mawāhib al-Jalīl Šarḥ Sīdī Khalīl*, quoted in Arabi, 1997, p. 220). On usurious transactions, the famous Mālikī jurist and philosopher Ibn Rušd (d. 595/1198) informs us that Mālik Ibn Anas invalidated contracts which are formally admissible due to usurious pretexts (*dharāʾiʿ rabawīya*). However, in contrast to Mālik, 'al-Shāfʿī does not consider suspicious transactions, taking into account for the validity and invalidity of sales only what the parties stipulate and state with their *tongues* and the *appearance* of their acts' (Ibn Rušd, *Bidāyat al-Mujtahid wa Nihāyat al-Muqtaṣid*, quoted in Arabi, 1997, p. 220, note 56; my italics).

The concept of *khiyār* (or *ikhtiyār*), which we mentioned in the previous section with regard to the Ḥanafīs, is well recognized in the Mālikī treatises as well, where it conveys the outcome of a free decision among different options (Santillana, 1938, p. 39). Here, the centrality of the *niyya* is shown in the requirement of a free and conscious intention, in order to enter the contract; in case of duress, for instance, the act exists in its *arkān* but cannot produce any effect, since 'he who is under duress does not follow his own intention, but that of the person responsible for the duress; . . . the declaration is merely apparent' (*ibidem*, p. 41): 'he who is under duress does not have the *niyya* to do what he is obliged to do; rather, he has the intention of doing the contrary' (*ibidem*, p. 47; see section 3.4.4 in this chapter).

The different positions of the four Sunnī schools on the psychological formation of the contract can be summarised following Arabi and through Diagram 2.

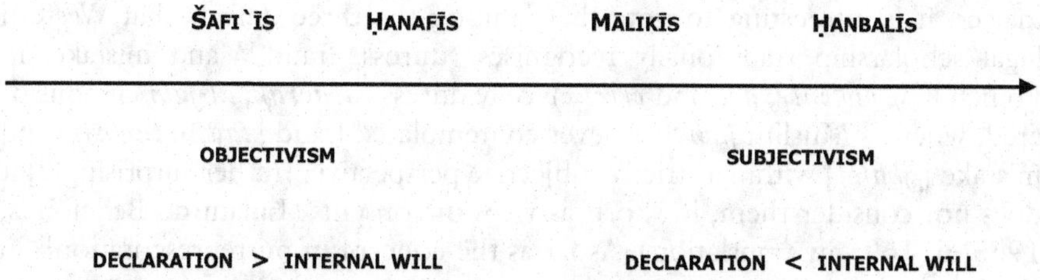

Diagram 2 Objectivism and subjectivism in the Sunnī schools (author's elaboration)

> [T]he Ḥanafīs and the Shāfiʿīs tend to ignore the ultimate aim of the contracting individual if that aim is neither stated in the terms of the contract nor evident from the circumstances surrounding the transaction; by contrast, the Mālikīs and the Ḥanbalīs go beyond the apparent expressions of intent, addressing the real motive underlying the transaction even if the latter are not mentioned in the contract.
>
> (Arabi, 1997, p. 210)

Significantly, the preferences of the schools for an objective or subjective approach mirrors their positions with regard to contractual freedom and the validity of attached clauses (Diagram 1, section 3.4.2), where the doctrinal divergences between the Ḥanafīs and the Šāfiʿīs, on the one hand, and the Mālikīs and the Ḥanbalī, on the other, are coherently maintained.

Furthermore, the relevance of the psychological formation of the contract in its different components (*niyya*, *qaṣd*, *khiyār*, and *riḍā*) also matches with the positions of the schools on legal artifices (*ḥiyal*; sing. *ḥīla*), whose validity depends mainly on the objectivity of interpretation, despite the illegal purpose that they seek to achieve; as Schacht explained, they can be seen as the 'use of legal means [external declarations] for extra-legal ends [illicit purposes]. . . . The 'legal devices' enabled persons who would otherwise, under the pressure of circumstances, have had to act against the provisions of the sacred Law, to arrive at the desired result while actually conforming to the letter of law' (1964, pp. 78–79). As *ḥiyal* is a core subject matter to understand the interplay between contractual theory(*-ies*) and commercial practice(*-s*) in Islamic medieval trade, their study is postponed to Chapter 4 (section 4.2.3).

3.4.4. The vices of consent (duress, ikrāh*; fraud,* tadlīs*; mistake,* ghalaṭ*), misrepresentation, and the doctrine of* al-khiyārāt

The psychological formation of the contract in Islamic law can find further evaluation through the survey of the vitiating factors of the consent. On this matter, it is interesting to note that, among the three defects that Western legal scholarship traditionally recognises (duress, fraud,[17] and mistake; in French law, *violence*, *dol*, and *erreur*), only duress (*al-ikrāh*; *al-jabr*) is considered, whereas Muslim *fiqh* 'has never contemplated fraud [*tadlīs, taghrīr*] and mistake [*ghalaṭ*] within a strictly subjective perspective; [rather surprisingly] it does not consider them, in short, as vices of consent' (Linant de Bellefonds, 1965, p. 169; my translation). As far as the concept of misrepresentation[18] in English contract law is concerned, the term does not find direct correspondence in Muslim *fiqh*, where the function of protection of the innocent party from deceit and fraud is mainly covered, as we will see later, by the doctrine of *al-khiyārāt*.

I would like to focus preliminarily on duress (*ikrāh*) as a vitiating factor of the free manifestation of the will. Once again, the Sunnī schools diverge in their assessment of the validity of the contract vitiated by duress (for a comparative perspective of English and Islamic law, see Al-Fadl, 1991; for a general overview and reference to modern legislation, Rayner, 1991, pp. 245–253). According to the majority of the Ḥanafī jurists, the contract, though existent, is corrupted, defective (*fāsid*), and consequently, voidable, as sound consent (*riḍā*) is a prerequisite for the validity of the *'aqd*. By contrast, the Mālikīs consider the act affected by duress valid (*ṣaḥīḥ*) but non-binding (*ghayr lāzim*). More precisely, the Ḥanafīs distinguish between constraining (*mulji*) and non-constraining (*ghayr mulji*) duress in relation to the role of free choice (*khiyār*).

> The first type (compelling duress) nullifies consent [*riḍā*] and vitiates free choice [*khiyār*]. The second type (non-compelling duress) nullifies consent [*riḍā*] but does not vitiate free choice [*khiyār*]. . . . Ḥanafī jurists argued that consent, as in being content or pleased with one's decisions, is often lacking even without duress or with minimal duress . . . any amount of duress is liable to negate consent. But only serious or compelling duress will also spoil choice.
>
> (Al-Fadl, 1991, pp. 127–128)

With regard to the Šāfi'īs and the Ḥanbalīs, they classify the contract affected by duress as inexistent (*bāṭil*) – i.e. void (Linant de Bellefonds, 1965, p. 170; Al-Fadl, 1991, pp. 140–141), since it affects the validity of the *tarāḍī* (agreement). But their arguments on the point are markedly dissimilar. For the Ḥanbalīs, the fundamental problem lies in the lack of a sound *niyya* (subjectivism); due to the vitiated *niyya*, the *tarāḍī* is vitiated as well, the contract lacks its *rukn*, and it is therefore inexistent. For the Šāfi'īs, instead, duress negates the existence of the agreement as an external fact which must be valid in its material occurrence, with marginal consideration, as previously remarked, of the *niyya* (objectivism) (see section 3.5.2 in this chapter).

Moving now to the other two vitiating factors of the consent, unlike duress, '[m]istake [*ghalaṭ*] is given the least consideration among the impediments to consent [reporting al-Sanhūrī's position] . . . [t]he principles of *Ghalaṭ* are certainly not to be found in any systematically theoretical exegesis among the Sharī'a authorities' (Rayner, 1991, pp. 175–176). Regarding fraud, '*tadlīs* is itself generally considered not to have been of purely Islamic origins . . . *taghrīr* and *tadlīs* do not constitute regular "impediments" or "*vices du consentement*"' (*ibidem*, pp. 204–205). The great Egyptian jurist Al-Sanhūrī confirms how, in contrast to the Western legal tradition,

> Islamic jurisprudence recognizes all three kinds of defects, but in an inverse order. Most prominent of all is its treatment of duress (*ikrāh*), which is accorded a separate and explicit analysis. Fraud (*tadlīs*) comes in the second place, after duress . . . as a source of defective transactions in its own right, and some schools identify it by this very term. On the other hand, error (*ghalaṭ*) is the least prominent of contract defects in Islamic law, as it is the most subjective type of defect.
>
> (Al-Sanhūrī, *Maṣādir*, quoted in Arabi, 1995, p. 156)

This inverse order can raise two questions for the Western lawyer visiting the city of the *'aqd*. 1) First, how are duress, fraud, and mistake thought of in Muslim *fiqh*? Are they conceived as subjective defects of the contract or defects affecting the *tarāḍī* as 'speech act,' 'occurrence of word' (*qawl*)? 2) Second, if *tadlīs* and *ghalaṭ* are given limited attention in classical treatises, does this imply that Muslim jurisprudence *thinks* of the matter of the sound manifestation of personal consent (*riḍā*) differently from Western legal tradition?

1) As far as the first question is concerned, Arabi notes that, in Muslim jurisprudence,

> a defect in the contract is considered as enjoying greater legal significance the more objectively it is induced. . . . By this criterion, error is the most subjective of the three categories, since, being a subjectively fostered illusion, it does not arise from any direct external cause. Fraud, which is charged with more legal effect than error, though dependent on a subjective blindness of sorts, is none the less critically linked to an external source of deception. The most objective type of legally defective contract is that obtaining under duress, where the threats of death, bodily harm, or imprisonment render the contract null and void (*bāṭil*) (Arabi, 1995, p. 156).

As we will shortly see, within this objective approach, fraud, and mistake/error (as well as the notion of misrepresentation) seem to be substituted by the doctrine of the 'option' (*khiyār*; pl. *khiyārāt*) to enter the contract in the doctrinal elaboration of Muslim scholars.

2) The term *khiyār* indicates, for the Ḥanafīs, 'the fact of tending towards an object and wanting it' (Ibn-'Ābidīn) and it is distinguished from consent, *riḍā* (defined by Al-Taftazānī as 'the result of the *ikhtiyār*'). All the schools

attribute relevance to the topic of *al-khiyārāt* in relation to the enforceability of the contract, to guarantee the sound approval of the transaction.

In the attempt to explain why error and fraud do not receive particular attention by the *fuqahā'*, Linant de Bellefonds notes that the issue of the invalidity of the contract due to *tadlīs* and *ghalaṭ* is not *thought* of by Muslim scholars as a vice of the *riḍā*; with this aim, on the contrary, it is replaced by the theory of *al-khiyārāt*, aimed at assuring the valid 'choice' of the contracting parties, so to protect them from any prejudice that may derive from unsound engagements (1965, pp. 213–215). Linant de Bellefonds specifies that any valid act (fulfilling all its *arkān* and the *śurūṭ* determined at Law),

> does not definitively bind the actor(s) if it comprises an option (*khiyār*) . . . for the contracting parties to cancel the act unilaterally. The word *khiyār* implies a choice . . . the beneficiary has the choice between two alternatives: to ratify the act, which becomes definitively binding, *lāzim*, or rescind it, and the act will be deemed never to have existed.
>
> (Linant de Bellefonds, 1965, p. 309; my translation)

Options are either conventional or legal; the former are added by the parties as terms of the contract (*khiyār aś-śarṭ* – 'stipulated' or 'conditional' option, option of condition – and the *khiyār at-ta'yīn* – option of 'designation,' faculty of choosing among several objects); the latter are automatically recognized by Law, independently from their insertion in the agreement (*ibidem*, p. 309; see also Rayner, 1991, p. 306; for instance, guarantee against defects, 'option for defect,' *khiyār al-'ayb*). Following Linant de Bellefonds, one can argue that legal options replace both the category of mistake/error (*khiyār al-ghalaṭ*, which is absorbed within the topic of the stipulated option, *khiyār aś-śarṭ*: see specifically on this point, Linant de Bellefonds, 1965, pp. 383–385) and fraud (*khiyār al-tadlīs*), thus fulfilling the function of protecting the contracting parties from unsound agreements. The doctrine of *al-khiyārāt* certainly shows strong similarities with that of misrepresentation in English contact law, since they both have the function of providing protection against any deception in the formation of the agreement. With this same aim, other examples are the faculty to control the matter that is not present at the *majlis* ('option of inspection,' *khiyār al-ru'ya*) and the *khiyār al-waṣf* (the choice due to the absence of a desired quality in the object).

The *khiyār aś-śarṭ* is an important element to understand the nature of the *'aqd*. Its validity is recognised by all the schools on the basis of the *ḥadīth*: '"The Prophet said to Habbān al-Anṣārī, who was complaining of being cheated in his transactions: When you buy or sell, at the moment of sale make a declaration to the effect 'that there shall be no cheating (*Lā khilāba*) and I reserve for myself the Option for three days"' (quoted by Rayner, 1991, p. 309; see also Linant de Bellefonds, 1965, p. 312). The 'option life' (*waqt al-khiyār*) of three days is strictly imposed by Ḥanafīs[19] and Šāfi'īs, while the

Ḥanbalīs admit any term, provided that the parties express clearly in the contract the duration; the Mālikīs make the validity of the option dependent on the needs of the parties and the nature of the contract (Linant de Bellefonds, 1965, pp. 316–317). With the *khiyār aš-šarṭ* 'either one or both parties to a contract may insert a condition . . . giving them an option . . . to either cancel or ratify the sale' (Rayner, 1991, p. 309). It must be noted that the effectiveness of the contract is subordinated solely on the choice of the beneficiary of the *khiyār aš-šarṭ* to ratify the exchange. This leads to two corollaries. First, the *khiyār aš-šarṭ* cannot be said equivalent to an invalidity due to mistake, as an initial error is not a requirement for its exercise. Second, the *fuqahā'* do not allow making the contract dependent on some future uncertain events through the insertion of a *khiyār aš-šarṭ*, since this would correspond to *gharar* (see later, section 3.5.4), with the consequent invalidity of the act (Linant de Bellefonds, 1965, p. 313); consequently, the *khiyār aš-šarṭ* does not correspond to a condition precedent of common law. Comparing the analysis of the *khiyār aš-šarṭ* in the *Aṣl* by the Ḥanafī al-Šaybānī (d. 189/804) with that in the *Mudawwanah al-Kubrā* by the Mālikī Saḥnūn (d. 240/855), D'Emilia remarks how for both the classical *fuqahā'* the contract is not binding (*lāzim*) for the option holder until his unilateral consent (*riḍā*) to the exchange is given; during the option life (*waqt al-khiyār*), the beneficiary of the option can examine the property (so that the option holder can decide carefully about the exchange, avoiding any mistake); the consent must be external, as mere internal consent (*riḍā' bi'l-qalbi*) is void (*bāṭil*) (D'Emilia, 1957, pp. 634–635).

In accordance with D'Emilia, Bellefonds gives a twofold interpretation of the *khiyār aš-šarṭ*, both as a remedy against wrongful engagements and as a means to enjoying a period of reflection before concluding the contract (this explains why the option is called, especially by the Mālikīs, *šarṭ at-tarawwā*, 'condition of reflection') (1965, p. 313).

On this point, another interpretation can be advanced. Although the *khiyār aš-šarṭ* can certainly be used by the beneficiary as a means of self-protection, in order to evaluate carefully the utility of the *'aqd* (and consequently avoid any error), it also gives the holder the power to cancel or ratify his approval of the contract, without the need to justify his decision in reference to defects or hidden elements unknown at the moment of the consent. Hence, depending solely upon the will of the holder, the *khiyār aš-šarṭ* appears to be a whimsical condition. Considering this, a) what is the effect of the *khiyār aš-šarṭ* on the enforceability of the *'aqd*?; and b) what is the chronological position of the *khiyār aš-šarṭ* in the formation of the agreement (*tarāḍī*)?

a) With regard to the first point, in the Ḥanafī doctrine the contract affected by an option of stipulation is valid but subject to ratification (the final rational/voluntary acceptance of the act by the beneficiary); thus, the *fuqahā'* describe it as not-yet-binding (*ghayr lāzim*) or suspended (*mawqūf*). More precisely, the binding effects of the two sides of the *'aqd* are regarded separately. The only effect (*ḥukm*) which is suspended is that of the contractor who has reserved for himself the option. The other party, on the contrary, is already bound from the time of the conclusion of the contract. Hence, the contract is *mawqūf*, on the one side; *lāzim*, on the other side (Linant de Bellefonds, 1965, p. 322; Rayner, 1991, p. 317). The dual nature of the optional contract, non-binding for one party and binding for the other, is testament to the perpetuation in Islamic law of a unilateral construction which is common in the laws of antiquity (although soon abandoned in favour of a bilateral construction). This point is underlined by Schacht in relation to the etymology of *ījāb* (offer): '*ījāb*, making something *wājib*, means etymologically not "to offer" but "to make definite, binding, due", and this reflects a different, unilateral construction of the contract' (1964, p. 22); it is also remarked by Zysow ('*ījāb* . . . seems to reflect a stage of law in which sales were affected by unilateral conveyances:' 1985–86, p. 75).

b) What is the exact temporal collocation of the faculty of choice? The *khiyārāt* cover a spectrum of time which is located between the formation of mutual consent, *tarāḍī*, and the definitive effectiveness of the contract, which is suspended until the final ratification of the *'aqd*: 'there is therefore life between the formation of the contract and its consensual or forced end. This life corresponds to particular rights for the parties which operate in Islamic law of options such as "time out" on the contract, a time for reassessment' (Mallat, 2007, p. 279). This is a clear peculiarity of Islamic contract law in comparison with Western law.

> In Western systems the contract itself is sacrosanct because all the necessary investigations and calculations are made, or are deemed to have been made, prior to the conclusion. In the Islamic system the procedure is virtually reversed. The first essential is to get the contract off the ground, to create the legal tie or *'aqd*, by mutual agreement. Then follows the time for reflection to ascertain whether or not the proper expectations of the parties are to be realised, and if they are not, to exercise the option to break the tie or rescind the contract. At this stage the Islamic *'aqd* is, comparatively, little more than a declaration of intent. Only when the wide-ranging and elaborate system of options is exhausted does the contractual commitment become fully imperative and legally binding (Coulson, 1984, pp. 73–74).

On the quality of *al-khiyārāt* as a means for later reassessment (hence covering aspects that in Western legal systems relate more to the idea of fraud, mistake/error, or misrepresentation), two final points can be advanced. First, what Šāfi'īs and Ḥanbalīs indicate in their treatises as 'option of the contractual session' (*khiyār al-majlis*: i.e. the faculty for the parties to revoke the offer or acceptance just given during the contractual negotiations, *majlis*; see next section) does not specifically entail a faculty of choice. In fact, since a valid contract doesn't exist until the parties have left the meeting (Linant de Bellefonds, 1965, p. 310, note 4), the distribution of contractual rights (*ḥuqūq al-'aqd*) is not yet definitive, so there is no need for a choice to ratify or annul it. Second, the faculty of reassessment that *fiqh* provides can in general be interpreted (as previously suggested) as a means of safeguarding against any defects of the exchanged properties, as proven by the so-called *khiyār al-ʿayb* (option for defect):

> under Islamic commercial law, the seller in a sale and purchase agreement is under an obligation to allow the buyer to inspect or examine the fitness of the goods to be sold not only before the conclusion of the agreement but also after. If there is any defect in the goods, regardless of whether this defect is discovered before or after the conclusion of the agreement, Islam then grants the option (*khiyar*) to the buyer either to continue with the agreement or to rescind.
>
> (Billah, 1998, pp. 278–279)

3.5. The construction of the *ʿaqd* as consensual transfer of properties

Any human action finds its legal status in the rule (*maḥkūm bihi*); next to its moral classification (the *al-aḥkām al-khamsa* of the *forum internum*), the *šarʿī* act is judged in its performance (*forum externum*; see section 3.3.2 of this chapter) as part of divine creation. It is precisely regarding this performance that the *ʿaqd* can reveal an underlying unity in *fiqh* doctrinal elaboration.

In fact, if the relevance of the intention (*niyya*) varies in the assessment of worldly transactions (*muʿāmalāt*) from the subjectivism of Mālikīs and Ḥanbalīs to the objectivism of Šāfiʿīs and Ḥanafis, the way of considering the contract in Muslim *fiqh* shows some deep connotations of meaning in the construction of the 'legal reality' of Islam, in the intersection between divine creation and human agency, which is common to all the *madhāhib* in their non-identity with Western law-religion. Maintaining the metaphor of the city, one may think that the 'material construction' of its 'buildings' occurs through some tangible elements, each necessary for the valid conclusion of the contractual relation between the parties; and namely, the external expression (*ṣīghah*) of the intentions of the parties within the contractual session (*majlis*) (section 3.5.1); and the valid manifestation of an offer (*ījāb*) and a convergent acceptance (*qabūl*) for an agreement (*tarāḍī*) to be reached (section 3.5.2). Furthermore, while the contractual building lies on the 'ground' of its subject matter, its 'bricks' are properties (*amwāl*) whose type affects the rules to be applied for the stability of the construction (section 3.5.3); last but not least, fundamental principles to keep the 'equilibrium' of the building – namely, the prohibitions of *ribā*, *gharar* and *maysir* (section 3.5.4) – must be met.

*3.5.1. Expression (*ṣīghah*), verbalism, and the unity of negotiations (*majlis al-ʿaqd*)*

For the contract to exist, the *niyya* finds its material outcome in the external expression, an utterance (*ṣīghah*) of the intent. The *ṣīghah* can be described as the manifestation of the *animus contrahendi* (*qaṣd*), in the rational choice (*khiyār*) to express the consent (*riḍā*). The external form (*ṣīghah*) is 'the material fact, the perceptible expression, that is to say, the words or the gesture or the act, even if negative [silent], which is the body that shapes the intentions of the contracting parties' (Santillana, 1938, p. 20; my translation).

For the manifestation of the intention any form (*ṣūra*) is valid. The lack of formalism is a peculiar aspect of Muslim *fiqh*, which has never fixed formal procedures to enter the contract (such as the Roman *stipulatio* or the English covenant). While *fiqh* tends to insert commercial transactions into a list of nominate contracts, at the same time, it avoids formalism nearly entirely.[20] This aspect, according to Frank Vogel, 'is a particularly striking result sociologically, because all legal systems were once supposed to evolve from formalism toward abstract obligation, reaching the latter only at advanced stages' (2006, pp. 31–32). This does not apply, however, to matters for which the Law asks for specific *formulae* (words, gestures . . .), such as marriage (*nikāḥ*), repudiation (*ṭalāq*), or in the case of acts of worship (*ʿibādāt*).

At the same time, Vogel notes how there is 'a covert sense in which, in several schools at least, formalism re-enters. This results from scholars' adoption of a certain "objective" approach to the interpretation of the declarations of the parties. The classical and extreme statement is that of al-Shāfiʿī, who claims to give legal judgements only by what is apparent, and never by what is hidden' (*ibidem*, p. 32). The objective approach of the Šāfiʿīs (and the Ḥanafīs) in dealing with the psychological formation of the contract has been previously discussed, in opposition to the subjectivism of the Mālikīs and the Ḥanbalīs. In fact, this is an aspect that differs from the need for specific forms to make the agreement enforceable; the lack of formalism appears to be a common element for all the schools, since no specific *ṣīghah* is required to make the *ʿaqd* enforceable (the objective approach of the Šāfiʿīs and Ḥanafīs refers to the interpretation of the declaration, not to the need for specific *formulae* in Islamic contract law).

There are, indeed, two other elements that may suggest a subtle formalism, and which deserve further attention to understand the rationales of the *ʿaqd* in relation to Islamic *dīn* as Muslim *bíos*: 1) the preference given to oral contracts with respect to written agreements or contracts concluded by performance (despite the general recognition that written documents correspond to oral declaration, *al-kitāba ka-l-ḥitāb*) – a tendency that Chehata describes under the label of 'verbalism;' 2) and the need for a unique session for the validity of the contract (*majlis al-ʿaqd*).

1) With regard to the idea of 'verbalism,' Chehata remarks how in Muslim *fiqh*, despite the lack of any need for special solemnities (in form of gestures, rituals . . .),

> words [must be . . .] pronounced. There is a special formalism that we call "verbalism". This is a memory of the ancient magical might of the verb, of the ritual word that obliges. It is the *ṣīgah*. This *ṣīgah* may have different forms or *ṣūra*, but its existence is necessary. The intention that

> is expressed through other means, such as the movement of the head, will not oblige. . . . The written document itself does not oblige without the pronunciation of the words.
>
> (Chehata, 1969, p. 110; my translation)

Although Chehata relates 'verbalism' to the power of the words, no 'ritualism' exists in *fiqh* contract law; words 'are necessary only as expressions of the internal will. They do not have any own inherent power, like in ancient Roman law' (Linant de Bellefonds, 1965, p. 124; my translation). If, according to Zysow, '[t]he basis for requiring that contracts be formed by a verbal exchange of offer and acceptance is not entirely clear' (1985–86, p. 70), an interpretation of verbalism may be advanced in relation to the centrality of the Word in the acoustic space of Islam. As seen in Chapter 2, the action of the believer becomes a *materialisation* of the divine Word in his agency:

> the divine law is a manifestation of the divine Word. The implication of this statement for ethics is that the human being as an ethical being is a being of the word. . . . Humans can therefore not be adequately understood in their ethical dimension as already constituted beings "before the Law" who are then asked to find out by which means they will reply. Or rather, they can be understood in this way only because the law as a particular manifestation of the divine Word constitutes them *by way of word*.
>
> (Stelzer, 2008, p. 169)

If the ethical nature of the action is grounded on the *Word*, verbalism, in the material occurrence of the contract, *re*-presents the divine will by echoing the Law through human (verbal) *words*. There is an additional element to be taken into consideration here when looking at the *ʿaqd* as manifestation of Islamic *dīn*. Verbalism requires the sentences to be expressed in the past or present tense; the future tense does not determine the formulation of a valid contract: 'according to the texts, the past tense obliges without the need for considering the intention. This intention will be investigated in the case of use of the present tense' (Chehata, 1969, p. 111, my translation; on the matter, see also Linant de Bellefonds, 1965, pp. 123–134). With regard to the Ḥanafī *madhhab*, al-Kāsānī remarks how

> [t]he present-tense form [of a contract of sale] is that the seller says to the buyer "I sell this thing to you for such and such [an amount]" and intends [with this] an offer of contract (*nawā al-ījāb*) and the buyer says . . . "I buy this thing from you for such and such [an amount]" and intends [with this] an offer of contract (*nawā ījāb*) . . . this satisfies the requirements [of a valid contract] (*yatimmu al-rukn wa yanʿaqidu*), however we consider the intention (*al-niyya*) here.
>
> (Kāsānī, *Kitāb Badāʾiʿ al-Ṣanāʾiʿ*, quoted in Powers, 2006 p. 109)

The passage is significant for three reasons. First, al-Kāsānī refers to a double-offer (*ījāb*) instead of an offer plus acceptance to describe the contract of sale, a point which will be further discussed in the next section (3.5.2); second, he explicitly refers to the present-tense form; third, he underlines the need to investigate the *niyya*, which is generally superfluous for the Ḥanafīs. A reference to Arabic grammar may help to clarify the point. As noted by Böwering,

> a vision of God acting instantaneously in the world as the sole true cause [see Chapter 2] . . . also proved akin to Arabic grammar, which lacks genuine verbs for "to be" and "to become". Neither does Arabic employ the tenses of past, present, and future. Instead, it uses verbal aspects of complete and incomplete, marking the degree to which an action has been realized or it yet to be realized without distinguishing precisely between present and future.
>
> (Böwering, 1997, p. 60)

Arabic grammar distinguishes between the perfect verb (*al-māḍī*), which refers to a complete action in the past, and the imperfect verb (*al-muḍāriʿ*), which describes an incomplete event, occurring in the present or in the future. Marking the completion of the action through the perfect tense secures, for the Muslim jurist, the performance of the action (*kasb*) and so the attribution of responsibility for the *mukallaf*; there is a 'performative' outcome in the use of the perfect verb.[21] In contrast, the present or future tense (imperfect verb) do not fully bind the contracting parties in relation to the acquisition (*kasb*) of the action created by God. 'For this reason, the law requires that both offer and acceptance be couched in the past tense to indicate finality, rather than in the future tense, which is promissory ('*ida*)' (Zysow, 1985–86, p. 75). What we find in the Islamic *ʿaqd* is not a model of executory contracts with promises to be performed in the future; on the contrary, it is an executed exchange (on this specific point, see section 3.5.2 in this chapter). It is within this background that the need for investigation of the intention (*niyya*) of the parties (due to possible ambiguity due to the lack of the use of past tense) can be explained in the passage by al-Kāsānī.

Within the discussion of the relevance of verbalism in Muslim *fiqh*, for all juristic schools, the contract is binding according to the use of the word (*qawl*), and specifically, in the form of a verbal offer (*ījāb*) and a verbal acceptance (*qabūl*). In this regard, the Ḥanafī Sarakhsī describes any declaration as a 'fact of the tongue' (*fiʿl al-lisān*); a 'speech act' (Chehata, 1971, p. 171). The fact that contracts are primarily oral rather than written, as already remarked, is clear evidence of the centrality of the *Word* in the rationales of classical *fiqh* as manifestation of Islamic *dīn*. *Inter praesentes*, the oral agreement is necessary and cannot be replaced by a written document, since it is the fact of the tongue (*fiʿl al-lisān*) that obliges (*lāzim bi-ʾl-qawl*). Written agreements can replace orality only *inter absentes*, where the rule 'written documents correspond to oral declarations,' *al-kitāba ka-l-ḥitāb*, finds application. Thus, '[w]riting the contract is neither legally necessary nor, according to *fiqh* manuals, even legally efficacious' (Powers, 2006, p. 101). Even though it was customary practice in medieval trade for documents to be widely used in commercial transactions, 'the jurists never modified their attitude toward written documents. . . . The personal word of an upright Muslim was deemed worthier than an abstract piece of paper or a piece of information subject to doubt and falsification' (Wakin, 1972, p. 6). The matter will find further elaboration when locating the *'aqd* in the reality of medieval Muslim societies (see specifically section 4.2.2).

2) Not only must a verbal offer (*ījāb*) be followed by a verbal acceptance (*qabūl*), but these declarations must occur at the (same) time and place of the *majlis al-'aqd*, 'contractual meeting' or 'session' (Mallat, 2007, pp. 271–276). All the schools require that the declarations happen in the same spatial and temporal fragment (unity of time and space); a contract that is made in violation of this rule is not merely invalid (*fāsid*), but inexistent, *bāṭil.* The requirement is so strong that for the Ḥanafīs the contract becomes an indivisible entity, to the extent that:

> its construction replicates this unity. Unity of the act: thus, a single contract cannot involve two or more *negotia*. Unity of time: the contract must be concluded in the same temporal session. Unity of place: the contract must be concluded in the same spatial place. . . . To conclude, the contractual phenomenon must occur within the modality of the 'three unities'.
>
> (Chehata, 1969, p. 104; my translation)

The doctrine of the *majlis al-'aqd* is common to all the four Sunnī schools, with marginal divergences on the modalities of the contractual meeting.

> The principle is that the offer must be accepted by the other party during the same contractual session. The contractual session happens in the place where the two parties meet; it begins when the offer is emitted; it lasts till the two parties leave. It finishes, moreover, when one of the two parties declares his intention not to continue the negotiation. All the schools agree on these points; the divergences emerge on the following four questions: A. does the contractual session end only when the two parties leave? B. must the acceptance follow the offer immediately? C. is the party who offers bound by his offer and must he maintain it till the end of the contractual session? D. last (and this is the most serious issue), may the person who has already accepted withdraw his statement before the end of the session?
>
> (Linant de Bellefonds, 1965, p. 148; my translation; for a comparative investigation of these issues, see *ibidem*, pp. 148–154)

Interestingly, the claim of the unity of the contractual meeting is applied (fictitiously) even when the contracting parties are physically absent, with the contract being concluded by written documents or messages (*kitāba* or *risāla*). All the rules regarding the contractual session *inter praesentes* are applied, *mutatis mutandis*, to the meeting *inter absentes*: the contract is always concluded at the place and time of the acceptance, when mutual consent (*tarāḍī*) has been manifested (*ibidem*, pp. 154–156; Chehata, 1969, p. 119).

Similarly to verbalism, the need for a unique session for the validity of the contract finds its rationale within the conceptual construction of the *ʿaqd* in relation to Islamic *dīn*. When inserted in the *Wor(l)d* of Islam, shaped by the everlasting creativity of God in time, 'words' and 'contractual session' are conceived in the light of a *unity of the act in the time and space* of God's creation; the performance of the action must be complete (and so 'completed' in space and time) for the contract to exist. Hence, as the words must be reported according to the perfect verb of Arabic language, so the declarations must be unified in the *majlis al-ʿaqd*. For this reason, the violation of the requirements of the *majlis al-ʿaqd* renders the contract inexistent. The unity of the *majlis al-ʿaqd* also explains why the Šāfiʿīs and Ḥanbalīs admit an 'option of the contractual session' (*khiyār al-majlis*) – i.e. the faculty for the parties to revoke the offer or acceptance just given during the contractual negotiations.[22] As long as the *majlis* is open, there is not yet a valid contract, and each of the parties can abandon the negotiations without legal consequences.

3.5.2. *Offer* (ījāb) *and acceptance* (qabūl) *in the* tarāḍī*: what is the nature of the agreement in Muslim* fiqh*?*

As in common and civil law, in the theory of the *ʿaqd*, the convergence between an offer (*ījāb*) and an acceptance (*qabūl*) in the agreement (*tarāḍī*) gives rise to an enforceable contract. But how do offer and acceptance relate in Muslim *fiqh*? If the *tarāḍī* is itself a 'craft of work' which depends on the local knowledge of Muslim jurisprudence (see section 3.1 in this chapter), does it create obligations binding human wills, as in the civilian tradition, or enforceable promises by means of consideration, as in common law? Or something else?

A fundamental starting point for the discussion can be found directly in the Qur'ān: 'Oh ye who believe! Do not consume your property among yourselves in vanities *(bi-al-bāṭil*): but let there be amongst you traffic and trade by mutual good-will [*tijaratan ʿan tarāḍin minkum*]' (Q. 4:29). This *āyat* shows an opposition between consuming, devouring, squandering properties unjustly (the term applied here is precisely *bāṭil*, which refers, as we know, to the 'nullity,' 'inexistence' of the action) and legitimate (*ṣaḥīḥ*) trade (*tijārah*) by 'mutual consent between the parties' (*ʿan tarāḍin minkum*). Accordingly, the *tarāḍī*, as the empirical manifestation (*ṣīghah*) of the convergence between two assents – *riḍā* – in the offer (*ījāb*) and acceptance (*qabūl*), represents a constitutive element (*rukn*) of any *ʿaqd*.

But what is its 'value' in Muslim *fiqh*? If no sound (*ṣaḥīḥ*) contractual building can exist without the *tarāḍī*, the 'ground' on which this building subsists cannot be identified as an 'act of (human) will' creating legal obligations (as it is in the tradition of civil law); rather, it consists in the 'external occurrence' of the agreement itself in the transaction. In other words, it is more a matter of rational choice than a matter of will; not by chance, its Arabic root is not that of *irāda*, 'will' (*R-W-D*, 'volition,' 'wish,' 'desire') but of *riḍā* (*R-Ḍ-Y*), which refers to the idea of 'approval,' in the sense of being pleased with one's decision. The *tarāḍī* is mainly a matter of human rationality (*'aql*); it is the conscious and rational commitment to adhere to the rules of the contract (*aḥkām al-'aqd*) as established by Law, by an *animus contrahendi* (*qaṣd*) that leads to the rational choice (*ikhtiyār*) of expressing consent (*riḍā*).

Thus, even if the notion of *tarāḍī* certainly implies a bilateral convergence of offer (*ījāb*) and acceptance (*qabūl*), it does not entail an obligatory (civil law) construction. 'It is not formed by an exchange of promises but an exchange of grants,' according to Zysow; a point 'which may reflect a pre-Islamic stage in which sales were unilateral conveyances' (1985–86, p. 76). Whereas John Makdisi considers Zysow's use of the term 'grant' ambiguous (1999, p. 1653, note 85), its meaning can be derived from the differentiation that he makes between promises and grants, as mentioned previously. Since the idea of the 'exchange of promise' is interpreted by Zysow as an aspect of 'our modern law,' being 'future-oriented' (*ibidem*, p. 75) in standard executory contracts, the notion of 'grant' supposedly relates to a transfer of properties that the parties confirm in the contract; something 'past-oriented' that is ratified; in other terms, the result of a conveyance that has been executed. Hence, the nature of the *tarāḍī* differs essentially from the doctrine of consensualism of civil/common law both in relation to its time construction and the role of human will. As regards time, it is oriented to the past (executed exchange of grants) and not the future (executory exchange of promises, or obligation to be performed). Regarding the role of the will, it does not embrace the notion of 'consensualism' as the 'source' of the transfer of titles; the binding force of the *'aqd* lies, in fact, on the equivalence of the countervalues (see the following). Although the Qur'ān speaks of 'trade by mutual good-will,' 'mutual consent' (Q. 4:29: *an tarāḍin*), Schacht remarks significantly that 'this is not used as a technical term, as appears from sura ii.233, and the concept of agreement or *consensus* as such does not enter into the Islamic theory of contracts' (1964, p. 22, note 1).[23]

In this regard, Hamid (1977) prefers to translate *tarāḍī* as 'mutual assent,' not 'mutual consent.' Unsurprisingly, the Arabic word that would render literally the idea of 'agreement' (*ittifāq*)[24] does not appear with reference to the *'aqd* in classical texts. As Chehata points out 'the term *ittafaqā* can be found [in Šaybānī] only once. But it does not refer to the agreement of wills. The text deals with the burden of proof, in case of agreement or disagreement of the parties on the qualities of the object of the sale' (1971, p. 164; my translation). Challenging the bilateral construction of the contract (offer and acceptance) as standard rule, Schacht remarks how the original nature of the *'aqd* was probably unilateral.

> The essential form of a contract in Islamic law consists of offer and acceptance (*ījāb* and *qabūl*). . .. This juridical construction, however, disagrees with the terminology because *ījāb*, making something *wājib*,

> means etymologically not 'to offer' but 'to make definite, binding, due', and this reflects a different, unilateral construction of the contract which is well known from other systems of law. It seems, therefore, that a unilateral construction was superseded by the bilateral one[.]
>
> (Schacht, 1964, p. 22)

This unilateral construction of the *'aqd* adds another point of reflection regarding the doctrine of the *khiyār*, as the rational expression of adherence to the agreement, and highlights how the principle of consensualism[25] cannot be immediately applied in the context of Muslim *fiqh*. In the space of Islam, the *'aqd* is not the autonomous outcome of human wills converging in the *tarāḍī*: 'the act does not exist thanks to the will of the person' (Chehata, 1970b, p. 126), as in the tradition of civil law. On the contrary, Muslim jurisprudence concentrates on the rational approval (an 'assent') of the transfer of goods by the parties; the agreement is primarily *a fact of intellect, not of will* (it is an '*acte de raison*' according to Chehata: *ibidem*), where the *ṣīghah* embodies the intention (*niyya*) to adhere to the Law through the material pronunciation of words.

In the Ḥanafī school, for instance, Qudūrī asserts that the juristic act is 'a rational act led by a specific intention;' but 'the intention is not the will that creates the act as in our modern law. In Islamic law it simply promotes the declaration following reflection (act of intellect). And it is the declaration itself that brings about legal effects' (Chehata, 1971, pp. 168–169; my translation). In the same way, Sarakhsī, in his *Mabsūṭ*, explains that 'the juristic act exists in the fact that a declaration has been pronounced' (*ibidem*, pp. 170–171); it is a manifestation of rationality expressed in an outer declaration and, even if supported by intention, 'it is clear that . . . at the base of the juristic act there is not the notion of a will as creator of rights' (*ibidem*). Accordingly, the *tarāḍī* is made by the factual correspondence between two declarations, not by the meeting of convergent wills in the agreement. This correspondence 'binds' (*'aqada*) the contracting parties to the contractual effects (*ḥukm al-'aqd*) of the transaction; when the conditions established by Law are met, the *tarāḍī* determines a new allocation of property rights (*ḥuqūq al-'aqd*), not the rise of legal obligations in the sense of the civil law tradition.[26] On one topic Muslim scholarship expresses a unanimous position:

> every effect which derives from the declaration is produced following the way established by law; and not the way desired by the parties. The contract is a "cause" (*sabab*) established by law, whose deriving effects (*ḥukm*) are, in the same way, defined by law. From the *animus* required as a necessary condition for the effectiveness of the declaration – to the *voluntas* conceived as the substratum of the juristic act, there is a tremendous gap.
>
> (Chehata, 1970b, pp. 128–129; my translation)

In summary, in the theory of the *ʿaqd*, human intention and rationality, not the autonomous will of the parties, determine a novel allocation of *ḥuqūq*, according to the rule established by God (*ḥukm*). The contract does not create obligations binding the contracting parties; the rights (*ḥuqūq al-ʿaqd*) are effects established by God (*ḥukm al-ʿaqd*). The enforceability of the contract does not derive from the binding force of the *tarāḍī* within the frame of consensualim (*solus consensus obligat*), but it is established by Law in the agency relationship between God and His believers (on the point see also the conclusive reflections of this chapter: section 3.6).

3.5.3. The subject matter (maḥall) *of the contract* (al-maʿqūd ʿalayhi)*: exchanging properties* (amwāl)*, either* ʿayn *or* dayn*, in relation to the* dhimma

As seen before (section 3.3.3), any *šarʿī* act is grounded on certain *arkān* (the divine injunction; the capacity of the agent; and the 'place', *maḥall*, of the juristic relation) and it is dependent on certain conditions (*šurūṭ*) for its validity.

The specific 'place,' *maḥall*, the 'ground' on which the *ʿaqd* stands, consists of '[the subject matter] upon which the contract is stipulated' (*al-maʿqūd ʿalayh*), the contract being upon it (*ʿalayh*). This is what in French law is defined as the *objet du contrat* and Santillana renders as *id de quo est contractum* (1965, p. 16: lit. 'that which [the parties] are negotiating about'). More precisely, *al-maʿqūd ʿalayh* in Muslim *fiqh* can refer both to the contractual terms, clauses, and subject-matter of the agreement, as well as to the properties (*amwāl*, sing. *māl*) that are exchanged. Keeping the metaphor of the building (see beginning of section 3.5), the *maḥall* may be thought as the 'ground,' the 'surface' where the *ʿaqd* stands – a construction whose materials (the 'bricks') are the properties to be exchanged, while the agreement (*tarāḍī*) between the parties is the 'labour,' the human 'workforce' that constructs the edifice.

On the topic of the *objet du contrat*, the elaboration by Muslim scholars ranges from a detailed regulation of property law to a 'preoccupation with maintaining the balance between the diverse effects resulting from legal acts in conjunction with their efforts to prevent all aleatory or usurious transactions' (Rayner, 1991, p. 131, quoting Linant de Bellefonds, 1965, p. 184).[27] In particular, Linant de Bellefonds specifies four requirements (1965, p. 185; similarly, Zahraa, 1998, p. 271):

1. the goods must exist at the time of the contract;
2. it must be something capable of being possessed, of certain delivery or capable of being executed immediately (in case of an obligation for performance);
3. it must be licit, legal (*mubāḥ*);
4. it must be clearly determined as regards its genus, species, quality, and value.

These requirements can be better specified as follows.

1. The *objet* must exist at the time of the conclusion of the contract (principle of existence of the object).

'This requirement . . . has as its purpose the protection of the parties to the contract against any risk through hazard or *gharar* likely to cause imbalance of the benefits' (Comair-Obeid, 1996, p. 336; for the notion of *gharar*, 'uncertainty,' see next section, 3.5.4). For instance, it is illegal to sell the fruit which has not yet appeared on the tree. The requirement is grounded on the following *ḥadīth*: 'Abū Dāwūd recites an *ḥadīth* that Ibn Ḥazm asked to the Prophet: 'A man asked me to sell him something that I did not have; should I go and buy it from the market?' The Prophet replied: 'Do not sell what you do not have'' (Rayner, 1991, p. 133).

> As far as the *ḥadīth* is concerned, it contains nothing to invalidate the sale of a non-existent object. What the *ḥadīth* denotes is the prohibition of the sale of an existing object that the seller himself does not own. The full scenario of the *ḥadīth* is self-explanatory. . . . Al-Kāsānī pointed out that Hakīm Ibn Hizām used to sell goods that he did not own by taking the price from a prospective buyer, then he would go to the market to purchase the goods, and then he would deliver them to the buyer. This scenario was brought to the attention of the Prophet (pbuh) who then stated the wording of the *ḥadīth* translated above. This scenario clearly shows that it is the ownership but not the existence of the goods that has been addressed by the Prophet's *ḥadīth*.
>
> (Zahraa and Mahmor, 2002, p. 386)

However, classical sources also remark how 'the goods must be already in existence at the time the contract of sale is concluded and that the sale of a not-yet-existing (*ma'dūm*) object is void' (*ibidem*, p. 380);[28] in relation to the doctrine of *gharar*, this suggests that 'the absence of uncertainty and doubt regarding the qualitative and quantitative description of the subject matter as well as the safe availability rather than the existence of the subject matter is the prime concern for the validity of the contract of sale' (*ibidem*, p. 397).

2. It is not sufficient that the object exists: 'for the juridical act to be valid the article must be available for immediate delivery' (principle of certainty of delivery) (Comair-Obeid, 1996, p. 337).

This relates to another *ḥadīth* of the Prophet, which prohibits 'the sale by a seller of that which is not in his possession' (*bayʿ al-ʿinsan ma laysa ʿindah*). Vogel notes how the Ḥanafis radically prohibit any sale of non-existent objects, while the Ḥanbalīs tend to require only the certainty of delivery (for instance,

Ibn al-Qayyim limits *gharar* to the 'inability to deliver the sale object') (Vogel, 2006, p. 68).

3. The *objet* must be licit (*mubāḥ*) (principle of legality).

Linant de Bellefonds specifies that the reference to a general principle of legality cannot be found in Muslim *fiqh* (1965, p. 194). Jurists, in contrast, enumerate the necessary conditions for the validity of the contract of sale: the transferred property (*māl*) must be capable of benefit, pure (*ṭāhir*) and not prohibited by *Šarīʿah* (*ibidem*). The sale of something which gives no benefit makes the *objet* inexistent and the contract void (*bāṭil*). Hence, things that by their very nature cannot be of private benefit (the air, the sea, rivers, lakes, grass, . . .) are not valid *objet*. Religious limitations are numerous in Muslim *fiqh* and comprise the notion of 'purity' (*ṭahāra*); examples of unlawful – *ḥarām* – objects are alcoholic drinks, pork, hazard games (see *ibidem*, pp. 197–204).

4. The subject matter must be clearly determined regarding its genus, species, quality, and value, when a tangible thing is under contract; similarly, when it refers to a performance, it must be precisely determined as to its nature and its value. The issue of the precise determination of the subject matter can lead either to a lack of certainty which results in nullification (*fāsid*) of the contract, or to a non-serious uncertainty which implies a *khiyār at-taʿyīn* (option of specification: section 3.4.4). In the latter case, when the contract comprises different options of choice, the parties have a right of specification within a certain time period.

As noted, in the doctrinal elaboration of Muslim scholars, the *objet*, the subject-matter (*maḥall*) of the contract, has primary relevance, so as to maintain a balance between the legal effects of the transaction and avoid the risk of usurious and aleatory outcomes (see Rayner, 1991, p. 131). More in general, this importance can be explained because the *objet* is itself the 'ground' where the agreement (*tarāḍī*) can validly stand; offer and acceptance 'are understood as performatives; that is, as constitutive, dispositive utterances . . . [by which] the parties are creating immediate entitlements in each other . . . by transfer of title to goods' (Zysow, 1985–86, p. 75). If these dispositive utterances define the human 'workforce' of the parties in the construction of the agreement, the 'surface' upon which the contract lies is an exchange of goods, that must relate 'as much as possible to the here and now' (*ibidem*, pp. 76–77), a point which explains the prohibition in Muslim *fiqh* of aleatory contracts (involving elements of uncertainty and risk with an outcome in the future: see later, *gharar*), as well as the executed (rather than executory) nature of the Islamic *ʿaqd*.

The 'bricks' for the construction of the contractual edifice are the properties that are exchanged. The concept of property (*māl*, pl. *amwāl*) is fundamental to understand the *ʿaqd* in Muslim *fiqh*,[29] where 'ownership [*milk*] is not a 'right', in the modern sense of the term . . . ownership is integrated in the thing' (Chehata, 1973, p. 178; my translation). Chehata's remark can be better understood by maintaining our metaphor of the contractual building in the city of the *'aqd*. Since everything in Islam belongs to God, that ownership is 'in the goods,' as ownership is embedded in the properties that are sold and constitute the 'bricks' provided by God to human beings for commercial transactions. In other words, they are not 'rights' of the 'labourers' who are participating in the construction of the contract; *amwāl* enjoy, somehow, a tangible connotation as physical entities that are transferred in the transaction. Consequently, in their discussion of the notion of *milk*, Muslim scholars focus on the qualities of the goods and of the subject matter (see the foregoing), not on the 'rights' of the parties as subjects of the transaction; these are not 'owners' (in the modern sense of the term) but, more precisely, agents performing God's will.

According to Vogel, *māl* (property) is any existent thing to which human nature inclines (2006, p. 27); for Anderson, it is everything that has commercial value, 'whose corporeal, usufructuary and other rights of any kind the exchange of which is customary are to be regarded as property (*māl*) of commercial value' (Anderson, 1975, p. 103; see also Islam, 1999). It must be physically possessable (*qabḍ*, taking of possession) and disposable by the property holder (act of disposition, *taṣarruf*); moreover, property can relate to the 'substance' of the thing (*raqaba*) or to its 'use' or 'usufruct' (*manfa'a*, pl. *manāfi'*). The centrality of the concept of *māl* in the conceptualisation of the *'aqd* is witnessed by the fact that a variety of contractual rules in all the juristic schools depend on the existence of the goods either as *property hic-et-nunc* (*'ayn*: specific visible thing) or *property-in-the-future* (*dayn*: literally 'debt,' subsisting 'in the *dhimma* of the counterparty') (Cattelan, 2013, p. 194).[30] This distinction recalls, to a certain extent, the dichotomy '*choses in possession*' – '*choses in action*' in common law, which distinguishes 'tangible personal property' from 'personal rights of property' that can be claimed by action, and not by taking physical possession. But the pair *'ayn – dayn* of Muslim *fiqh* does not really translate either the couple *chose in possession – chose in action* of common law, or the pair *corps certain – chose de genre* of civil law (Cattelan, 2013, p. 196). The bricks of the city of the *'aqd*, once again, prove to be made of a distinct material.

In fact, the concept *'ayn* (pl. *a'yān*; whose meaning is 'eye,' the organ of sight; but also the functional result of the ability to see, the object that is seen: Van de Bergh, 1975), by embodying the ideas of individuality, specificity and present existence (Brunschvig, 1976c, p. 303; the brick 'here and now,' as suggested also by Zysow, 1985–86, p. 75), identifies in Muslim *fiqh* the tangible *property hic-et-nunc* (*corps certain*) (Cattelan, 2013, p. 191). By contrast, the concept of generic thing, part of a genre (*jins*), something fungible (*chose de genre*) opposed to the thing-itself (*'ayn*), is expressed in Muslim *fiqh* in various ways:

- *mithl* (pl. *amthāl*) connotes the 'equivalent' of something; the thing can be replaced by another of the same genre, number, measure or weight; if

there is no equivalent (*mā lā mithl lah*) the thing is necessarily *ʿayn* (*ibidem*, p. 192);
- the *chose de genre* is also called *shay'* (or *māl*) *fī dh-dhimma*, 'property in the *dhimma*,' the legal personality of the counterparty; interestingly, as Brunschvig notes (1976c, p. 304), the thing-itself is opposed here not to the thing as part of a genre but to the thing as bound to the responsibility of a person; from an objective matter, we move to a subjective *locus* (*maḥall*);
- this shift becomes even more evident with the concept of *dayn* (pl. *duyūn*), whose literal meaning is 'debt,' but also 'credit,' and which describes something intangible at present because generic, not 'actualised' yet as '*ayn* or existent only in the future. In this sense, *dayn* indicates the debt (as passive side of a credit) and the credit (as active side of a debt); accordingly, Islamic scholars distinguish the creditor as holder of *dayn* (*lahu dayn*: the credit *belongs to* him) from the debtor as owing the *dayn* (*ʿalayhi dayn*: the debt being stemming from him, being *upon* him) simply with the use of different prepositions (Cattelan, 2013, p. 192).

It is in the fundamental linkage that 'exists between the concept of *dayn* as debt/credit and the legal personality, *dhimma*, of the debtor, where, until the transfer, *dayn* properties are necessarily located' (*ibidem*, p. 195) that the nature of *dayn* in Muslim *fiqh* can find proper explanation and be distinguished both from the *chose in action* of common law and the obligation of civil law.

On the one hand, the notion of *dayn* also relates to *dīn* (as we have remarked in section 2.3) in the sense of a debt, credit, obligation that renders part of Islam as a religious community by means of a human liability which indirectly reflects the judgement (*dīn*) of God. In this context, Zahraa and Mahmor remark how 'in Islamic legal terminology, the term *dayn* is used to denote debt. Although *dayn* in some sense is defined as *māl* (property) that *someone owes* to *another*, it is sometimes used in a much wider sense as a reference to an abstract or religious liability that is established against a person' (2001, p. 224).

On the other hand, when interpreted within the dyad *ʿayn – dayn*, the notion of debt departs from the Western idea of obligation (a legal duty for the individual) to embrace a material connotation as a kind of property *already owned* by the creditor: 'the debtor owes it to him either now [as generic thing, still to be individualised as *ʿayn*] or in the future [either as generic – *dayn fī dh-dhimma* – or specific thing – *dayn fī l-ʿayn*]' (Vogel, 2006, p. 27). As Hiroyuki Yanagihashi puts it, *dayn* refers neither to the obligation nor to the credit (/ debt): 'to be exact, the term '*dayn*' refers to the *object* of an obligation or credit' (2004, p. 173; italics added); it is a 'brick' that must still be added to the edifice, which is owed by the counterparty and necessary to maintain the equilibrium of the construction. Within this background, 'the notion of *dayn* intrinsically embodies an idea of temporality as a credit relation . . . , where the debt/credit is not primarily conceived as a burden for the subject, but as a property (intangible at present) *already owed* by the creditor but *not yet received* in concrete form (and for this reason, *still* in the *dhimma* of the debtor)' (Cattelan, 2013, p. 193).

Accordingly, the *dhimma*, 'legal personality' (but whose meaning also involves an idea of care, conscience, responsibility, protection, security) can be thought of as the 'wheelbarrow' ('[t]he metaphor is of a physical place in the individual under obligation': Vogel, 2006, p. 28) through which the debtor transports *dayn* bricks that already belong to the creditor but are temporarily *upon* the debtor; as evocatively said by the Mālikī Khalīl Isḥāq (d. 767/1365) in his *Muhtaṣar*, 'they are not *of* him, but weigh *upon* him [i.e., over his *dhimma*]' (quoted by Santillana, 1938, p. 2). In this light, Chehata compares it to a 'plate' (*assiette*): the *dhimma* is not a 'link' between the creditor to the debtor but a 'repository' (*réceptacle*),[31] a 'container' of *dayn* properties. '*Mais, à la verité, la* dhimma *ne se confond point avec l'obligation: elle en est proprement l'assiette. La* "fides" *engagée, l'objet du droit existera dans le réceptable de droits qu'est la personne. . . . La* dhimma *n'est pas que le lien qui unit le créancier au débiteur, elle en est surtout le réceptacle*' (Chehata, 1977, p. 238). My metaphor of the 'wheelbarrow' adds a more dynamic dimension to this representation, stressing the role of the Muslim believer as 'God's agent,' 'workforce' (not owner) in performing the contractual construction. The conceptual interdependence between *dayn* properties and *dhimma* (the wheelbarrow where bricks are temporarily located to be taken to the site of the *'aqd*) is also proven by the fact that *'ayn* properties (keeping the metaphor, 'bricks already on site') never fall into the *dhimma* (Chehata, 1977, p. 238).

> Pour les obligations *'ayn*, on ne parle pas de *dhimma*. Déterminé dans son individualité, l'objet d'une obligation *'ayn* est toujours *certum*. Si le débiteur refuse de livrer, ce n'est pas son patrimoine qui en répondra. Comme pour toute obligation de faire, la seule inexécution ne donne pas droit à des dommage-intérêts.
>
> (Chehata, 1969, p. 172; in identical terms, Delcambre, 1981, p. 207)

In summary, if, for the 'place' (*maḥall*), the 'ground,' upon which the contract lies (*al-ma'qūd 'alayh*) *'ayn* bricks are already available-on-site (they are materially existent *hic-et-nunc*), *dayn* bricks (existent physically *in-the-future* and now as debt/credit) are temporarily located in a wheelbarrow, the *dhimma* (legal personality) of the debtor, under obligation to bring them to the creditor (who already owns them), since they are needed for the equilibrium of the construction. As Brunschvig remarks, it is in this 'contrast between the thing that for now is present ["*l'objet actuellement present*"] and the subject who endures ["*le sujet qui dure*," hence his *dhimma*, guaranteeing the debts]' (1976b, p. 322, my translation) that we can shed light on the pair *'ayn* – *dayn* in the Muslim legal tradition.

3.5.4. *The equilibrium of the contract and the doctrines of* **ribā, maysir,** *and* **gharar**

The general title of this section (3.5), referring to the construction of the *'aqd* (from which the metaphor of the 'contractual building' employed in these pages derives), implicitly points to one of the major peculiarities of the Islamic contract: something that can be described as a *material* approach that leads Muslim jurists to concentrate more on the outer occurrence of the exchange rather than on its psychological background.

Of course, this does not deny that intention (*niyya*) and the other psychological dimensions (*irāda*, *qaṣd*, *khiyār*, *riḍā*) are essential for the valid formulation of consent – with significant divergence between the objectivism of the Šāfi'īs and Ḥanafīs and the subjectivism of the Mālikīs and Ḥanbalīs (as explained in section 3.4.3). Rather, what is *absent* in Muslim *fiqh* is the conception of the contract as the outcome of human will underpinning the civilian theory of obligation, grounded on the *autonomie de la volonté*; in Islamic law, the centrality of will is replaced by a rational assent, an approval (*riḍā*) of the *'aqd* that must be expressed by the parties in its outer manifestation (*ṣīghah*). On the one hand, this aspect moves the coordinates of the contract more towards human intellect, rationality, reason (*'aql*) rather than that of intention (*niyya*) (on this point, see section 3.6 in this chapter); on the other hand, all the elements that this book has already underlined (the limits to the parties' contractual freedom, at 3.4.2; the vices of consent, replaced by the theory of *al-khiyārāt*, at 3.4.4; the external formation of the agreement, 'verbalism,' in the unity of negotiations, at 3.5.1; the conditions related to the *objet* in relation to the *dhimma* of the person, at 3.5.3), should lead the visitor to the city of the *'aqd* to pay special attention to the material qualities of its contractual building.

This is not to say that the 'human workforce' is neglected in the elaboration of Muslim scholars; although the idea of autonomy is marginalised, an agreement is certainly necessary in its outer (verbal) occurrence (*ṣīghah*). At the same time, God (the Master Architect of all the universe, providing believers with guidance – *Šarī'ah* – also for the construction of the *'aqd*) has revealed a broad set of binding rules to guarantee the 'stability,' the 'safety' of the building for His agents. It is in this context (by maintaining the *'aqd* within the local knowledge of Muslim *fiqh* as a 'craft of space:' section 3.1) that the prohibitions of (1) (unlawful) gain, increase, addition, enrichment (*ribā*, usually rendered with 'interest,' 'usury'); (2) 'uncertainty' (*gharar*, also 'risk,' 'hazard,' 'speculation') as to whether or not a contractual obligation will be performed; and (3) 'gambling' (*maysir* or *qimār*)[32] can find their precise meaning.

These rules can be conceived as the conditions for the 'architectural stability' of the contractual building; they guarantee the balance, the equilibrium of the contract – and, in the end, its safety for the contracting parties. In this light, both the concept of *māl* (section 3.5.3) as something material and tangible and the 'reality' of any right (*ḥaqq*) as depending on God's will (*ḥukm*) (Chapter 2) not only explain the centrality of the *objet* in Muslim *fiqh* but also reaffirm the significance of the underlying doctrines of *ribā*, *gharar* and *maysir* as cornerstones for the stability of the contractual edifice.

- Ribā

Fundamental provisions regarding *ribā* ('illicit increase') can be found in the second *sūra* of the Qur'ān, verses 275–281, particularly in relation to the opposition of *ribā* to legitimate trade (*al-bayʿ*, lit. 'sale,' broadly interpreted with reference to any kind of commerce).

> (275) Those who devour usury will not stand except as stands one whom the Evil One by his touch hath driven to madness. That is because they say: "Trade is like usury" [*al-bayʿu mithlu ar-ribā*], But Allāh hath permitted trade and forbidden usury [*'aḥalla Allāhu al-bayʿa wa-ḥarrama ar-ribā*] [. . .]. (276) Allāh will deprive usury of all blessing, but will give increase for deeds of charity: for He loveth not creatures ungrateful and wicked. (277) Those who believe, and do deeds of righteousness, and establish regular prayers and regular charity, will have their reward with their Lord: on them shall be no fear, nor shall they grieve. (278) O ye who believe! Fear Allāh, and give up what remains of your demand for usury, if ye are indeed believers. (279) If ye do it not, take notice of war from Allāh and His apostle: but if ye turn back, ye shall have your capital sums: deal not unjustly, and ye shall not be dealt with unjustly. (280) If the debtor is in difficulty, grant him time till it is easy for him to repay. But if ye remit it by way of charity, that is best for you if ye only knew. (281) And fear the Day when ye shall be brought back to Allāh. Then shall every soul be paid what it earned, and none shall be dealt with unjustly.

Other relevant passages can be found in Q. 3:130 ('Ye who believe! Devour not usury, doubled and multiplied; but fear Allāh; that ye may really prosper') and Q. 4:161 ('That they took usury, though they were forbidden; and that they devoured men's substance wrongfully; – We have prepared for those among them who reject Faith a grievous punishment'). For the opposition *ribā*/charity, next to Q. 2:276–277, see also Q. 30:39 ('That which ye lay out for increase through the property of (other) people, will have no increase with Allāh: but that which ye lay out for charity, seeking the countenance of Allāh (will increase): it is these who will get a recompense multiplied'). As far as the *Sunna* is concerned, it is reported that the Prophet said: '*Ribā* is of 73 types. The least of them is like a man having sexual intercourse with his mother' (*Ibn Mādja*; *Ḥākim*); 'The Messenger of God cursed the one who consumes *ribā*, the one who makes it be consumed, its inscribed, its two witnesses' (*Muslim*; *Bukhārī*); 'Gold for gold, silver for silver, wheat for wheat, barley for barley, dates for dates, salt for salt, like for like, equal for equal, hand to hand. If these types [*aṣnāf*] differ, then sell them as you wish, if it is hand to hand' (*Muslim*). For the divergences among the juristic schools on the extension of the prohibition of *ribā* and their interpretation, the most comprehensive source in the English language remains the book by Nabil Saleh (1992a, pp. 11–43). With regard to the historical reconstruction of the early Islamic law of property in the 7th–9th centuries CE, Yanagihashi has convincingly shown, through the study of the rules that led to the formation of the doctrine of *ribā*, that 'the prohibition had been established as a general principle that governs the Islamic law of property in the first decades of the eighth century, i.e. just before Abū Ḥanīfa and Mālik emerged as representative authorities in their respective regions' (Yanagihashi, 2004, p. 300).

• Gharar

The term *gharar*, usually translated as 'risk,' 'hazard,' 'uncertainty,' expresses in Arabic the idea of a (potential) danger of loss due to the incorporation of risk in the transaction (hence affecting the safety of the contractual construction).

> In the case of *gharar* . . . I would like to argue that a good translation already exists in the term 'risk'. The term risk (Italian: *risco* [*rectius*, *rischio*]; French: *risque*) is derived from the Latin roots *re* = back and *secare* = cut, thus reflecting the potential for a sailor to have his ship cut by hitting a rock. In other words, 'risk' means 'danger of loss'. This is precisely the meaning of the Arabic term *gharar*. . . . The origin of the term is the three-letter past tense verb *gharra* [*GH-R-R*], meaning 'to deceive'. Thus, the *Encyclopedia of Jurisprudence* . . . states that *tadlīs* = cheating (in trade) and *ghabn* = fraud and deception are among the categories of *gharar*. The type of uncertainty regarding future events which constitutes *gharar* may be one-sided or two-sided, and it may be intentional or unintentional. However, in all of the definitions that follow, one thing is common: the incorporation of risk.
> (El-Gamal, 2001, pp. 4–5; see also El-Gamal, 2006, pp. 58–62)

While the term *gharar* does not appear in the Qur'ān, the *Sunna* reports that the Prophet 'forbade the sale of an escaped slave or animal, the sale of a bird in the air or a fish in the water, the sale of what the vendor is not in a position to deliver, . . . the sale of the young still unborn when the mother is not part of the sale, the sale of milk in the udders and the sale of the stallion's sperm' (Saleh, 1992a, p. 106) because of the fear of *gharar*. Numerous *aḥādīth* relate to the matter, especially with regard to the existence of the *objet* (see section 3.5.3): 'The Prophet has forbidden the sale in which uncertainty (*gharar*) exists' (*Muslim; Ibn Mādja; Abū Dawūd; Al-Tirmidhī*). 'The Prophet forbade sale of . . . the "stroke of the diver" [*ḍarbat al-ghā'is*, apparently, sale in advance of the yield of a diver's dive, whatever it was]' (*Ibn Mādja*). 'Do not buy fish in the sea, for it is *gharar*' (*Ibn Ḥanbal*). 'The Prophet forbade sale of what is in the wombs, sale of the contents of their udders, sale of a slave when he is runaway, . . .' (*Ibn Mādja*). 'The Prophet forbade the sale of grapes until they become black, and the sale of grain until it is strong' (*Bukhārī; Muslim; Abū Dāwūd; Tirmidhī*). 'Whoever buys foodstuffs, let him not sell them until he has possession of them' (*Bukhārī*). 'He who purchase food shall not sell it until he measures it [*yaktālahu*]' (*Muslim*) (*aḥādīth* quoted in Vogel, 2006, p. 23; for a detailed explanation, see Saleh, 1992a, pp. 62–106).

- Maysir/Qimār

> O ye who believe! Intoxicants and gambling [games of chance: *maysir*], (dedication) of stones, and (divination by) arrows, are an abomination, – of Satan's handiwork: eschew such (abomination), that ye may prosper. Satan's plan is (but) to excite enmity and hatred between you, with intoxicants and gambling, and hinder you from prayer: will ye not then abstain?
>
> (Q. 5:90–91)

According to some commentators, this verse refers to a complex game played at the time of the Prophet, 'by which lots were drawn for parts of a slaughtered camel with those who lost paying for all its cost.[33] Most declare the term . . . [*maysir*] to refer to gambling generally' (Vogel, 2006, p. 13, note 53). In the *Sunna*, the word *qimār* is more common to define the concept. Sayyiduna 'Abd Allāh ibn 'Umar says: '*maysir* is the *qimār*.' Sayyiduna Abū Hurayra narrates that the Prophet said: 'Whosoever says to another: "come let's gamble" should give in charity [as a form of expiation for intending to gamble]' (*Bukhārī*).

Proceeding with order to consider how revealed sources have been interpreted in *fiqh* legal tradition to guarantee the stability of the contract, Muslim scholars interpret *ribawwi* transactions as invalid due to an unbalanced distribution of rights (the building was erected unstable, and so it risks falling down), either on the grounds of a quantitative inequality at present (*tafāḍul*) or because of a delay (*nasā'*, *nasī'a*, *naẓira*). Thus, in the case of monetary exchange (contract of *ṣarf*), the values must be identical and the transfer of possession immediate on both sides in order to avoid any illicit excess (*ribā 'l-faḍl*, '*ribā* of excess'). In addition to this, any unjustified delay in the performances is forbidden, such as *ribā 'l-nasī'a* ('*ribā* of delay').[34] In their classifications, the *fuqahā'* also refer to *ribā al-jahiliyya* ('pre-Islamic *ribā*'), occurring when the giver offers the taker at the maturity date two alternatives: to settle his debt (*dayn*) or to increase it two-fold. This was a customary practice in the pre-Islamic era, which is directly prohibited in the Qur'ān (Q. 3:130; see foregoing quote).

Mahmoud El-Gamal advances an economic explication of *ribā* (2000; see also El-Gamal, 2006, pp. 49–57) by describing it in the light of a 'symmetric relation,' an equality between the countervalues that guarantees equity in the transaction thanks to a 'quantitative equilibrium' among the parties (Cattelan, 2009). This concept can be well illustrated through the equilibrium between the sides of a building under construction, whose bricks must be balanced quantitatively. Next to the metaphor of the *ʿaqd* as a building under construction, another explanatory image is offered by Andrey Smirnov in his article about the comparison between the Western and the Islamic conception of justice (already mentioned in Chapter 2). Smirnov highlights how the essence of any right (*ḥaqq*) in Islam is to think about 'a sort of substance that has constant volume, of which some parts may happen to be not where they belong, not in the due place; and justice means the necessity of returning them to where they should be' (1996, p. 344). Any *ḥaqq* relates to what is 'real,' 'true,' 'just' as established by God when conceived in the unity of the two sides (active and passive) of the legal transaction (the symmetric relation that gives stability to the building). Accordingly, Smirnov alludes to the archetype of the scales as symbol of justice to remark that while 'Western thinking is concerned with the pans of the scales and their contents' (to the extent that the two side of the transactions are conceived one independent from the other), 'for classical Islamic thought the stress lies on the central balancing pivot' (*ibidem*, p. 346), so that it is the balance of the building that defines the inner validity of the contract.

> It is making one equal to the other (equality between two necessarily *separate* entities) that is important in the first case, and theoretical discussion tries to determine the accuracy of this equalizing. . . . In the second case it is the fact of balancing the opposites that is important, this balance being reached by means of the centering and mediating pivot; the theoretical task is to find out how the two might be linked to form a balanced unity and what the conditions are for such a linkage.
>
> (*ibidem*, pp. 346–7)

The metaphor of the scales and of its pans can shed light over the concept of *ribā* as conceived in Muslim *fiqh* in the following terms: the validity of the *ʿaqd* depends on the maintenance of an equilibrium (Smirnov's 'balanced unity;' El-Gamal's 'symmetric relation') between the contracting parties. Therefore, any (unlawful) increase, addition, (illicit) gain (*ribā*) on the one pan makes its legal construction defective, either in an exchange at present (*ribā ʾl-faḍl*, *ribā* of excess) or when it affects the responsibility of the *dhimma* of the debtor (*ribā ʾl- nasīʾa*, *ribā* of delay). This interpretation of *ribā* in terms of 'balanced unity,' 'equilibrium,' 'symmetry' is also confirmed by al-Kāsānī, in a passage where he describes the purpose of any bilateral commutative exchange in terms of equality of the counter-values (already quoted at 3.4.1).

> Equality . . . is the aim of the contracting parties (*al-musāwāt* . . . *maṭlūb al-ʿāqidayn*). . . . The entirety of the sold object is to be considered equivalent to the entirety of the price (*kull al-mabīʿ yuʿtabar muqābalan bi-kull al-thaman*), and the entirety of the price equivalent to the entirety

of the sold object. Any increment (*ziyāda*), whether in price or in the object which has no corresponding equivalent, would be an additional value without compensation . . . and this is the meaning of usury (*ribā*).

(al-Kāsānī, *Badā'i' al-Ṣanā'i' fī Tartīb al-Sharā'i'*, reported by Arabi, 1997, p. 208)

The passage can further clarify the doctrine of *ribā* in Muslim *fiqh*.

First, the prohibition is referred by the *fuqahā'* only to synallagmatic contracts (*mu'āwaḍāt*), where each party is bound to provide something to the other, not to liberal acts (*at-tabarru'āt*); in this sense, it shares some similarity with the doctrine of consideration in common law. In a *ḥadīth* narrated by Jabir bin Abdullāh and reported by *Bukhārī*, it is recorded that the Prophet repaid the debt that he owed to Jabir and he gave him an extra amount; the scholars explain that a borrower is free to pay an extra amount on the principal sum providing that the act is gratuitous and not stipulated as a condition of the borrowing (such a payment would be *ribawwi*).

Second, *ribā* is described in most legal manuals as one of the principles governing contracts in general within the chapter on sales – the sale being, *bay'*, the archetype of any commutative contract in Muslim *fiqh*. In this regard, the widespread translation of *ribā* in Western scholarship as 'usury' and 'interest' becomes misleading (if not erroneous), since the application of the doctrine is not limited to money lending (contract of *qarḍ*: 'loan of money and of other fungible objects which are intended to be consumed,' Schacht, 1964, p. 157) or money exchange (the contract of *ṣarf*). In fact, since 'the prohibition requires a balance between the value of the subject matter and its consideration' (Yanagihashi, 2013), it finds a much larger application beyond the ban of interest in the loan (as in the unjustified enrichment of the exchange of fungible things of the same genre; the illicit profit due to the delay of the performances; . . .). Not by chance, the concept of *ribā* is not opposed to the legitimate lending of money, but more in general to 'trade/selling' in the Qur'ān: Q. 2:275: 'God permitted trade and forbade *ribā*' (*'aḥalla Allahu al-bay'a wa-ḥarrama ar-ribā*).

Third, the recognition that 'the Arabic term is usually held to constitute something wider than the mere prohibition of excessive interest' (Rayner, 1991, p. 267) explains why the concept of *ribā* can apply (as noted previously) to any unlawful increase with no corresponding consideration at present (*ribā 'l-faḍl*). Accordingly, Schacht (2012) defines *ribā* in the *Encyclopedia of Islam* as 'increase in' or 'addition to' (the content of a pan, in the metaphor of the scales); in its widest interpretation, it is 'any unjustified increase of capital for which no compensation is given.' In line with these interpretations, one of the most comprehensive definitions of *ribā* has been given by Nabil Saleh in the following terms:

[r]ibā, in its Shari'ah context, can be defined . . . as an unlawful gain derived from the *quantitative inequality of the counter-values* [italics

added] in any transaction purporting to effect the exchange of two or more species (*anwaʿ*, sing. *nawʿ*), which belong to the same genus (*jins*) and are governed by the same efficient cause (*ʿilla*, pl. *ʿilal*). Deferred completion of the exchange of such species, or even of species which belong to different genera but are governed by the same *ʿilla*, is also *ribā*, whether or not the deferment is accompanied by an increase in any one of the exchanged counter-values. That being the case, usurious transactions were classified into two categories: (a) *ribā ʾl-faḍl* [*ribā* of excess], which is produced by the unlawful excess of one of the counter-values as described above, and (b) *ribā ʾl-nasīʾa* [*ribā* of delay], which is produced by delaying completion of the exchange of the counter-values, as also described above, with or without an increase or a profit.

(Saleh, 1992a, p. 16)

Similarly to *ribā*, the prohibitions of *gharar* and *maysir* are conceptually related to the nature of the exchanged properties (not to the intentions of the parties). More precisely, one could say that, whereas the prohibition of *ribā* affects the balance, the equilibrium, the stability of the contractual building, those of *gharar* and *maysir* are related to the 'quality' of the 'material' of its construction (see on this point Cattelan, 2009). A defective structure of the *ḥuqūq al-ʿaqd*, in fact, (a) may also depend on the non-sufficient determination of the content of the pans, due to ignorance (*jahāla*) of some aspects of the transaction or the non-existence (*ʿadam*) of the object (*gharar*), or (b) may derive from an agreement on gambling or an aleatory contract (*maysir*). In both cases the 'materials' used for the contractual building become intrinsically fragile, risky, dangerous for the parties (keeping the metaphor of the building, one could say that the concrete is defective; the bad quality of the cement deprives the construction of its solidity, independently of any proportionality, equality, equilibrium that is pursued under *ribā* instructions).

Literally meaning fraud (*al-khidʿa*), *gharar* in transactions has often been used in the sense of risk, uncertainty and hazard. . . . *Gharar* . . . includes both ignorance over the material attributes of the subject matter and also uncertainty over its availability and existence. Al-Sarakhsī has thus stated that *gharar* in a contract or transaction exists when its consequences are hidden and unknown to the contracting parties (*al-gharar mā yakūnu mastūr al ʿaqībah*).

(Kamali, 1999, p. 200)[35]

Similarly, Zahraa and Mahmor point out that 'the Arabic word *al-gharar* means danger (*al-khatar*), that denotes the exposure to perish [the building's collapse] without prior knowledge' (2002, p. 384). They refer to Al-Sarkhasī, Al-Šīrādhī, and Al-Ramlī, who define *gharar* as 'what the consequence of which is hidden or unknown' (*mā kāna mastūr al-ʿāqibah*) (*ibidem*, p. 385) and provide a list of ten cases affected by *gharar* by Ibn Juzay.[36]

Both the doctrines of *gharar* (lack of knowledge, uncertainty, danger of loss) and *maysir* (gambling) further testify to the 'material' approach of Muslim *fiqh* towards the *'aqd*. In the case of *gharar*, the lack of sufficient knowledge of the subject matter deprives the construction of the *'aqd* of necessary solidity; its *material* is defective, since the matter itself is hidden, unknown, or insufficiently known to the contracting parties. Thus, according to Saleh, 'all sorts of transactions where the subject-matter, the price or both, are not determined and fixed in advance [lack of disclosure], are under a suspicion of *gharar* according to Sharia standards' (Saleh, 1992a, p. 63). After the examination of the explanatory examples and definitions reported by the traditions of each school, he concludes that

> observance of the following three rules should, in principle, avert *gharar* in any give[n] transaction: (a) There should be no want of knowledge (*jahl*) regarding the existence of the exchanged counter-values. (b) There should be no want of knowledge (*jahl*) regarding the characteristics of the exchanged counter-values or the identification of their species or knowledge of their quantities or of the date of future performance, if any. (c) Control of the parties over the exchanged counter-values should be effective.
>
> (*ibidem*, p. 66)

The rules on *gharar* and their effects on the validity of the contract vary in the literature, in relation to their impact on the 'solidity' of the contract. In this regard, Kamali indicates four conditions for *gharar* to have legal consequences.

> The first of these is that it must be excessive, not trivial. A slight *gharar*, such as *gharar* in the sale of similar items which are not identical at one and the same price is held to be negligible. Second, that it occurs in the context of commutative contracts (*'uqūd al-mu'āwaḍāt al-māliyyah*), thus precluding *tabarru'āt*. Third, that *gharar* affects the subject matter of contract directly, as opposed to what may be attached to it (e.g. in a cow, it is the animal itself, not its yet to be born calf). Fourth, that the people are not in need of the contract in question. Should there be a public need (*ḥājjat al-nās*) for it, *gharar*, even if excessive, will be ignored. This is because satisfying the people's need takes priority by virtue of the Qur'ānic principle of removal of hardship (*raf' al-ḥaraj*). The Sharī'a thus validates *salam* (advance purchase) and *istisnā'* (manufacture contract) regardless of the *gharar* elements therein, simply because of the people's need for them.
>
> (Kamali, 1999, p. 201)

In the light of this, Kamali notes how '[*g*]*harar* can be summarised to occur into four main varieties on account respectively of uncertainty and risk pertaining to the existence of the subject matter, or over its availability, uncertainty over the quantities involved, and lastly of uncertainty over timing of completion and delivery' (*ibidem*, p. 210).

Moving from the prohibition of *gharar* to that of *maysir*, the risk of intrinsic uncertainty regarding the outcome of the contractual construction becomes even higher in the case of aleatory transactions, which result in a random distribution of properties among the contracting parties. Metaphorically speaking, in this situation, the parties bet on the very subsistence of the contract; issues of equilibrium, stability, balance (*ribā*), as well as of solidity (*gharar*) are then overcome by the structural insecurity (*maysir*) of the building. In this sense, *maysir* equals *qimār*, a word which stems from the root *Q-M-R*, indicating 'that which increases at times and decreases at other times' (and so *qamar* is the Arabic for 'moon'); the *'aqd* shakes as if there was an earthquake, and its security is marginalised in favour of the advantage of one party (who may increase his wealth from the ruin of the house) at the expense of the other. Due to this structural insecurity, contracts affected by *maysir* are always deemed void, inexistent (*bāṭil*).

3.6. A unity of diversities: *fiqh* pluralism and the totality (3L) of the *'aqd* as the performance of God's will

From the role of intention (*niyya*) and rationality (*'aql*) (section 3.4) to the construction of the contract between divine creation and human agency (section 3.5), this chapter has guided our journey in 'crafting the place' of the *'aqd* as a work of local knowledge (section 3.1) that specifically belongs to Muslim *fiqh*. The journey has developed through a dialectical comparison with Western (civil/common) law (section 3.2), highlighting the inherent normative pluralism that belongs to the interpretation of the revelation by the Muslim juristic schools. It is in this unity of diversities that the meaning of the Islamic contract may find at this point a full disclosure of its *own* conceptual map, within an acoustic place where divergences and contradictions coexist as intrinsic manifestation of Islamic *dīn/bíos* (section 3.3) in the different ways of walking (*madhāhib*) along the Path towards salvation (*Šarī'ah*).

After visiting the city of the *'aqd* along the itineraries of the *madhāhib*, we can report to the *Arab Girl* some conclusive remarks about the nature of the Islamic contract.

In the search of orientation, the problem of how to craft the *'aqd* as a space of local knowledge has led our investigation to conceive the 'city' as a signifying practice, with the *'aqd* itself being a vehicle of legal meaning; a medium of Islamic *nomos* (see Introduction). For us, the riddle of the Sphynx of Thebes has taken the form of the question 'what is the meaning of the *'aqd* as a signifying practice in Muslim legal tradition?'

Moving away from the bias embedded in the representation of *fiqh* as a decadent system of law, as mirrored in the improper corpus of Gérôme's *Almeh*, still at the borders of the city (section 3.3.3), we have advanced the preliminary definition of the *'aqd* as an act of disposal (*taṣarruf*) of property rights (*ḥuqūq*). The investigation of *fiqh* normative pluralism has shown the coexistence of a plurality of different interpretations in an *iurisdictio* where legal opinions are ramified and cases proliferate in their distinction, moving from unified principles: a multiplicity of voices where the geometric (visual) space of Western law is replaced by a 'sacred law without *corpus*' (section 2.4.5). It is precisely within this logic that the ***unity of diversities*** of the *'aqd* must be located: within a ***totality*** (the third level, 3L, in Bhaskar's dialectic) that this chapter has studied by comparing the Western and Islamic legal traditions in a reciprocity of ***absence*** and ***presence*** (as metaphorically depicted in the coexistence of *Two Towers*: section 3.2). Dealing with this ***totality***, the search has highlighted how the ***diversity of contractual rules*** testifies, in fact, to the ***unity*** of the Islamic contract when coherently located in the interaction between law and religion in Muslim jurisprudence. Hence, the third level of Bhaskar's dialectics can explain how the lack of a general theory of contract law in the treatises of *fiqh* is coherently underpinned by a logic which is not grounded on the presence of spatial separation, as in the Temple of Western modernity (section 2.2). By contrast, the place of the *'aqd* in the acoustic space of Islam ***unifies*** its construction in Muslim legal tradition as expression of Islamic ***dīn***, through the conception of the transaction according to pillars (***arkān***) and conditions (*šurūṭ*) that define the 'place' (***maḥall***) of the *šar'ī* act as an instrument of salvation for the believer.

Within the space of Islamic ***dīn***, it is not the free will of the parties to make the contract binding. On the contrary, it is the adherence to the Law, the performance of God's will, that renders the *'aqd* valid and enforceable. As discussed in section 3.5.2, the agreement (***tarāḍī***), grounded on the verbal coincidence between offer and acceptance (*ījāb* and *qabūl*), does not equal the idea of mutual consent of the civil law tradition. Quite the opposite – the idea of 'agreement or ***consensus*** as such does not enter into the Islamic theory of contracts' (Schacht, 1964, p. 22), to the extent that neither the word 'agreement' (*ittifāq*) nor the verb 'to come to an agreement' (*ittafaqā*) are used in *fiqh* sources in the sense of 'coincidence of wills' (Chehata, 1971, p. 164); in the same way, the human will (*irāda*) never appears in classical texts in relation to the Western modern idea of consent.

In a world ruled by God's will in any instant of the creation, where *ījāb*, making something ***wājib***, 'means etymologically not "to offer" but "to make definite, binding, due"' (Schacht, 1964, p. 22), the agreement (***tarāḍī***) is neither promissory nor obligatory; rather, it assumes the connotation of a mutual assent, approval of the parties (Hamid, 1977) to the conferral of properties (Zysow, 1985–86) according to the rules already established by Law, in a conceptual framework where man's rational component overrides the role of the human will. It is this rational component that plays a fundamental role in the construction of the *'aqd* (the 'reason,' *'aql*, of the human beings, responsible agents of God); correspondingly, the fundamental nature of the *'aqd* is not that of a contract-consent (civil law) nor of a contract-bargain (common law) (see back, section 3.3), but of a performance of God's will.

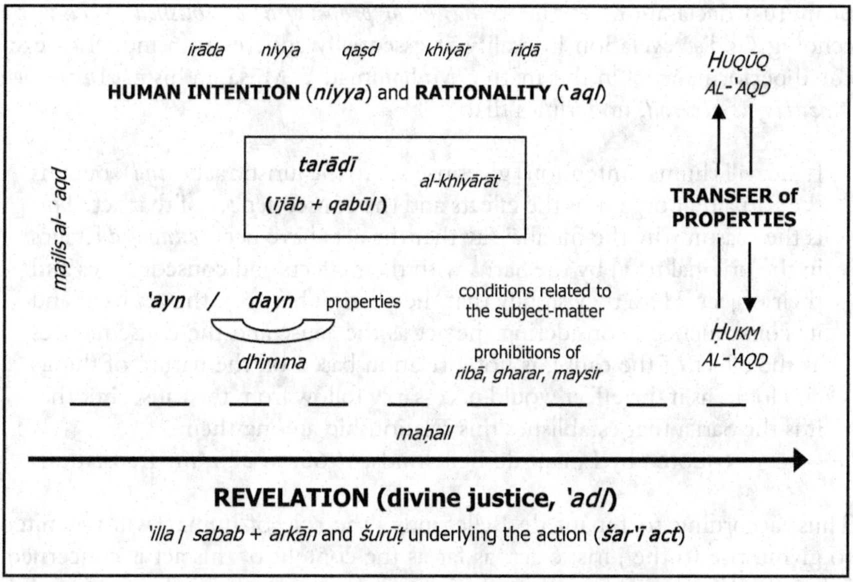

Diagram 3 The *ʿaqd* as conceived in the tradition of Muslim *fiqh* (author's elaboration)

Diagram 3 provides a conclusive representation of the various components of the *ʿaqd*, whose *unity* resides in the performance of God's revelation by the Muslim agent. As suggested, the reader may imagine the contractual construction as a building whose various components operate in harmony to reach justice in the transfer of properties: a divine justice (*ʿadl*), which has been revealed in God's rule (*ḥukm*) and made *real* by means of man's right (*ḥaqq*).

At the end of our visit to the city of the *ʿaqd*, before examining what transformations it has experienced over the centuries (Chapter 4), our conclusions can be supported by referring to some great scholars, whose positions summarise the contents of our investigation.

As remarked in these pages, the *ʿaqd* is not a consensual agreement that is a source of obligations, but a disposition by words (*taṣarruf al-qawliyya*) (materially expressed in a *ṣīghah*) whose legal effect (*ḥukm*) is already established by God. The point is confirmed by the great Egyptian jurist al-Sanhūrī, who notes how 'the centre of a contract . . . [is] its subject matter and not an obligation. . . . [The contract is] the connection of an offer with an acceptance, not necessarily with the view of creating obligations but of bringing a change to the status of the subject matter' (Sanhūrī (1954–1959), *Maṣādir al-Ḥaqq fī l-Fiqh al-Islāmī*, quoted in Hassan, 2002, p. 261).

The very root of the Islamic *ʿaqd* is not the exchange of promises or obligations (as it is, respectively, in common law and civil law), but the concurrence of mutual declarations in the *exchange of property as established by Law*; by echoing God's revelation in reality, it essentially adheres to a model of executed performance. On this matter, Muḥammad Y. Mūsā, in his *al-Amwāl wa Naẓariyyat al-ʿAqd*, underlines that

> [t]he will [human intention] gives rise . . . to the juristic act (*ʿaqd*), but it is the Šarīʿa that organises the effects and the consequences of that act. This is the reason why the fuqahā' say that the acts have been *endowed* [italics in the original text] by the Šarīʿa with their effects and consequences and their object. Here they signify that the relation between the act itself and its consequences, considering the act as the cause and the consequences as the effect of the cause, is not a relation based on the nature of things and logic, as if the effect would necessarily follow from the cause, but that it is the Šarīʿa that establishes this relationship among them.
>
> (quoted by Linant de Bellefonds, 1965, p. 225; my translation)

Thus, according to Linant de Bellefonds, 'the role of human will is limited to giving rise to the juristic act; as far as the content of this act is concerned, it has already been fixed by the Šarī'a, and the human being has no possibility either to modify it, or to enlarge it or even to limit its effects' (*ibidem*; my translation).

In line with the interpretation of this book, Chafik Chehata also remarks how

> [i]n Islamic law, a contract is . . . [formed] by two declarations made by each of the contracting parties. Once formed, all its legal effects follow, inescapably. It is not the "will" of the parties making the declarations which gives the contract its binding character. The declaration itself is an evident, fundamental fact; in turn, it presupposes a rational act. Thus, at a more philosophical level, *the declaration implies, rather, something more of reason than of will.* Once the conditions for the formation of the contract are fulfilled, the consequences follow as a *matter of law. Islamic law attributes no power to the will to create obligations. For this reason, there can be no doctrine of "autonomy of will".*
>
> (Chehata, 1970a, p. 139 – italics added; in similar terms, Chehata, 1970b, pp. 139–140)

Moreover, dealing with the role of the *objet*, Chehata adds that

> [t]he decisive element of the legal relation lies in the object. The object takes place between the two persons who enter into the relationship through it. This relationship, of which the object is the specific term, is constituent of the right. The title that founds the right of the subject is the reason which establishes a link of belonging between him and the object.

> Once this relationship has been concretely realised, a state of adjustment and of equilibrium must rule: everything in its [due] place.
>
> The subject ruled by Law is certainly obliged towards the other party but his obligation has no other object than the thing or the act which is due. He is less tied to the other party than obliged towards an objective performance.
>
> The presence of an object between the contracting parties is the feature of the contractual relationship. It gives to the contract its objective nature: through it the concrete realization of the effects of the contract establishes not only an equilibrium among the persons, but it creates a 'state of things' [settlement of entitlement], a social state, properly said.
>
> (Chehata, 1968a, p. 141; my translation)[37]

This explanation coherently matches the essence of the right (*ḥaqq*) in Islam as 'a sort of substance that has a constant volume, of which some parts may happen to be not where they belong, not in the due place; and justice means the necessity of returning them to where they should be' (Smirnov, 1996, p. 344; see section 3.3.3).[38] Accordingly, it can be said that the contracting parties enter the contract *by means of* the *object*, and the doctrines of the (civilian) *cause* and (English) consideration are replaced by a principle of *equivalence of the counter-values* (Chehata, 1969, pp. 67–70).

> Broadly, Islamic law finds the binding force of a contract in the notion of equivalence of performances. Therefore, contracts containing reciprocal obligations are the only ones which are wholly irrevocable. The gift is essentially revocable. The same applies to the loan of a movable or an immovable, partnership, bailment, and gratuitous agency. It is this notion of mutuality which explains the Islamic theory of interest. Interest of any kind, at any rate whatever, whether for a loan or in any other circumstance is prohibited, so to speak, by definition.
>
> (Chehata, 1970a, p. 140)

Notes

1 Introductory note to the exhibition *Talking Maps*, displayed at the Bodleian Weston Library in Oxford from 5 July 2019 to 8 March 2020 – which I visited in August 2019.

2 The role of legal texts in defining how law works in a certain society will be further explored in Chapter 4, with specific reference to the notion of 'textual polity' by Brinkley Messick (1993).

3 To the extent that 'the most obvious shaping factor, in any work of Islamic law, is its engagement with the past of a particular tradition, and its loyalty to it' (Calder, 1996, p. 980).

4 The *Aṣl* is only one of the six volumes known *as ẓāhir ar-riwāya*, 'the authorised version' of al-Šaybānī's writings, which still today represents the core of the Ḥanafī *madhhab* (and is usually opposed to a similar number of other works known as *ghayr ẓāhir ar-riwāya*, 'the unauthorised version').

5 The term is also employed to describe liberal (*tabarru'āt*) or unilateral acts (e.g. guarantee), as well as juristic acts (e.g. testament) or the *'aqd* of marriage (*nikāḥ*).

6 In other words, it is not the idea of bargain that fosters the contract of civil law, but rather, the recognition of man's freedom as the 'value' that makes a promise binding to the person through consent. Consequently, a donation is a contract in civil law, as expression of free will, but not in common law, due to the lack of consideration. I take the notions of contract-bargain and contract-consent from an article by A. G. Chloros (1968), specifically pp. 139–140.

7 In particular, Decock explores the role of *causa* in relation to how Christian theologians re-adapted the doctrine of 'just price' to give 'just foundation' to equality in contractual matters.

8 For instance, H. Patrick Glenn, in his book *Legal Traditions in the World* (2000), distinguishes the tradition of civil law by speaking of 'the centrality of the person' and that of common law in relation to an 'ethic of adjudication' (see respectively, Chapter 5 and Chapter 7).

9 On this point, see Schacht, 1964, pp. 124–133; Milliot, 1953, pp. 207–230. Louis Milliot relates the concept of *ahliyya* directly to that of *dhimma*, '*la qualité qui lui* [the person] *permet de faire ce à quoi elle a droit ou est oblige . . . C'est la capacité, privilege et charge, inseparable de la nature humaine et inevitable*' (1953, p. 221).

10 Arabi specified that this Prophet's saying can be found

> in the third/ninth century *ḥadīth* collections of al-Bukhārī (*al-Jāmi'al-Ṣaḥīḥ*, Beirut n.d.; p. 2) and Muslim (*Ṣaḥīḥ al-Imām Muslim*, Cairo: 1344 AH; p. 1907). As it has numerous applications in daily life, and especially in acts of worship, it later came to be designated as one of the generic fundamental rules of the law (*qawā'id al-shar'*).
>
> (1997, p. 211, note 29)

11 On this point, Linant de Bellefonds criticises al-Sanhūrī, who identified the notion of 'cause' in Muslim *fiqh* as equivalent to that of the *motif determinant* of French scholarship; in reality,

> *les quelques solutions grapillées ici et là, que l'on tente laborieusement d'expliquer par un recours à la notion de cause finale, n'ont pas assez de densité pour qu'il soit possible d'affirmer que le Fiqh a fait de la cause un élément indispensable à la validité de l'acte juridique.*
>
> (1965, p. 295; for a comparative investigation, pp. 281–305)

On the problem of the *autonomie de la volonté*, see also Linant de Bellefonds, 1958b; on the purposive approach by al-Sanhūrī, see here, Chapter 4.

12 The concept of *sabab* as the immediate purpose (*al-gharad al-mubašar*) of the contract (Art. 165 Jordan Civil Code) or the motive (*ba'ith*) that causes the contracting parties to enter the contract (Art. 176, par. 2, Kuwaiti Civil Code) appears in the legislation of Arab countries influenced by Western models (Saleh, 2001, pp. 349–350).

13 For a concise investigation of the topic with reference to the legislation of Arab countries, with its divergence from classical Islamic law, see Saleh, 2001.

14

> The underlying principle in contracts and stipulations is permissibility [*ibāḥa*] and validity. Any [contract or stipulation] is prohibited and void only if there is an explicit text or a *qiyās* [analogy] (for those who accept *qiyās*) proving its prohibition and voiding.
>
> (Ibn Taymiyya; quoted by Vogel, 2006, p. 29)

15

> No contract is nullified except due to its own terms. . . . Sale contracts are not nullified on grounds of pretext or evil intention (*niyyat sū'*). . . . Thus if a man

> buys a sword intending to kill with it, the sale is permissible; though the intention is not admissible, it does not invalidate the sale. . . . The Book, followed by the Sunna and the general judgment of Islam, all indicate that contracts have legal effect according to their manifest content and are not invalidated by the intention of the parties.
>
> (Šāfiʿī, *Kitāb al-Umm*, 7 vols. (Cairo, 1325 AH), vol. 7, 270, quoted in Arabi, 1997, p. 210)

> The principle I follow is that any contract which is valid in appearance, I do not nullify (*anna kull ʿaqd kana ṣaḥīḥan fi'l-ẓāhir lam ubṭilhu*) on grounds of suspecting the parties: I validate it by the validity of its appearance; I take their intention to be reprehensible (*akrah lahumā al-niyya*) if – were it made explicit – that intention would invalidate the sale.
>
> (*ibidem*, p. 212)

16 Nevertheless, as recognised both by Linant de Bellefonds (1965, pp. 293–294) and Arabi (1997, pp. 214–215), the notion of relevant 'determining motive,' as final aim of the parties (the Western *cause*), finds relevance in the classification by the Ḥanafis of liberal acts (*tabarruʿāt*); that is to say, outside the genre of synallagmatic contracts (*muʿāwaḍāt*). The distance from bilateral transactions is also remarked by the terminology used; in fact, the notion used for liberal acts is not *niyya*, but *maqṣūd* ('aim,' 'purpose'). Accordingly, as Linant de Bellefonds notes, 'Kāsānī, in his outline of the rules of the sale, the specimen of contract par excellence, avoids the word *maqṣūd*' (1965, p. 295; my translation).

17 Fraud (*dol*) refers to every artifice by which a person deceives another for the purpose of concluding a contract. Fraud includes fraudulent misrepresentation or any other conduct that nullifies the apparent consent between the parties, due to bad faith.

18 In English contract law, misrepresentation refers to any false statement of fact that induces the other party to enter the contract. As a vitiating factor it allows the innocent party to rescind the contract (which is voidable, not void). While a mistake is inadvertent, a misrepresentation is often wilful and intentional, made with the intention to deceive (an exception in English law is the case of innocent misrepresentation).

19 More precisely, the limit is strictly imposed by Abū Ḥanīfah but not by his two followers, aš-Šaybānī and Abū Yūsuf (D'Emilia, 1957).

20 For some exceptions, see Linant de Bellefonds, 1965, pp. 126–129; Santillana, 1938, pp. 20–21.

21 In this regard, Messick notes how

> [i]n Arabic, verbs in this tense have a 'past' form and are analyzed this way by the Arab grammarians. For the western Arabist, however, the grammatical category for this tense is known as the 'Perfect', and in such contexts the preferred translation for what I have rendered as 'I sold' would be a modified present or 'performative' form, such as 'I hereby sell'. I have rendered these verbs in the past tense in English in an attempt to follow the Islamic jurists, for whom marking the completing of the legal act is a central analytic feature.
>
> (2001, p. 157, note 14)

22

> Here the Mālikīs and Ḥanafis hold that once a contract has been concluded by corresponding offer and acceptance, neither of the parties may retract their declarations, whether or not the *Majlis* has been terminated. Contrastingly, the Ḥanbalīs and Shāfiʿīs regard such declarations as provisional for the duration of the *Majlis.*
>
> (Rayner, 1991, p. 109)

23 Q. 2:233, in fact, deals with the matter of weaning ('The mothers shall give suck to their offspring for two whole years, if the father desires, to complete the term') by 'mutual consent' (*an tarāḍin*); nevertheless, the sense is not that of a 'agreement as source of obligations,' but of a pact.

24 Wehr (1979) renders the meaning as 'coincidence, congruence, congruity; agreement; conformity . . . ; covenant, compact, convention, contract:' p. 1272; *ittifāq* as verbal noun derived from the VIII form of the root *W-F-Q*, 'to be right, proper, suitable, fit, appropriate,' and hence, *ittafaqa*, 'to agree, come to an agreement, reach an agreement . . . ; to make a contract, conclude an agreement': *ibidem*, p. 1271.

25 *Solo consensus obligat*: the agreement, without the need for special formalities, is sufficient to make the contract legally binding – with the immediate transfer of ownership in the property of goods.

26 In the same terms, Chehata remarks how

> *[l]e* 'aqd *en droit musulman, n'est pas tant un acte générateur d'obligations, qu'un acte juridique créant une nouvelle situation de droit ou modifiant une situation préexistante. Le vendeur sera naturellement tenu de livrer la chose vendue, de même que l'acquéreur devra en payer le prix. Mais ces obligations ne sont pas considérées comme les effets* (ḥukm) *du contrat, mais proprement comme les droits du contrat* (ḥuquq al-'aqd).
>
> (Chehata, 1960, p. 328)

27 Linant de Bellefonds remarks how

> the fuqahā' have established a set of rules which . . . for their breadth and meticulousness contrast with the few and concise prescriptions . . . [of] Western systems, where all this is often reduced to the assertion that the object must be possible and in commerce.
>
> (1965, p. 184; my translation)

'Just to give an example, Kāsānī, *Badā'i'*, . . . devotes not less than 15 pages, size in-quarto, to three conditions that the object has to fulfil . . . : to exist, to be deliverable, to be licit' (*ibidem*, p, 184, note 1; my translation).

28 The *fuqahā'* admit two explicit exceptions to the rule: the future contract *salam* (authorised directly by the Prophet) and contract to manufacture, *istiṣnā'* (admitted by *istiḥsān*) (Linant de Bellefonds, 1965, pp. 186–191; Rayner, 1991, p. 134–138).

29 The sacred nature of properties, whose Owner is only God, is remarked in many passages of the Qur'ān (see for instance Q. 2:188; Q. 4:29; Q. 7:128; Q. 57:5; Q. 4:32).

30 In this section I re-elaborate the contents of my research on the concepts of *'ayn* and dayn, as published in *Arab Law Quarterly* (Cattelan, 2013). I am grateful to the journal for the permission to reproduce.

31

> *Dhimma* is generally defined as a presumed or imaginary repository that contains all the rights and obligations relating to a person. It is like a container that embraces all the financial and other rights and obligations in the present and the future. Al-Zarqa' presents *dhimma* 'as a juristic container presumed in a person in order to encompass all its debts and obligations that are related to it'. . . . *Dhimma* might continue to exist after the death of the person up to the time when all its rights and obligations are settled.
>
> (Zahraa, 1995, pp. 203–204)

32 The words *maysir* or *qimār* are used in *fiqh* with the same meaning, although only the word *maysir*, referring to a form of game (see in the main text), appears in the

Qur'ān, while *qimār*, deriving from the root *Q-M-R*, refers to what increases at times and decreases at other times.

33 In this sense, in his *Dictionary*, Wehr describes *maysir* as 'an ancient Arabian game of chance (forbidden by the Qur'ān) played with arrows without heads and feathering, for stakes of slaughtered and quartered camels.'

34 The *ḥadīth*

> [g]old for gold, silver for silver, wheat for wheat, barley for barley, dates for dates, salt for salt, like for like, equal for equal, hand to hand. If these types [*aṣnāf*] differ, then sell them as you wish, if it is hand to hand

covers *ribā* in sales of two kinds:

> with delay, and immediate (hand-to-hand). The first is called *ribā* of delay (*ribā 'l-nasī'a*), applying to credit transactions, and the second is called *ribā* of excess (*ribā 'l-faḍl*), applying to barter and currency exchange.
>
> (Vogel, 2006, p. 19)

35 A comprehensive collection of the various juristic definitions of *gharar* is provided by El-Gamal: 'Al-Qarāfi . . . states: "The origin of *gharar* is that which is not known to occur or not (e.g. birds in the sky or fish in the water). On the other hand, that whose existence is known, but whose characteristics are unknown (e.g. when a seller sells that which is hidden in his sleeve), it is called *majhūl* (unknown). Thus, the definitions of *gharar* and ignorance are each more general in some respects and less general in other respects . . . This is the reason for the [legal] scholars' differences over the nature of *gharar* and *jahālah* (ignorance)." We may contrast this definition with those collected in Al-Zuḥaylī: 1. Al-Sarakhsī of the Ḥanafī school defines *gharar* thus: "*gharar* is that whose consequences are hidden". 2. Al- Shīraāzī of the Shafi'ī school said: "*gharar* is that whose nature and consequences are hidden". 3. Al-'Isnawī of the Shafi'ī school said: "*gharar* is that which admits two possibilities, with the less desirable one being more likely". 4. 'Ibn Taymiya of the Ḥanbalī school said: "*gharar* is that whose consequences are unknown". His student 'Ibn Al-Qayyim said: "it is that which is undeliverable, whether it exists or not". 5. 'Ibn Ḥazm of the Ẓāhirī school said: "*gharar* is where the buyer does not know what he bought, or the seller does not know what he sold". 6. Dr. Al-Zuhayly's summary definition is thus: "*gharar* sale is any contract which incorporates a risk which affects one or more of the parties, and may result in loss of property". 7. A more explicit definition by Professor Muṣṭafā al-Zarqā' is the following: "*gharar* is the sale of probable items whose existence or characteristics are not certain, due to the risky nature which makes the trade similar to gambling". That final definition by Professor al-Zarqā' seems to be the most appropriate one to use. It subsumes all the other definitions as special cases, and makes explicit that the payoffs from the *gharar* exchange are rendered risky by the probable nature of some of its cornerstones (in terms of existence or characteristics)' (El-Gamal, 2001, pp. 5–6).

36

> (1) difficulty in performing delivery of the subject matter; (2) lack of sufficient knowledge (*jahl*) regarding the type of the price or the subject matter; (3) lack of sufficient knowledge regarding the characteristics of the price or of the subject matter; (4) lack of sufficient knowledge with regard to the quantum of the price or the quantity of the subject matter; (5) lack of sufficient knowledge with regard to the date of future performance; (6) two sales in one transaction (*bay'atān fī bay'atin*); (7) the sale of what is not expected to revive; (8) *Bay'al-ḥaṣāh*, which is a type of sale whose outcome is determined by the throwing of a stone; (9) *Bay'al-munābadhah*, which is a sale performed by the vendor throwing a cloth at the buyer and concluding the sale transaction without giving the buyer the opportunity to properly examine the object of the sale; (10)

Bayʿal-mulāmasah, where the bargain is concluded by touching the object of the sale without examining it.

(Zahraa and Mahmor, 2002, p. 387)

37 Significantly, Chehata uses in the passage the phrase '*l'assujetti au droit*' (he who is subjected to the law) and not '*sujet de droit*' (subject of law) (Chehata, 1968a, p. 141) (for my translation of *maḥkūm lahu* as 'ruled subject,' see section 3.3.1).

38 In an article dedicated to the possible influence that classical Islamic law had on the origins of the English system of common law, John Makdisi concentrates specifically on the existence of a legal imbalance, and the need to re-establish an equivalence:

> [t]he passing of ownership of the object of sale upon the conclusion of the contract created a legal imbalance. . . . This imbalance required the buyer to give up the price to the seller in order to restore balance between the parties. In this situation, Islamic law operated on a principle of equivalence. The imbalance was the source of the contractual obligation on the buyer to pay the price.
>
> (Makdisi, 1999, p. 1652)

References

Abd-Allah, U.F. (2008) Theological dimensions of Islamic law. In: Winter, T. (ed.) *The Cambridge Companion to Classical Islamic Theology*. Cambridge: Cambridge University Press, pp. 237–257.

Ahmed, S. (2016) *What Is Islam? The Importance of Being Islamic*. Princeton and Oxford: Princeton University Press.

Al-Fadl, K.A. (1991) The common and Islamic law of duress. *Arab Law Quarterly*. 6(2), pp. 121–159.

Anderson, J.N.D. (1975) Islamic law and structural variations in property law. *International Encyclopaedia of Comparative Law*. II.

Arabi, O. (1995) Al-Sanhūrī's reconstruction of the Islamic law of contract defects. *Journal of Islamic Studies*. 6(2), pp. 153–172.

Arabi, O. (1997) Intention and method in Sanhūrī's *fiqh*: cause as ulterior motive. *Islamic Law and Society*. 4(2), pp. 200–223.

Arabi, O. (1998) Contract stipulations (*shurūṭ*) in Islamic law: the Ottoman Majalla and Ibn Taymiyya. *The International Journal of Middle East Studies*. 30(1), pp. 29–50.

Bhaskar, R. (1993) *Dialectic: The Pulse of Freedom*. London: Verso.

Billah, M.M. (1998) *Caveat emptor* versus *khiyar al-ʿaib*: a dichotomy. *Arab Law Quarterly*. 13(3), pp. 278–299.

Bodleian Library (2019) *Talking Maps*, exhibition. Online Introduction. Available at: www.bodleian.ox.ac.uk/whatson/whats-on/upcoming-events/2019/july/talking-maps. Accessed 2 August 2019.

Böwering, G. (1997) The concept of time in Islam. *Proceedings of the American Philosophical Society*. 141(1), pp. 55–66.

Brunschvig, R. (1976a) Devoir et pouvoir: histoire d'un problème de théologie musulmane. In: Brunschvig, R. (ed.) *Études d'Islamologie*, Vol. I. Paris: Maisonneuve et Larose, pp. 179–220.

Brunschvig, R. (1976b) Théorie générale de la capacité chez les hanafites médiévaux. In: Brunschvig, R. (ed.) *Études d'Islamologie*, Vol. II. Paris: Maisonneuve et Larose, pp. 37–52.

Brunschvig, R. (1976c) Corps certain et chose de genre dans l'obligation en droit musulman. In: Brunschvig, R. (ed.) *Études d'Islamologie*, Vol. II. Paris: Paris: Maisonneuve et Larose, pp. 303–322.

Buskens, L., and Dupret, B. (2015) The invention of Islamic law: a history of Western studies of Islamic normativity and their spread in the orient. In: Pouillon, F., and Vatin, J.-C. (eds.) *After Orientalism: Critical Perspectives on Western Agency and Eastern Re-Appropriations*. Leiden and Boston: Brill, pp. 31–47.

Calder, N. (1996) Law. In: Nasr, S.H., and Leaman, O. (eds.) *History of Islamic Philosophy*, Part II. London: Routledge, pp. 979–998.

Cattelan, V. (2009) From the concept of *ḥaqq* to the prohibitions of *ribā*, *gharar* and *maysir* in Islamic finance. *International Journal of Monetary Economics and Finance*. 2(3–4), pp. 384–397.

Cattelan, V. (2013) Property (*māl*) and credit relations in Islamic law: an explanation of *dayn* and the function of legal personality (*dhimma*). *Arab Law Quarterly*. 27(2), pp. 189–202.

Chehata, C. (1960) ʿAqd. In: Bearman, P., Bianquis, T. *et al.* (eds.) *Encyclopaedia of Islam*, 2nd ed. Leiden: Brill and Paris: Maisonneuve et Larose.

Chehata, C. (1968a) Le concept de contrat en droit musulman. *Archives de Philosophie du Droit*. 13, pp. 129–141.

Chehata, C. (1968b) Le contrat en droit musulman. *Zeitschrift für Vergleichende Rechtswissenschaft*. 70, pp. 81–96.

Chehata, C. (1969) *Théorie Générale de l'Obligation en Droit Musulman Hanéfite: Les Sujets de l'Obligation*. Paris: Éditions Sirey.

Chehata, C. (1970a) Islamic law. In: *International Encyclopedia of Comparative Law, Vol. II, The Legal Systems of the World, Their Comparison and Unification, Ch. 2, Structure and the Divisions of the Law*. Leiden: Martinus Nijhoff Brill; Tübingen: J.C.B. Mohr Siebeck, pp. 138–142.

Chehata, C. (1970b) *Droit Musulman: Applications au Proche-Orient*. Paris: Dalloz.

Chehata, C. (1971) *Études de Droit Musulman*. Travaux et Recherches de la Faculté de Droit et des Sciences Économiques de Paris. Paris: Presses Universitaires de France.

Chehata, C. (1973) *Études de Droit Musulman, 2 / La Notion de Responsabilité Contractuelle: Le Concept de Propriété*. Paris: Presses Universitaires de France.

Chehata, C. (1977) Dhimma. In: Bearman, P., Bianquis, T. *et al.* (eds.) *Encyclopédie de l'Islam*, 2nd ed., Vol. II. Leiden: Brill and Paris: Maisonneuve et Larose, p. 238.

Chloros, A.G. (1968) The doctrine of consideration and the reform of the law of contract: a comparative analysis. *The International and Comparative Law Quarterly*. 17(1), pp. 137–166.

Comair-Obeid, N. (1996) Particularity of the contract's subject-matter in the laws of the Arab Middle East. *Arab Law Quarterly*. 11(4), pp. 331–349.

Coulson, N.J. (1984) *Commercial Law in the Gulf States: The Islamic Legal Tradition*. London: Graham and Trotman.

Cover, R.M. (1983) The Supreme Court, 1982 term – Foreword: *nomos* and narrative. *Harvard Law Review*. 97(1), pp. 4–68.

Decock, W. (2013) *Theologians and Contract Law: The Moral Transformation of the Ius Commune (Ca. 1500–1650)*. Leiden: Brill.

Delcambre, A.-L. (1981) Dayn. In: Bearman, P., Bianquis, T. *et al.* (eds.) *Encyclopédie de l'Islam*, 2nd ed., Supplément Livraison 3–4. Leiden: Brill and Paris: Maisonneuve et Larose, pp. 206–207.

D'Emilia, A. (1957) Il khiyār ash-sharṭ nel *Aṣl* di Shaybānī. *Rivista degli Studi Orientali.* 32, pp. 633–640.

Eagleton, T. (1991) *Ideology: An Introduction.* London: Verso.

El-Gamal, M.A. (2000) *An Economic Explication of the Prohibition of Ribā in Classical Islamic Jurisprudence.* Proceedings of the Third Harvard University Forum on Islamic finance, Center for Middle Eastern Studies, Harvard University, Cambridge, MA, pp. 3–8.

El-Gamal, M.A. (2001) *An Economic Explication of the Prohibition of Gharar in Classical Islamic Jurisprudence.* Paper presented at the 4th International Conference on Islamic Economics, Leicester, 13–15 August 2000. Also in Islamic Economic Studies, 2001. 8(2), pp. 29–58.

El-Gamal, M.A. (2006) *Islamic Finance: Law, Economics and Practice.* Cambridge: Cambridge University Press.

El-Hassan, A.W.A. (1985) Freedom of contract, the doctrine of frustration, and sanctity of contracts in Sudan law and Islamic law. *Arab Law Quarterly,* 1(1), pp. 51–59.

Geertz, C. (1983) Local knowledge: fact and law in comparative perspective. In: Geertz, C. (ed.) *Local Knowledge: Further Essays in Interpretive Anthropology.* New York: Basic Books, pp. 167–234.

Glenn, H.P. (2000) *Legal Traditions in the World: Sustainable Diversity in Law.* Oxford: Oxford University Press.

Hallaq, W.B. (1985–1986) Legal reasoning in Islamic law and common law: logic and method. *Cleveland State Law Review.* 34, pp. 79–96.

Hamid, M.E. (1977) Mutual assent in the formation of contracts in Islamic law. *Journal of Islamic and Comparative Law.* 7, pp. 41–53.

Hassan, H. (2002) Contracts in Islamic law: the principles of commutative justice and liberality. *Journal of Islamic Studies.* 13(3), pp. 257–297.

Islam, M.W. (1999) *Al-mal*: the concept of property in Islamic legal thought. *Arab Law Quarterly.* 14(4), pp. 361–368.

Jackson, S.A. (1996) *Islamic Law and the State: The Constitutional Jurisprudence of Shihāb al-Dīn al-Qarāfī.* Leiden: Brill.

Kamali, M.H. (1999) Uncertainty and risk-taking (*gharar*) in Islamic law. *IIUM Law Journal.* 7(2), pp. 199–216.

Linant de Bellefonds, Y. (1958a) Volonté interne et volonté déclarée en droit musulman. *Revue Internationale de Droit Comparé.* 10(3), pp. 510–521.

Linant de Bellefonds, Y. (1958b) L'autonomie de la volonté en droit musulman. *Revue Algérienne, Tunisienne et Marocaine de Législation et de Jurisprudence.* 74(2), pp. 87–111.

Linant de Bellefonds, Y. (1965) *Traité de Droit Musulman Comparé, 3 Vols. Vol. 1, Théorie Générale de l'Acte Juridique.* Paris and La Haye: Mouton & Co.

Linant de Bellefonds, Y. (1977) Fāsid wa-bāṭil. In: Bearman, P., Bianquis, T. *et al.* (eds.) *Encyclopédie de l'Islam,* 2nd ed., Vol. II. Leiden: Brill and Paris: Maisonneuve et Larose, pp. 849–852.

Makdisi, J.A. (1999) The Islamic origins of the common law. *North Carolina Law Review.* 77, pp. 1635–1739.

Mallat, C. (2007) *Introduction to Middle Eastern Law.* Oxford: Oxford University Press.

Messick, B. (1993) *The Calligraphic State: Textual Domination and History in a Muslim Society.* Berkeley: California University Press.

Messick, B. (2001) Indexing the self: intent and expression in Islamic legal acts. *Islamic Law and Society.* 8(2), pp. 151–178.
Milliot, L. (1953) *Introduction à l'Étude du Droit Musulman.* Paris: Recueil Sirey.
Pollock, F. (1911) *Principles of Contract: A Treatise on the General Principles Concerning the Validity of Agreements in the Law of England*, 8th ed. London: Stevens and Sons.
Powers, P.R. (2006) *Intent in Islamic Law: Motive and Meaning in Medieval Sunnī Fiqh.* Leiden and Boston: Brill.
Ranouil, V. (1980) *L'Autonomie de la Volonté: Naissance et Évolution d'un Concept.* Travaux et Recherches de l'Université de droit, d'Économie et de Sciences Social de Paris. Paris: Presses Universitaire de France.
Rayner, S.E. (1991) *The Theory of Contracts in Islamic Law: A Comparative Analysis with Reference to the Modern Legislation in Kuwait, Bahrain and the United Arab Emirates.* Arab and Islamic Laws Series. London, Dordrecht and Boston: Graham & Trotman.
Rosen, L. (2000) *The Justice of Islam: Comparative Perspectives on Islamic Law and Society.* Oxford: Oxford University Press.
Said, E.W. (1978) *Orientalism.* London and Henley: Routledge & Kegan Paul.
Saleh, N. (1990) Definition and formation of contract under Islamic and Arab laws. *Arab Law Quarterly.* 5(2), pp. 101–116.
Saleh, N. (1992a) *Unlawful Gain and Legitimate Profit in Islamic Law: Ribā, Gharar and Islamic Banking*, 2nd ed. London: Graham & Trotman.
Saleh, N. (1992b) Are the validity and construction of legal acts affected by cause (*sabab*)? (A comparative study under Islamic and Arab laws). *Arab Law Quarterly.* 7(2), pp. 116–140.
Saleh, N. (1998) Origins of the sanctity of contracts in Islamic law. *Arab Law Quarterly.* 13(3), pp. 252–264.
Saleh, N. (2001) Freedom of contract: what does it mean in the context of Arab laws? *Arab Law Quarterly.* 16(4), pp. 346–357.
Sanhūrī, A.R.A. (1954–1959) *Maṣādir al-Ḥaqq fī l-Fiqh al-Islāmī, Dirāsa Muqārina bi-l-Fiqh al-Gharbī* (*The Bases of Right in Islamic Law, a Comparative Study with Western Law*), 6 Vols. Cairo: Jāmi'ah ad-Duwal al-'Arabiyya.
Santillana, D. (1938) *Istituzioni di Diritto Musulmano Malichita con Riguardo Anche al Sistema Sciafiita*, Vol. II. Roma: Istituto per l'Oriente.
Schacht, J. (1964) *An Introduction to Islamic Law.* Oxford: Clarendon Press.
Schacht, J. (2012) Ribā. In: Bearman, P., Bianquis, T. *et al.* (eds.) *Encyclopaedia of Islam*, 2nd ed. Leiden: Brill and Paris: Maisonneuve et Larose. Online edition. Accessed 15 March 2019.
Smirnov, A. (1996) Understanding justice in an Islamic context: some points of contrast with Western theories. *Philosophy East & West.* 46(3), pp. 337–350.
Stelzer, S.A.J. (2008) Ethics. In: Winter, T. (ed.) *The Cambridge Companion to Classical Islamic Theology.* Cambridge: Cambridge University Press, pp. 161–179.
Van de Bergh, S. (1975) 'Ayn. In: Bearman, P., Bianquis, T. *et al.* (eds.) *Encyclopaedia of Islam*, 2nd ed. Leiden: Brill and Paris: Maisonneuve et Larose.
Van Ess, J. (1970) The logical structure of Islamic theology. In: Von Grunebaum, G.E. (ed.) *Logic in Classical Islamic Culture, First Giorgio Levi della Vida Biennial Conference, Near Eastern Centre, University of California, Los Angeles, May 12, 1967.* Wiesbaden: Otto Harrassowitz, p. 23 ff.

Vogel, F.E. (2006) Contract law of Islam and the Arab Middle East. In: *International Encyclopedia of Comparative Law, Vol. VII, Contracts in General*, Chapter 7. Tübingen: Mohr Siebeck; Dordrecht, Boston and Lancaster: Martinus Nijhoff Publishers.
Wakin, J.A. (1972) *The Function of Documents in Islamic Law*. New York: State University of New York Press.
Wehr, H. (1979) *A Dictionary of Modern Written Arabic (Arabic-English)* (ed. by Cowan, J.M.), 4th ed. Wiesbaden: Harrassowitz.
Yanagihashi, H. (2004) *A History of the Early Islamic Law of Property: Reconstructing the Legal Development, 7th-9th Centuries*. Leiden: Brill.
Yanagihashi, H. (2013) Contract law. In: Fleet, K., Krämer, G. *et al.* (eds.) *Encyclopaedia of Islam*, 3rd ed. Leiden: Brill. Accessed 18 February 2020.
Zahraa, M. (1995) Legal personality in Islamic law. *Arab Law Quarterly*, 10(3), pp. 193–206.
Zahraa, M. (1998) Negotiating contracts in Islamic and Middle Eastern laws. *Arab Law Quarterly*. 13(3), pp. 265–277.
Zahraa, M., and Mahmor, S.M. (2001) Definition and scope of the Islamic concept of sale of goods. *Arab Law Quarterly*. 16(3), pp. 215–238.
Zahraa, M., and Mahmor, S.M. (2002) The validity of contracts when the goods are not yet in existence in the Islamic law of sale of goods. *Arab Law Quarterly*. 17(4), pp. 379–397.
Zysow, A. (1985–86) The problem of offer and acceptance: a study of implied-in-fact contracts in Islamic law and common law. *Cleveland State Law Review*. 34(1), pp. 69–77.

4 Realities of the Muslim world

Changing contexts over time

Moving from the revelation of *Šarīʿah* to the tradition of *fiqh*, our voyage has proceeded by means of strategies of translation (Chapter 2) and comparison (Chapter 3) to discover the *ʿaqd* in the acoustic space of Islam. More precisely, following Bhaskar's dialectic, Western contract law has been connected to Muslim *fiqh* (*The Two Towers* in their reciprocal coexistence) by exploring the plural itineraries of the ***madhāhib*** (section 3.2) within a domain of ***totality*** (3L), whose different elements (such as 'A' and 'B') are always connected.

'Totalities are systems of internally related elements or aspects. A [for us, Western contract law] may be said to be internally related to B [Muslim *fiqh*] if it is a . . . condition for the existence . . . of B, whether or not the converse is the case (i.e. the relation is symmetric)' (Bhaskar, 1994, p. 75). By thinking of the contract in the Muslim legal tradition, the Western traveller must cross a bridge of translation (section 2.5) where ***presence*** and ***absence*** coexist in mutual ***non-identity***. If the biblical myth of Babel highlights that law exists only in the form of specific laws (see section 2.1), '[t]ranslation builds bridges between . . . [laws] . . . [and] permits and encourages adaptation to new cultural contexts and needs: it changes . . . [laws] as it bridges them' (paraphrasing Richard Ovenden in Duncan, Harrison *et al.*, 2019, p. 7). The work of comparison allows the traveller to go across the bridge from West to East, keeping the two sides united in the process of discovery.

This point can make more explicit two fundamental corollaries of Bhaskar's concept of ***totality*** that our search has already indirectly touched on. First, 'all investigation has the practical character of a relational dialectic, in which the investigator is in principle part of the totality she describes' (Bhaskar, 1994, p. 77). The original invitation made at the beginning of Chapter 1 of this book about 'knowing ourselves' (the famous maxim *gnōthi seauton*, inscribed in the pronaos of the Temple of Apollo in the city of Delphi) as manifestation of a specific law-religion experience is evidence of this inescapable relational dialectic.[1] Second, the description of the *ʿaqd* as a medium of Islamic ***nomos*** itself constitutes a sub-totality: when inserted in the flux of time and the variety of geographical contexts where Islamic law has been applied over the centuries, *fiqh* texts are themselves '***partial totalities***, constituted by external as well as internal and contingent in addition to necessary relations' (Bhaskar, 1994, p. 76).

DOI: 10.4324/9781315145761-5

In other words, while Chapter 3 has implicitly considered the 'place' of the *'aqd* as something static (as if its city could be inert in relation to the real life of human beings), the next step of our adventure consists in locating its evolution within time by contextualising *fiqh* literature in the dynamic flow of human events. In fact, far from being an abstract entity 'in the books,' the Islamic contract has always been part of the reality 'in action' of the Muslim world and beyond.[2] As its concrete performance has always been embedded in the lives of real people and practiced differently in space and time, it is in light of the changing reality of the *'aqd* that this chapter is going to address (and complete) the understanding of *fiqh* as 'a conceptual replica of social life, not necessarily aspiring to be either complete or practical, but balanced between revelation, tradition and reality' (Calder, 1996, p. 981). By locating the Islamic contract in its process of change over time, its transformation (from medieval trade to the modern law of Muslim countries and our contemporary times) will disclose how its reality has changed while maintaining elements of continuity with classical *fiqh*, which are re-emerging (while re-adapted) today, as we will see, in the transnational space of Islamic finance.

Of course, it is not the purpose of this chapter to provide a comprehensive account of the transformation of the *'aqd* in all the great synchronic and diachronic variation of contexts that it has experienced (an enterprise for which not even an entire library of social and anthropological studies would suffice). Rather, the evolution of the *'aqd* will be narrated here through some general (yet meaningful) sub-chapters – as if the *Arab Girl*, receiving us back after the tour of the city, were to tell us the story(*-ies*) of her city and its evolution; it is time, now, to listen to her.

4.1. Continuity, change, and transformative praxis (4D): *fiqh* and textual polities

'Islamic law is not that found in the books of the jurists, but rather the outcome of a malleable and sensitive application of rules in a complex social setting. . . . To know what . . . [the *'aqd*] was, therefore, is to know how actual Muslim societies of the past *lived* it' (Hallaq, 2009, p. 167).

The *'aqd* is not only a manifestation of God's revelation, nor just a topic of the legal tradition; it is a 'craft' that belongs to a social reality, and as such, its 'life' has always depended on the specific space and time of its occurrence. As remarked from the very beginning of this book, there is no general and uniform archetype of the *'aqd* spanning all the history of the Muslim world; rather, both its theory(-ies) and practice(-s) have always been affected by a multiplicity of factors inserted in social reality. Of course, if the investigation of the specific space(s) and time(s) of the Islamic contract cannot be undertaken in this book (historical materials as well as anthropological and ethnographic research would be needed for this aim), the metaphor of the *'aqd* as a city and the reference made to Rome in the Introduction can help us to draw some general reflections on the matter.

On the one hand, a city is never an abstract place; on the contrary, its buildings exist for being employed by people, and their construction is functional to social life. While, in the previous chapter, much attention was given to the 'rules' that are necessary for the valid construction of the *ʿaqd* (as a building for which certain kinds of material and work are needed to guarantee its stability), we now have to examine how these rules of construction have evolved over time to meet the new needs of the city's population.

On the other hand, if changes always imply a certain degree of separation from the past, aspects of continuity persist (the tradition of *fiqh*, from medieval times, still maintains its cultural and religious echo, as we will see). In a similar way, by visiting Rome, one can immediately feel the sense of continuity of a millennial enterprise, where the ancient ruins of the Roman Forum and the magnificence of the Colosseum continue to exist in a landscape that was subsequently affected by the architecture of the Church, the Baroque, modern and contemporary styles.

This is precisely what the Introduction to this book described by referring to a persistent continuity *in practice* of the Islamic contract, despite the changeable and plural nature of its *theories and practices* in time. Looking back at the bridge of translation from West to East that we mentioned in Chapter 2, the traveller should now make an additional effort by putting the *theories* of the *ʿaqd* in a changeable domain of commercial and social *practice* that has been affected by a plurality of endogenous (e.g. the rise of the modern state in Muslim countries) and exogenous factors (e.g. legal transplants from other legal traditions). So, in the history of the *ʿaqd*, the surface of amplification of God's Word in echoing divine revelation (see section 2.4.5) has changed over the centuries, with normative forces that have affected the nature of the contract in the Muslim world both by means of processes of law-making (e.g. the impact of codification in the colonial and post-colonial period: section 4.3) and adaptation to the globalisation of financial markets (section 4.4). In fact, the *ʿaqd* itself, at the very beginning of Islamic history, was not the result of the Islamic revelation alone but of local practices at the time of the Prophet (section 4.2).

More in general, the values of the contract in the Muslim world have always combined elements related to the performance of Islamic *dīn/bíos* (to which the elaboration of *fiqh* was addressed) with a variety of contextual factors, from local customs to the political interests of modernisation, and later, the commercial concerns of contemporary capitalism. Not by chance, the recognition of this intrinsic plurality has constituted one of the methodological tenets of our research of the Islam-Muslim-world (section 1.3.2) by adhering to Shahab Ahmed's invitation

> to conceptualize Islam in terms that map onto the human and historical reality wherein Muslims have authored and lived with contradiction *as Islam*, . . . [and . . .] to locate the logic of difference and contradiction as coherent with and internal to Islam – that is, to provide a coherent

> account of contradiction in and as Islam (*ibidem*) . . . [by drawing] attention to . . . the mutually constitutive relationship between Islam and Muslims: on how Islam makes Muslims as Muslims make Islam.
> (Ahmed, 2016, pp. 542–543)

In a publication dedicated to the variation of meaning of Islamic contract law from classical times to the present global economy (Cattelan, 2021), I stress how the social nature of norms go far beyond their letter in legal manuals and form part of the collective identity of the communities where they are applied, where their concrete life subsists. Their presence *in-time* embraces mutable contexts in the *transformative praxis* (and so *agency*) as fourth dimension (4D) of Bhaskar's dialectics.[3] Here, the focus on *change* that is distinctive in social sciences highlights the nature of negativity (2E) in terms of a process rather than a product, which allows the 'shaped possibility of becoming' (Bhaskar, 1993, p. 142), where '[t]he past shapes the present and therefore shapes, without determining, possible futures' (Norrie, 2009, p. 34). Understanding of the Islamic contract, then, requires looking at a *transformative praxis* in which real people (merchants, Muslim believers, and non-Muslims) participate and by which they are transformed, too, as agents in a *totality* (3L) of internally related elements.

The implications of the passing of time radically challenge the possibility of dealing with any trans-historical archetype of contractual rules (see Introduction). Since the normative space of the *'aqd* cannot be properly understood without locating its nature *in-time* as a socio-anthropological construction,[4] the 'bridge' of translation and comparison that we have crossed during our research must (metaphorically speaking) migrate from one age to another, in a conceptual exercise of continuity-through-change, where the 'imag(in)ing power of . . . [re-presenting the *'aqd*] is immersed in social reality and so subject to present (i.e., our presence *in-time*)' (Cattelan, 2021, p. 76). Moving the bridge of Babel (section 2.5) *in-time* requires, I believe, an additional power of imag(in)ing that can, fortunately, be inspired by one of the most famous poems of Nobel Laureate Wisława Szymborska (1923–2012); namely, 'The people on the bridge.'[5] In her poem, Szymborska comments on our 'odd planet,' whose inhabitants, in her opinion, 'are odd, too.' They 'are subject to time, but they won't admit it;' rather, they 'have their own ways of expressing protest' (Szymborska, 1996, p. 167). For instance, they make 'little pictures,' like the one printed by Japanese master Utagawa Hiroshige (1797–1858) ('a rebel . . . who, by the way, died long ago and in due course,' as Szymborska wittily remarks: *ibidem*, p. 168) under the title *Sudden Shower over Shin-Ōhashi Bridge and Atake* (1857) (Figure 4.1).

> At first glance, nothing special.
> What you see is water.
> And one of its banks.
> And a little boat sailing strenuously upstream.
> And a bridge over the water, and people on the bridge.

Figure 4.1 Sudden Shower over Shin-Ōhashi Bridge and Atake (print artwork by Utagawa Hiroshige, 1857; Metropolitan Museum of Art, New York)

It appears that the people are picking up their pace
because of the rain just beginning to lash down
from a dark cloud.

The thing is, nothing else happens.
The cloud doesn't change its colour or its shape.
The rain doesn't increase or subside.
The boat sails on without moving.
The people on the bridge are running now
exactly where they ran before.

It's difficult at this point to keep from commenting.
This picture is by no means innocent.
Time has been stopped here.
Its laws are no longer consulted.
It has been relieved of its influence over the course of events.
It has been ignored and insulted (Szymborska, 1996, pp. 167–168).

Expressing our own protest against the conceptual fallacy of any trans-historical representation of the *ʿaqd* (as already criticised previously), the next pages will look at the variance of meanings that the Islamic contract has experienced over the centuries as a sort of 'city in evolution,' whose buildings have changed in relation to the social transformations. Recalling the bridge of translation/comparison, we can use Hiroshige's *Bridge* as a metaphor for a translation/comparison *subject-to-time* that we are employing in the search for these meanings.

In particular, looking closer at the *ʿaqd* in the light of its transformative praxis, this chapter proposes to outline the story of its city through three main periods, which can indirectly reflect a diverse relation between law and religion in the textual tradition of *fiqh*, and the related variation(-s) in the production of contractual rules as specific expressions of alternative 'textual polities' in the social reality (see the following). Keeping our reference to the metaphor of the city, the material construction of its buildings (the contracts negotiated in the reality of the Muslim world) has historically followed patterns that have changed over time. As a natural result, the rules that Muslim jurisprudence has forged in echoing God's revealed Word have necessarily been adapted (hence, transformed) to different contexts. In fact, they have often been adopted in relation to purposes that have not been primarily the expression of Islamic *dīn* but sometimes more in line with commercial aims of practice, political/social preferences, and reasons of economic profit, in a constant interplay between theory and practice. Hence, the meaning of *fiqh* textual rules on the *ʿaqd*, which we examined in Chapter 3 as an expression of Islamic *nomos*, have continuously changed in the transformative praxis of the Muslim world.

The conception of texts as vehicles of legal meaning in the mutual interdependence between law makers, interpreters, and users belongs to the core of a well-known work of legal anthropology; namely, Brinkley Messick's *The Calligraphic State: Textual Domination and History in a Muslim Society* (1993).[6] With reference to the topic, Messick remarks how texts exist themselves in the 'interlocking of a polity, a social order, and a discursive formation' (Messick, 1993, p. 1), which arises through the bilateral conjunction 'between the literary processes behind the constitution of authority *in* texts and the social and political processes involved in articulating the authority *of* texts' (*ibidem*, p. 1; italics in the original text). Hence, within the textual polities of the Muslim world,

> [d]ocuments are mediations, their writers mediators, between the enduring text of *shariʿa* law and the particular events of the world. [It is in this frame that we can] . . . consider the problematic way documents fit the law to the world, and the world to law – rendering form historical and giving form to history.
>
> (Messick, 1989, pp. 26–27)

Looking at *fiqh* rules as specific documents inserted in a certain social reality – hence, part of determined textual polities *in-time* where society affects the formulation of contractual rules – has a double advantage. On the one hand, it permits us to underline how contractual rules have been differently thought of in their practices in the Muslim world over the centuries. On the other hand, it makes it possible to broaden the *non-identity* of law and religion to a multiplicity of social, political, and economic factors that have always contributed to the 'idea' of the Islamic contract beyond the canons of Muslim *bíos* and have also shifted its conceptualisation (as we will see) from an acoustic to a visual space in modern times, during the era of Western colonisation. In brief, the sub-totality of *fiqh* literature, when inserted in the flux of time, must be replaced by the broader totality of the *'aqd* in its transformative praxis (4D). Through the fourth dimension of Bhaskar's dialectic, our understanding of the *'aqd* will be modified as well; we will *listen to* it no longer as the 'product' of Islamic law and religion, but rather, as a 'process' (*rectius*, 'processes') of legal, social, political, and economic interactions that are all constantly interconnected in the Muslim world.

Feeling the 'rain' of reality while crossing Hiroshige's *Bridge*, three ages can be identified in the history of the Islamic contract: that of medieval times, which this book has labelled under the title of *Verbal Trade* (section 4.2); the period of codification under the influence of Western culture, under the semantics of the *Codified Norm* (section 4.3); and the contemporary world of the *Typewritten Market* (section 4.4), dominated by the forces of global capitalism. As we will see, each of these ages will show peculiar modalities of production and application of contractual rules that will also be interpreted as the expression (at a micro- and macro-level) of radical changes in the nature of Islamic law as a social construction.

4.2. *Verbal Trade*

The first chapter of the story that the *Arab Girl* can narrate about her city can be set in medieval Islam; more precisely, from the origins of the Islamic contract, with the revelation of God's Word to the Prophet, to the end of the pre-modern era and the radical change in the coordinates of the *'aqd* (hence, of its map: section 3.2) that occurred with the transplantation of Western legal culture to Muslim countries (see section 4.3 in this chapter).

To depict this age of the Islamic contract, three elements are noteworthy in terms of the contextualisation of its practice *in-time*: the 'foundation' of the city in a context which was originally non-Islamic (section 4.2.1); the nature of what we described as 'verbalism' (section 3.5.1) in relation both to the religious background of the *'aqd* and the function of documentary evidence in medieval trade (section 4.2.2); and how the *practice* of this *Verbal Trade* can be coherently linked to the contract *theories* of the juristic schools also in relation to the elaboration of legal devices (*ḥiyal*) (section 4.2.3). As we will see shortly, the alternative approaches to *ḥiyal* by Sunnī schools can demonstrate both the impact of verbalism in commercial practice and how legal stratagems were not exclusively the product of trade customs but the consistent expression of specific *fiqh* textual polities.

4.2.1. Pre-Islamic customs, formalism, and the origins of the ʿaqd

The period prior to the revelation of Islam is commonly described in Muslim belief as an age of 'ignorance' (*jāhiliyya*): the ignorance of the Truth, of the (right) Path to salvation (*Šarīʿah*), with the human being still lost in a moral desert. The radical transformation from the ethic of tribalism to the monotheistic revelation of Islam finds a comprehensive depiction in the book by Toshihiko Izutsu on the *Ethico-Religious Concepts in the Qur'ān* (2002, first published in 1966). In particular, Izutsu's attention focuses on the semantic transformation that pre-Islamic tribal values undertook, 'with modifications in form and substance' (2002, p. 16), so as 'to be incorporated into the new code of Islamic ethics' (*ibidem*).

Contractual rules that were present in the Arabian Peninsula underwent a corresponding dynamic of re-formulation, within a process which was not at all one of radical rejection but, on the contrary, of re-adaptation of local customs according to the Message of the revelation. Most of these rules were certainly related to customary commercial practices within the context of cultural pluralism and polycentricity (Salaymeh, 2016, is explicit on the point)[7] that was the 'cradle' of the birth of Islamic law as well as that of the Islamic contract. As also suggested by Schacht, '[o]ne of the most distinctive technical features of Islamic law, the juridical construction of contracts, possibly derived from ancient Near Eastern law and might have come to the Muslims through the medium of commercial practice in Iraq' (1964, p. 22).

It is in this context that, as we noted in Chapter 3, the original structure of the *ʿaqd* was unilateral rather than bilateral. This is highlighted by the etymology of *ījāb* (offer): '*ījāb*, making something *wājib*, means etymologically not "to offer" but "to make definite, binding, due", and this reflects a different, unilateral construction of the contract' (*ibidem*), as also remarked by Zysow ('*ījāb* . . . seems to reflect a stage of law in which sales were affected by unilateral conveyances': 1985–86, p. 75). It is interesting to note that both Schacht and Zysow underline how Islamic contractual rules did not emerge in a vacuum but (moving from certain customary practices that were semantically reshaped by the revelation of Islam) evolved towards a specific construction of the *ʿaqd* where its bilateral nature superseded elements of the exchange that, in the pre-Islamic tribal society, had involved 'formal conveyances effected by symbolic, irrational actions' (Zysow, 1985–86, p. 71).

Hence, correspondingly to the transformation of the previous tribal moral code to the values of Islamic ethics (Izutsu, 2002), contractual rules underwent a re-formulation, as a result of which those actions which were previously considered sufficient to bind the parties (according to the model of implied-in-fact contracts) were substituted by an express verbal exchange of offer and acceptance. 'Muslim jurists who required an express offer and acceptance regarded only these acts as sufficiently unambiguous to demarcate the legal character of the transaction in question' (Zysow, 1985–86, p. 71). Hence, in classical Islamic law (see section 3.5.1), gesture, writing, handshaking, or the delivery of property were no longer considered sufficient for the valid conclusion of the contract; rather, it was the verbal exchange of offer and acceptance that was required for the enforceability of the exchange. As noted by Zysow, there was a religious meaning in pre-Islamic formulas whose survival Muslim jurists could not countenance. 'The jurists who demanded an express offer and acceptance based this requirement on the premise that recognizing the passage of title by delivery alone would amount to condoning the survival of these pre-Islamic practices in a new form. For them, implied-in-fact contracts were not informal at all, but represented the recrudescence of formalism' (*ibidem*, pp. 71–2). These pre-Islamic formulas, therefore, were soon substituted by the requirement of verbal consent between the parties – which, in fact, can be considered itself a precise manifestation of the new religiosity of Islam, grounded on the centrality of the divine *Word*, within which human beings are constituted in their ethical existence as '*by way of word*' (Stelzer, 2008, p. 169; see back, Chapter 2).

4.2.2. *Verbalism and documentary evidence in Muslim medieval trade*

'Although put forward as a rejection of formalism, the requirement of an express offer and acceptance cannot itself escape entirely the label of formalistic' (Zysow, 1985–86, p. 72). An interpretation of the rules of verbalism in classical Islam has been already advanced in this book with reference to the construction of the contract (section 3.5.1). As already seen, Muslim jurisprudence requires the oral declaration of convergent statements in order to make the contract binding for the parties; furthermore, the use of the past tense of the verb is needed, and the declarations have to occur within the same contractual session (*majlis al-ʿaqd*) in order to guarantee the unity of the *ʿaqd*. In fact, if these rules were a reaction to the symbolism of the irrational practices of the pre-Islamic tribal societies, which held some sort of religious meaning, the need for a verbal offer and acceptance can itself be interpreted as the manifestation of Islamic *dīn/bíos* (replacing previous pagan forms). If the ethical nature of the action in Islam is grounded on the divine *Word*, verbalism reflects the moral dimension of the human being 'as already constituted beings "before the Law" who are asked to find out by which means they will reply . . . *by way of word*' (Stelzer, 2008, p. 169).

At the same time, moving here from the interaction between revelation and tradition to the practice of contractual rules in the reality of medieval trade, the rationale of verbalism may be further investigated in relation to what has been considered a striking paradox in the early economy of the Muslim world; namely, the contrast between the strong reliance on written documents by traders, on the one hand, and the lack of recognition of their value (either as a formality to conclude the contract or as documentary evidence) in classical Islamic law (on this point specifically, see Lydon, 2009).

Schacht (1964, pp. 18–19)[8] notes that what can be described as the 'lack of faith in paper' (a formula that he did not use explicitly but was later coined by

Lydon, 2009) may appear a contradiction with regard to the Qur'ān's explicit endorsement of the recording of contractual agreements (as in Q. 2:282: 'Believers, when you contract a debt for a fixed period, put it in writing'). With no doubt, the preference for legal evidence based on oral testimony constitutes a cornerstone of classical Islamic law.

> Orality . . . was central to Islamic legal systems that hinged upon a reliance on the memory of mortals despite the spread of Arabic literacy and the growing popularity of writing. The underlying principle in Islamic legal theory was the belief that the spoken word was the most "authentic" form of proof (Johansen, 1997, p. 337). Oral testimony and oath taking were superior forms of evidence to written documents that, aside from the possibility of being tampered with or decontextualized, were not necessarily clear representations of the truth or of an author's intent (Johansen, 1997, p. 361). Both oath taking and witnessing were acts inextricably tied to the first pillar of Islam, the profession of one's faith in God (*shahāda*).
>
> (Lydon, 2009, pp. 654–655)

In the light of these considerations, the preference for 'verbality' also with regard to legal proof (the denial of Islamic law of 'the validity of documentary evidence . . . [by] restricting legal proof to the oral evidence of witnesses:' Schacht, 1964, p. 82) can shed further light on the interaction between religion, legal tradition, and commercial reality in medieval Islam – where, even though documents were written down, 'calligraphy' could not supersede the authenticity of oral communication.[9]

In *The Calligraphic State* (1993), already quoted previously, Brinkley Messick investigates the role of handwritten legal documents produced in the 1970s in the town of Ibb, a provincial capital in Šāfiʿī Lower Yemen, as an expression of a 'textual polity' interlocking authority and transmission of meaning within a specific social order (see endnote 6 in this chapter). The discursive formation that is inherently connected to any literacy production is meant in Messick's research to highlight 'the relation of shariʿa text to social practice' (Messick, 1993, p. 4), moving from the *Word*, the 'Quran as paradigm, the genealogies of textual transmission . . . anchored in recitation' (*ibidem*, p. 6) to human actions *by way of words.* Although Messick's analysis deals with a local community of the 1970s, his conclusions are illuminating also for Muslim medieval times.

In this conceptual context, in fact, although the textual polity of the *ʿaqd* has radically changed from the classical *fiqh* of medieval trade to the process of codification in Muslim countries, and later, in the *lex mercatoria* of contemporary global finance, *fiqh* texts and contractual documents have always defined the specific normative space of Islamic legal practice within a double movement[10] (from the *Word* to the document and from the *world* to the text – where the document text 'mediates both the re-production of the Text and the incorporative 'translation' of the world:' Messick, 1989, p. 35).

The function of written documents as mediation between the *Word* and the *world* in the performance of *Šarīʿah* through 'verbal trade' reaffirms, once again, the rationales of the acoustic space of Islamic *dīn*, with the moral/legal commitment of the parties becoming 'material' through their spoken *words* (section 2.4.5). Therefore, in medieval trade, even though written documents were commonly accepted as substitutes for oral declarations between absent parties, *inter praesentes* the verbalisation of the intention was always required as primary 'evidence' of the commitment to the contract – which could not, on the contrary, be immediately deduced from written documents. *Verbalism*, in the end (and far from any contradiction or paradox), was the direct result of a normative universe grounded on an acoustic rationality that could not be confined within the visual boundaries of a written text.

In contrast to this, as we will see by referring to the *Codified Norm* of modern Muslim states (section 4.3) and the *Typewritten Market* of Islamic finance (section 4.4), the textual polities of the Islamic contract radically departed from this in successive periods of its history, giving rise to alternative forms of discursive relations. But, before moving to the next stages of evolution of the city of the *ʿaqd*, another dimension of the production of contractual rules in the practice of medieval trade must be discussed: that of the so-called 'legal devices' (*ḥiyal*, sing. *ḥīla*) and their function in the traditions of classical schools, in their scholarly elaboration aimed at translating divine revelation into the human reality of commercial affairs.

*4.2.3. Legal devices (*ḥiyal*): contractual theories-into-practices*

Dealing with the reality of the *ʿaqd* in medieval Islam, one of the most revealing areas of the interplay between *fiqh* textual traditions and real-life commercial practices is that of legal devices (*ḥiyal*, sing. *ḥīla*).[11]

For long time, *ḥiyal* have been interpreted in Western scholarship as major evidence of the gap between theory and practice in Islamic law, following the position by Joseph Schacht (see also the Introduction to this book, specifically endnote 13): '[t]he legal devices represented a *modus vivendi* between theory and practice: the maximum that custom could concede, and the minimum (that is to say, formal acknowledgment) that the theory had to demand' (1964, p. 80). In Schacht's interpretation, legal devices became the main proof of the history of Islamic law as deeply 'dominated by the contrast between theory and practice' (*ibidem*, p. 199), to the extent that, as 'Islamic law is conscious of its character as a religious,' 'it believes in a continued *decadence* since the time of the caliphs of Medina . . . and it takes the *corruption* of contemporary conditions for granted' (*ibidem*; italics added). Within Schacht's 'theory vs practice' paradigm, '[t]he admission of the validity of legal devices (*ḥiyal*) serves to counteract, in practice, the claims of the theory' (*ibidem*, p. 200).

The critical revision undertaken in this book regarding the *decadence* and *corruption* of the Islamic contract (here associated with the practice of *ḥiyal*, as opposed to *fiqh* ideal theory) was originally ignited by Gérôme's *Arab Girl*

(Figure 0.1) as a visual representation of Orientalism. In particular, the bias towards the *Almeh* has been reviewed through a dialectic of non-identity (Bhaskar) by 'listening to' Muslim *fiqh* in the normative pluralism (Ahmed) that characterises the acoustic space (McLuhan) of Islam.[12]

With this in mind, the re-consideration of the function of *ḥiyal* in Muslim medieval trade finds further coherence, as we will see shortly, when located in the broader context of *madhāhib* contract theories, especially in relation to the prevalence (or not) of the external declaration over the inner motive – what has been described in terms of Šāfi'ī/Ḥanafī objectivism in contrast to Mālikī/Ḥanbalī subjectivism (see section 3.4.3).

> In the Arabic language the term *ḥīla* (pl. *ḥiyal*) denotes any skilful device, expedient or stratagem employed to overcome a difficulty, either by evading or eluding an inconvenience or by ingeniously managing the problem from which it derives. In other words, a *ḥīla* is any means that successfully deals with a difficult situation by transforming a problematic occurrence into a fruitful result. As this helpful change may be unlikely to be achieved through ordinary means, a *ḥīla* can be seen as an extraordinary tool that is useful (or somehow necessary) when standard means appear inadequate to fulfil a particular objective.
>
> (Cattelan, 2017, pp. 247–248)

Challenging Schacht's interpretation, a seminal article by Satoe Horii raised the first radical critique of the theory-vs-practice paradigm, by agreeing 'with Chehata that the phenomenon of *ḥiyal* attests to the lively development of Islamic law rather than to its decadence; and with Wichard that *ḥiyal* were an integral part of Islamic law rather than devices to circumvent it' (Horii, 2002, p. 315).[13] While fully subscribing to Horii's position, I have further elaborated the point (Cattelan, 2017, pp. 265–270) and showed how the divergent positions of the schools regarding the relevance of the motive, in the light of objectivism/subjectivism, match with their approach towards legal artifices (on the point see also Vogel, 2006, p. 32). In particular, the validity of *ḥiyal* depends mainly on the objectivity of interpretation, despite the illegal purpose that they seek to achieve.[14] This position is also supported by Mohammad Hashim Kamali, in linking the issue of *ḥiyal* to the different approaches of the schools towards externality and intent:

> [s]ome differences of orientation in legal thought among the schools can be ascertained with reference to the manifest form as opposed to the essence of acts and conducts. While some are inclined to pay attention to manifest conformity to the letter of the law, other are inclined to credit the intention behind the act, and seek a closer link between the two. But this is indicative only of a general orientation in the sense that they are not mutually exclusive categories as the proponents of one do not deny validity of the other. The Ḥanafīs and Šāfi'īs tend to stress the

> externality of conduct without exploring the intent behind it whereas the Malikīs and Ḥanbalīs are inclined toward the latter. A consequence of this difference of attitude can be seen in the approval or otherwise of legal stratagems (*al-ḥiyal al-fiqhiyyah*).
>
> (Kamali, 1998, p. 65)

In this regard, the approval or rejection of *ḥiyal* by the schools cannot be simply related to a prevalence of the practice over the theory, as proposed by Schacht; the doctrinal background of the different tendencies of the Sunnī schools regarding *ḥiyal* is much more complex and testifies, rather, to an interdependence between theory(*-ies*) and practice(*-s*) of Islamic law in medieval commercial reality.

On the side of objectivism, *ḥiyal* legitimacy was generally recognised by the Šāfiʿīs, on the grounds that external words prevail over the morality of inner intention. Schacht remarks how, although Šāfiʿī and the first few generations of his school regarded *ḥiyal* as reprehensible, they recognised their legal validity. The success of Ḥanafī *ḥiyal* literature (see later) caused several Šāfiʿī authors, from the 4th/10th century onwards, to compose books on legal devices and to distinguish valid *ḥiyal* (the great majority) from those considered reprehensible or forbidden (Schacht, 1964, p. 81). Šāfiʿī scholars also criticised the Mālikī doctrine of *sadd al-dharāʾiʿ* (see as follows) because it gave primacy to *istiḥsān* (preference) over *qiyās* (analogy) and thus replaced *qiyās* – 'an authentic scholarly endeavour (*iğtihād*) that is guided by indicators found in the texts and which are therefore perceptible to jurists' (as 'things must be judged by their appearances') – with *istiḥsān* – a 'form of reasoning from what is not perceptible' (Horii, 2002, pp. 343–344) (see also Cattelan, 2017, p. 257).

Together with the Šāfiʿīs, the Ḥanafīs considered *ḥiyal* valid and developed them into a special branch of law, called *makhārij* – i.e 'exits,' a genre that was a genuine part not only of Ḥanafī practice but also of their theory; as demonstrated by Satoe Horii, 'the *makhārij* did not represent a genre that belongs exclusively to the sphere of practice rather than doctrine. Rather, they served to attest, from a practical point of view, what the legal doctrine prescribes' (Horii, 2002, p. 331). The assertion is supported by a list of texts devoted to *ḥiyal* by Ḥanafīs: the *Kitāb al-Makhārij fī al-Ḥiyal* by al-Šaybānī; a brief and partial commentary on this text by Muḥammad b. Aḥmad al-Sarakhsī (originally a part of his *Kitāb al-Mabsūṭ*); the *Kitāb al-Ḥiyal wa'l- Makhārij* by Aḥmad b. 'Amr (or 'Umar) al-Khaṣṣāf; the *Jannat al-Aḥkam wa-Junnat al-Khuāṣṣām* by Saʿīd b. 'Alī al-Samarqandī. This particular status of *ḥiyal* in Ḥanafī literature is also confirmed by Udovitch who quotes al-Šaybānī's treatise.

> In al-Shaybānī's treatise specifically devoted to legal fictions, we read: "I said: What is your opinion of two men wishing to form a partnership with their possessions, one of whom has merchandise worth five

thousand dirhams and the other merchandise worth one thousand dirhams? He said: Partnership in goods is not permissible. I said: What type of legal fiction can they employ which would make partners in the merchandise they possess? He said: Let the owner of the merchandise worth five thousand dirhams purchase five-sixths of his colleague's merchandise with one-sixth of his own. If they do this, they will be partners in accordance with their shares in the investment; the one whose merchandise is worth one thousand dirhams becomes a one-sixth owner of the combine investment, and his colleague becomes an owner of five-sixths of it."
(al-Šaybānī, *Kitāb al-Makhārij fī al-Ḥiyal*, quoted in Udovitch, 1970b, pp. 120–121)

In later Hanafite literature, this particular method of circumvention is incorporated into the very body of the legal codes and is usually presented immediately following the prohibition. So complete was the assimilation of this legal fiction into the body of Hanafite law that in several codes it is given without the designation of *ḥīla* and appears as an accepted feature of positive law. What is perhaps even more significant in relation to commercial practice is the inclusion of this legal fiction – without being so designated – in the earliest *shurūṭ* (legal formulary) works.
(*ibidem*, p. 121)

The prevalence given by the Ḥanafis to the appearance of the act, irrespective of the real intentions behind it, and the development of the genre of *makhārij* as a recognised field of doctrinal elaboration, stemmed not from a blind formalism but from a conception of the divine Law as beneficial for the agent; as a consequence, they developed the *ḥiyal* in order to provide legal 'remedies,' techniques to seek a 'utility,' for the practitioners belonging to the *madhhab*. The literature of *makhārij* was primarily directed to the removal of oppression (*ẓulm*), interpreted in the broader sense as referring 'not only to an injustice exerted against a person, but to any circumstances that cause any inconvenience in daily affairs' (Horii, 2002, p. 320); the *Šarīʿah* itself was interpreted by the Ḥanafis as a body of 'exits' to 'escape the unlawful in search of the lawful,' and to cover the principal necessities of human life (Q. 65:2: 'If anyone shows piety towards Allah, He will appoint for him a way out (*makhraj*)'). Hence, the *ḥiyal* were not intended to 'escape' the Law but, on the contrary, to 'escape the unlawful in search of the Law.' Of course, not all devices were lawful, but only those that did not cause prejudice to others. Specifically on this point, Šaybānī, influenced by the Kufan authority Ša'bī (d. between 103/721 and 110/728),[15] points out that 'a *ḥīla* can be employed only to pursue a lawful course, seeking to get rid of what is unlawful' (quoted in Horii, 2002, p. 323).

There is no harm in *ḥiyal* for lawful purposes. Indeed, *ḥiyal* are means by which one can escape from the unlawful to the lawful. As for [those *ḥiyal*] that belong to this category and the like, there is no harm. Only

> rejected are those [*ḥiyal*] by means of which one seeks to prejudice another's right, to disguise a falsehood, or to make things doubtful. As for the means [i.e., the lawful *ḥiyal* . . .] that we mentioned, there is no harm in them.
>
> (*ibidem*, p. 323)

The genre of *makhārij*, reflecting a utilitarian conception of law (in the sense of 'utility' for the goodness of the community in following *Šarī'ah*) remarks how

> *makhārij* are appropriate solutions in the sense that they are in accordance with the spirit of the law, and their primary purpose is to provide remedies for those who seek them. Put differently, the Ḥanafīs, defined the law primarily in terms of utility. *Makhārij*, therefore, were nothing special for the Ḥanafīs, but something intrinsic to jurisprudence, an integral part of it. What the Ḥanafīs call "*makhārij*" include all possible, justifiable means to solve a given problem within the range of doctrine . . . in Ḥanafī legal discussion, it is often difficult to distinguish "*makhārij*" from mere applications of certain prescriptions. The Ḥanafīs "prescribed" *makhārij* rather than invented special methods to circumvent legal prescriptions.
>
> (Horii, 2002, p. 322)

As far as the Mālikīs are concerned, they developed a similar doctrine to that of the *makhārij*, albeit from a different point of view; in fact, in accordance with their subjective perspective, they rejected the position that 'utility' is the 'essence of law,' attaching greater importance to the inner intention rather than the declared will in the qualification of legal acts. Their position differed from that of the Ḥanbalīs, who categorically rejected *ḥiyal* as formalistic stratagems to circumvent legal provisions, in evaluating legal devices through the principle of *sadd al-dharā'i'* – i.e. 'to block ways' (ways that are likely to result in an evil end).

This principle might be seen as the antithesis of *ḥiyal*, 'in the sense that it prevents unlawful legal acts committed for presumably illegal purposes, notwithstanding their lawful appearance' (*ibidem*, p. 343). But the Mālikīs did not totally reject *ḥiyal*, as shown in the fundamental *Mudawwana* by Saḥnūn (d. 240/855); some of the Ḥanafī *ḥiyal* are deemed to be invalid, while others acceptable, under proper revision, according to the principle of *sadd al-dharā'i'*. The principle itself 'did not lead . . . to solutions qualitatively different from those suggested by the Ḥanafīs' (*ibidem*, p. 357), in the attempt to balance the utility of the act and the morality of the action, which seems to be a constant of the Mālikī school. In fact, both Mālikīs and Ḥanbalīs concentrated on the moral background of the action – a tendency which explains their attention to the real intent, the logic of the principle of *sadd al-dharā'i'*, and the refusal of *ḥiyal* as formalistic (and consequently unlawful) devices.

The shift from benefit to morality in the evaluation of acts by the Sunnī schools does not match the thesis of the historical existence of only ‘one’ Islamic law. On the contrary, the positions of the *madhāhib* in the conceptualisation of the psychological formation of the contract (as summarised in Diagram 4) show the coexistence of a range of alternative positions. These positions were mainly ‘utilitarian’ in the case of the Ḥanafīs and the Šāfi‘īs, while ‘ethical’ for the Mālikīs and the Ḥanbalīs – a divergence that further confirms the normative pluralism of *fiqh* tradition.

The meaning of *ḥiyal* as core manifestation of the interplay of theories-practices in Islamic medieval trade emerges also from the consideration that ‘[w]ritten documents often formed an essential element of *ḥiyal*’ (Schacht, 1964, p. 83).

> The more complicated *ḥiyal* normally consisted of several transactions between the parties concerned, each of which was perfectly legal in itself, and the combined effect of which produced the desired result. Each transaction was, as a matter of course, recorded and attested in a separate document. Taken in isolation, a document recording a single transaction or an acknowledgement made by one of the parties might be used by the other party to its exclusive advantage and for a purpose contrary to the aim of the whole of the agreement. In order to prevent this happening, the official documents were deposited in the hands of a trustworthy person . . . or intermediary, together with an unofficial covering document which set out the real relationship of the parties to each other and the real purport of their agreement.
>
> (*ibidem*, p. 83)

The phenomenon of the use of written documents in relation to legal stratagems cannot be explored appropriately in this book, with reference to a great

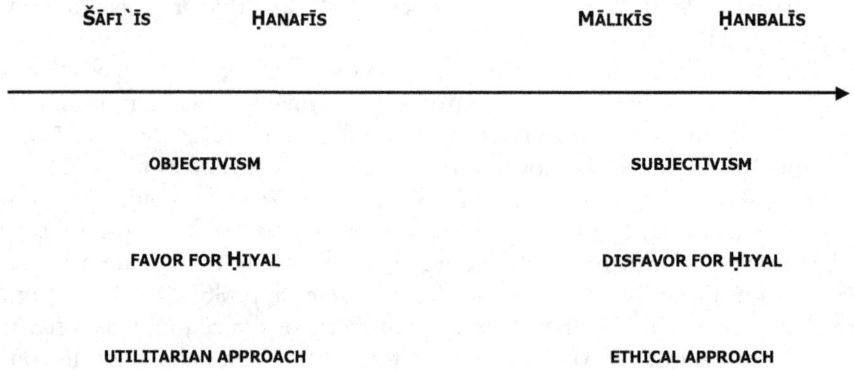

Diagram 4 Approaches by the Sunnī schools towards legal devices (*ḥiyal*) (author’s elaboration)

geographical and diachronic variance that could be interlinked to specific regional application of *fiqh* doctrinal elaboration. Other 'ages' of the *ʿaqd* still need to be narrated by the *Arab Girl*. Nevertheless, this employment of documents as essential instruments in legal practice suggests that we interpret the nature of Islamic medieval trade as specific textual polities where the role of Muslim jurisprudence (in ratifying *ḥiyal* or not) was not marginal, but rather, incisive. In fact, the approval/denial of the legitimacy of legal stratagems supports a theory-practice interplay where *fiqh* legal texts were contextualised in their own social realities and aimed at the solutions of practical commercial problems. Following Messick's terminology, in Muslim medieval trade, *fiqh* itself was 'a process of locating *Šarīʿah* in context, and its social anthropology worked in a "calligraphic", "handwritten" way by inserting the meaning of legal opinions in[to] a textual polity grounded on specific life-situations' (Cattelan, 2021, p. 82).[16]

In the next sections, we will see how the calligraphic polity of medieval *Verbal Trade*, located in the acoustic space of Islam, has been substituted during modern times by the realm of the *Codified Norm* and its visual geometry (section 4.3; for the distinction visual/acoustic space see section 1.3.3), and later, by the technology (and epistemology) of the *Typewritten Market* in the contemporary space of global finance (section 4.4). The transformative praxis of the *ʿaqd* through these different eras will conclude our analysis with some final reflections on the evolution of the 'design' of its city, with different physical layouts of the town, old and new, in relation to the historical variations of Muslim societies (section 4.5).

4.3. *Codified Norm*

With the rise of the modern era, a different chapter in the story of the *ʿaqd* started: a chapter in which the rules of 'verbalism' were replaced by those embedded in 'codified norms,' according to a semantics and a visual logic that replicated the *corpus iuris* of Western law.

4.3.1. The invention of a corpus *for Islamic law and the ʿaqd: Western transplants and the codification process in Muslim countries*

The image of the *corpus* has been widely employed in this book to refer to the deep assumptions underpinning Western visual rationality as well as their implications in the construction of the 'legal body' (*corpus iuris*) of Lady Justice (see Introduction). In modern times, the assumptions of systematisation, uniformity, continuity, and interconnection, which connote the visual space of Western modernity (see McLuhan, section 1.3.3), have found their most notable expression in the process of codification of law. Representing the law through codified texts does not constitute a neutral operation; on the contrary, texts of law (as highlighted in section 3.2) are themselves maps that narrate *who* people are though the normativity to which they subscribe. In other words, legal documents (and codes do represent the most peculiar manifestation of normativity in modern states) are not neutral media but are 'maps' that tell us a great deal about their makers, their recipients, and their function.

In fact, any medium of knowledge, as a system of representation, embodies a certain perspective, fixes a frame, and shapes similarities as well as contrasts; in brief, as stressed by McLuhan, the medium itself *is* the message, since it defines the content of the message (McLuhan and Fiore, 1967; see Chapter 1, endnote 14). If any mediated knowledge selects certain qualities of the referent while marginalising others, the transplant of legal codes from Western to Muslim countries during the period of colonisation, and later, through autonomous reception by the latter, has radically changed the 'referent' itself, which has been 'clothed' according to Western legal fashion.

Thus, it was through the codification process that the 'improper body' of the Islamic *ʿaqd* (the *Almeh* represented through an Orientalistic bias) 'has been dressed' in Western legal clothes (see section 3.1), acquiring a *corpus* that did not exist in *fiqh* classical times (section 2.4.5). As the Conclusion of this book will further remark, the substitution of the original acoustic rationality of Islam with the visual space of Western modernity *dis-located* the *ʿaqd* outside the Orient, reducing it to another stage of the Occident, 'a closed field, a theatrical stage affixed to Europe' (Said, 1978, p. 63). This new conceptual map moved the *ʿaqd* outside the *nomos* of Muslim jurisprudence, and the 'urbanity' of its city was profoundly reshaped according to Western coordinates (see later, section 4.5).[17]

The semantic transformation was so radical that Buskens and Dupret (2015) can rightly argue in their article that *this* 'invention of Islamic law'[18] entailed a 'process of knowledge formation' that moved the Muslim world towards 'alternative understandings of normativity and social order' (p. 31).[19] Although I subscribe to the perspective advanced by Buskens and Dupret, I believe that the concept of 'invention' (which certainly highlights a traumatic change in the nature of legal normativity in Muslim countries) can shed further light on the transformative praxis of the *ʿaqd* when inserted in the dialectical non-identity between Western and Islamic legal traditions (hence, when locating its understanding of the *Bridge* of Babel *in-time*). Moreover, the process of sematic 're-clothing' of the *ʿaqd* finds in Messick's notion of 'textual polity' a useful tool to uncover the relation between textual forms and legal norms that nurtured the passage from classical *fiqh* (a sacred law without *corpus*: section 2.4.5) to what Buskens and Dupret describe as an 'invention of Islamic law' by the assimilation of the form (the 'medium') of the Western *corpus iuris*. This transformation, if certainly induced by Western scholars, orientalists, and political powers, was at the same time enthusiastically embraced by local Muslim élites in translating original *ʿaqd* contractual categories into Western ones. On this matter, essential considerations are given by Messick with regard to the origins of a 'shariʿa-derived civil code,' the famous Majalla (or Mecelle), inspired by the literature of the Ḥanafī school, drafted by Ottoman reformers and issued in sixteen volumes from

1869 to 1876, with final promulgation in 1877 (Messick, 1993, p. 54). Puzzled by the discontinuity, non-linearity, and replication of overlapping rules in *fiqh* acoustic space, these reformers described Islamic normativity as 'an ocean without shores' (as reported by Liebesny, 1975, quoted in Messick, 1993, p. 54) – a metaphor that has some conceptual resemblance with the image of the echo advanced in this book (see section 2.4.5) and adheres to McLuhan's notion of the acoustic space as a 'space that has no center and no margin' (McLuhan, 1969).

> [The] innovative and contradictory character [of the Majalla] centered on the fact that it was "Islamic in content, but . . . European in form" [Liebesny, 1975, p. 65]. . . . Among Ottoman reformers, many of whom were astute observers of European society, the shari'a was considered archaic and unsuited for modern purposes. If "order" was the leitmotif of the reforms advocated, the shari'a had come to represent precisely the opposite: "disorder". . . . The authors of the *Majalla*, which was constructed exclusively of shari'a materials, likewise described these original texts as extremely difficult to work with. Their metaphor, again, was a boundless "ocean" "on whose bottom one has to search, at the price of very great efforts, for the pearls which are hidden there. A person has to possess great experience as well as great learning in order to find in the sacred law the proper solutions for all questions which present themselves" [Majalla, p. 4; quoted in Liebesny, 1975, p. 67].
>
> (Messick, 1993, pp. 54–55)

The rise of the codification process in Muslim countries in the 19th and 20th centuries (for a detailed account of this process of circulation of Western law see both Anderson, 1976; Castro, 1985) determined a dramatic departure from the original conceptualisation of rules in classical Islam: rules that were aimed at fostering the performance of Islamic *dīn* by the believer shifted into the stage of political control by the state. In other terms, while originally located in context-specific space, with Muslim scholars acting in close contact with the recipients of the norms, contractual rules became the object of a process of centralisation through their insertion in state codes as well as of procedures of bureaucratisation for their daily employment. The hermeneutical change of their meaning (within a transformative praxis where both the theory and the practice of these rules were radically affected by the rise of the modern state) went far beyond the 'contents' of normativity, touching deep elements of 'social power;' this core aspect legitimises the use of the notion of the 'invention of Islamic law' by Buskens and Dupret as the result of the process of Western transplants in the legal culture of the Muslim world. Within this radical change, with the acoustic space of Islam replaced by the visual space of state codification, the content of contractual rules moved from the original version of the *'aqd* in the manuals of Muslim *fiqh* to a style of formulation (within civil codes) and to contents that were clearly the outcome of Western influence; in summary, what was an 'acoustic Islamic law' (*fiqh*) became a 'visual Islamic law' through the form (the medium) of Western *corpus iuris*.

As remarked by Messick and already mentioned previously, the first and most significant example of this transformation (both of *content* and *context*) can be found in the Majalla, the Ottoman Civil Code (1877). Significantly, although intended as a compilation of the Ḥanafī school, the Majalla describes the contract as 'the contracting parties obligating themselves with regard [to] a given matter and binding themselves together with the same as a result of connecting an offer with an acceptance' (Art. 103; translation by Saleh, 1990, p. 105), using a general formula that is more in line with the civil law tradition rather than with the style of *fiqh* (where, as we know, a general definition of the *'aqd* is absent). Moreover, according to the Majalla, 'contracting is the connection of an offer with an acceptance in a lawful manner which marks its effect on the subject of that connection' (Art. 104; *ibidem*). One can immediately spot something of a discrepancy between the two Articles: Art. 103 focuses on the role of the contracting parties who 'oblige' themselves, a concept which is foreign to classical Muslim *fiqh*, while Art. 104 concentrates on the connection of offer and acceptance over the subject matter, more in line with the Islamic legal tradition. In fact, although the Western idea of 'obligation' doesn't belong to *fiqh*, Muslim reformers usually employed the concept of *iltizām* – a new legal usage translating the French '*obligation*.' But, as Chehata explains, while the classical term *wājib* referred to personal 'duty,' the word *iltizām* denoted in classical treatises the idea of obliging *themselves*, of 'self-obligation,' not that of an obligatory bond between the parties, as in the meaning of the French *obligation* (Chehata, 1969, p. 168; see also Vogel, 2006, p. 38). Art. 104, in contrast, seems to re-adopt the logic of *fiqh* classical treatises; here, the contract becomes the 'connection' of an offer (*ījāb*) and an acceptance (*qabūl*), which marks its effect on the 'subject matter' – i.e. the *objet* of the legal connection and not the subjects as contracting parties.

In the same way, the Egyptian Civil Code of 1949 defines the mechanism of contracting as follows: 'A contract is concluded, subject to any special formalities that may be required by law for its conclusion, merely from the moment that two persons have exchanged two concordant wills' (Art. 89; translation by Saleh, 1990, p. 105). The influence of the French-educated scholar al-Sanhūrī in the drafting of the Egyptian Code (which we will examine more closely in the next section) is undeniable in this provision. And the 'shadow' of al-Sanhūrī extended much further, placing the contract under the general heading 'Sources of obligations' in the Egyptian Civil Code (a clear signal of civil legal language belongs to the concepts of 'source' and 'obligation'). The same taxonomy is shown in the Iraqi Civil Code (1951) (Art. 73) and the Qatari Civil and Commercial Law of 1971 (Art. 7) (Saleh, 1990, pp. 105–106). A final example of hybridisation, quite similar to that of the Majalla, can be found in the Jordan Civil Code (1976): 'A contract is the connection and concurrence of an offer emanating from one of the contracting parties with an acceptance of the other party in a manner which affects the object of the contract and results in obligating each of the contracting parties with what was undertaken towards the other' (*ibidem*, p. 106).[20]

The influence of the Western definition of contract on the process of codification in Muslim countries can also be seen, alongside the idea of agreement as source of obligation, in the specific elements of the contract itself. For instance, the word *maqṣūd* assumes a remarkable role in the modern reconstruction of the original Ḥanafī doctrine on the role of *niyya* for the validity of the contract in the Majalla. Differently from classical Islamic law, where it was used only with regard to liberal acts (see Chapter 3, endnote 16), the 'determining motive' becomes a significant aspect of bilateral exchanges; accordingly, the text of the Prophetic *ḥadīth* '*innama al-aʿmāl bi'l-nīyāt*' ('acts are judged according to their intent') is replaced in Art. 2 of the Ottoman Majalla with the text '*al-umūr bi-maqāṣidihā*' ('actions are judged by their aims'); that is to say, in the version given by the Šāfiʿī jurist al-Suyūṭī (d. 911/1505; on this point, Arabi, 1997, p. 211 note 29) in order to justify the *ḥadīth*. The term reappears in Art. 3 ('in contractual matters, intent and meaning take precedence over wording and syntax;' that is to say, 'the criteria for contract rest on intent not on expression,' *al-ʿibra fil-ʿuqūd lil-maqāṣid wa-l-maʿānī lā bi-l-alfāẓ wa-l-mabānī*). In these passages, there is a clear transformation from the objective perspective of the Šāfiʿī and Ḥanafī schools on *niyya* (and the marginal importance of *maqṣūd*) to its emergence as a cornerstone of the theory of contracts in the Majalla.

A certain ambivalence can be found in the modern codifications of Arab countries, influenced by Western legal languages, also with regard to the notion of the *objet* of the contract, which becomes the 'object of the obligation' – mimicking the language of the French legal tradition. So, Arts. 127–130 of the Iraqi Civil Code adopt the notion of 'subject-matter of the obligation';[21] Art. 167 of the Kuwaiti Civil Code requires that the 'object of obligation' should be something possible at the moment of the conclusion of the contract, failing which the contract is to be considered *bāṭil*; Art. 187 of the Yemeni Civil Code states that the 'object of the obligation' should satisfy the following conditions: 1) it should respect the legal *Šarīʿah* conditions of the contract; 2) it should exist at the time; 3) it should be concrete; 4) it should be possible to exchange or sell it (for other examples, see Comair-Obeid, 1996, pp. 344–349).

4.3.2. *Embodying the West: Sanhūrī's reformulation of* sabab *and* ghalaṭ *in the Egyptian Civil Code*

The embodiment of Western law through the process of codification in Muslim countries, with the consequent 'invention' of a new textual polity in the form of 'Islamic law' (a label which suits the modern era of visual rationality, while *fiqh* relates better to 'Islamic law' in the acoustic space of Islam), can find a paradigmatic example in the Egyptian Civil Code of 1949.

The conceptual distance between the civilian doctrine of the *autonomie de la volonté* and the Islamic notions of *ʿilla* (*divina voluntas* in the qualification of the action) and *sabab* (efficient cause) has already been highlighted in section 3.4.1. In particular, we have seen how the notion of *cause* in French law as the 'purpose of the action' ('the sum of all external and internal motives which induce a party to conclude a legal act as well as the aim which is intended to be achieved through the legal act:' Saleh, 1992, p. 116) is absent in classical *fiqh*: 'the word cause (*sabab*), understood as inducing motive, is seldom employed in the classical law treatises. What is found instead is *niyya* or *qaṣd*, that is, the intention of the contracting parties in bilateral contracts and of the one party in unilateral undertakings' (*ibidem*, p. 121). In Chapter 3 we have also noticed how the vice of mistake, *ghalaṭ*, 'is given the least consideration among the impediments to consent . . . [t]he principles of *ghalaṭ* are certainly not to be found in any systematically theoretical exegesis among the Sharīʿah authorities' (Rayner, 1991, pp. 175–176) (see section 3.4.4).

The intention of the present section is to re-analyse the problems of the 'cause' and the conception of 'error' in classical *fiqh* by focusing on their civilian re-interpretation by one of the most influential Arab jurists of the last century, the great scholar ʿAbd al-Razzāq Aḥmad al-Sanhūrī (1895–1971). Sanhūrī played a fundamental role in drafting the Egyptian Civil Code of 1949,[22] whose provisions, under his coordination, were reproduced in the Syrian Civil Code of the same year (1949). Moreover, he also contributed to the new Iraqi Code promulgated in 1951 and effective in 1953 (for a reconstruction of the reception of Western legal models in Arab countries, see Castro, 1985). His work, as a lawmaker, comparatist, and reformer, was animated by the purpose of modernising Islamic classical law, thanks to the application of Western categories, after a doctorate in French civil law at the University of Lyon (1921–1927) (for an interpretation of this approach in the light of al-Sanhūrī's theory of state, see recently Ayoub, 2022).[23] The purposive approach of al-Sanhūrī clearly emerges in his *magnum opus*, the scrupulous analysis of the provisions of the Egyptian Civil Code held in the *al-Wasīṭ* (*The Intermediary*, 1952–1970, 10 volumes). Moreover, it is explicitly declared as methodological tool in the Preface of his *Maṣādir al-Ḥaqq fī l-Fiqh al-Islāmī* (*The Bases of Right in Islamic Law*, 1954–1959, 6 volumes).[24]

> The distinction between personal rights and material rights is essential in Western law; this distinction is the spinal column of Western laws as they derive from Roman law. . . . We are therefore dealing with one of the most important and most critical subjects of Western law, attempting to treat it in Islamic law. In doing this, we place Islamic law side by side with Western law in what is essentially important and in what is critical though hidden. *We treat Islamic law using the methods of Western law*, investigating whether there is in Islamic law personal rights and material rights as these are understood in Western laws derived from Roman law.
>
> (quoted in Arabi, 1995, p. 155, note 6; italics added)

Sanhūrī's aim of treating Islamic law through Western methods can be clearly seen in his re-formulation of the categories of error (*ghalaṭ*) and cause (*sabab*) (on this topic, both Arabi, 1995, 1997) by the incorporation of foreign civil law elements, directly drawn from his doctoral education in France.[25] The French backbone of al-Sanhūrī's legal approach is testified to in his reference to the doctrine of the *autonomie de la volonté* in *al-Wasīṭ* to the Egyptian Civil Code:

> The draft does not sacrifice the collective interests of society for the interest of individual freedom, nor does it consecrate *autonomie de la volonté* as the locus of all contractual relations. By contrast, the draft code attempts to achieve a balance between the interests of the individual and the collective. By the same token, the draft code does not allow the strong party in a contractual relation to injure the interests of the weaker party under the guise of individual freedom; the code does not licence individuals, regardless of their economic and social power, to abuse weak parties. . . . In this manner our draft code has come to champion social justice and embody the latest achievements of the twentieth century, the refinements of our times, and the civilisation of our age.
>
> (Sanhūrī, 1952–1970, *Al-Wasīṭ*, Vol. I, pp. 184–186, quoted in Shalakany, 2001, p. 219; see also pp. 220–221)

As noted by Shalakany, the Arabic terminology to render the phrase *autonomie de la volonté* (*mabda' sulṭān al-irādah*) is derived from French jurisprudence, and Sanhūrī's socialist approach to the principle builds on a long tradition of critique by progressive jurists, already incorporated by the Egyptian jurist in his first doctoral thesis (Shalakany, 2001, p. 219, note 56). The idea of social justice as naturally embedded in the *Šarī'ah*, paired with the purpose of modernising the new Egyptian Civil Code, constitute the main interpretative elements to understand Sanhūrī's work as lawmaker.

Within this frame, we can better understand, first, Sanhūrī's modernist reformulation of subjective error (*ghalaṭ*) in Islamic contract law. As recognised by Schacht and shown in the present work (section 3.4.4), '[a]mong the defects of declarations, error is taken into a limited account. . . . As regards fraud, there is little inclination to protect the victim. . . . The doctrine of duress (*ikrāh*) is more developed' (Schacht, 1964, p. 117). The position is expressly subscribed by al-Sanhūrī too.

> Islamic jurisprudence recognizes all three kinds of defects, but in an inverse order. Most prominent of all is its treatment of duress (*ikrāh*), which is accorded a separate and explicit analysis. Fraud (*tadlīs*) comes in the second place, after duress; fraud is recognized as a source of defective transactions in its own right, and some schools identify it by this very term. On the other hand, error (*ghalaṭ*) is the least prominent of contract defects in Islamic law, as it is the most subjective type of defect.
>
> (Sanhūrī, 1954–1959, *Maṣādir* . . ., Vol. 2, p. 112, quoted in Arabi, 1995, p. 156)

The narrow importance of the category of mistake has already been interpreted within the logic of Islamic law, where 'a defect in the contract is considered as enjoying greater legal significance the more objectively it is induced' (Arabi, 1995, p. 156; see back, Chapter 3). But, departing from this logic, Sanhūrī's 'modernist reading presents [the concept of mistake] under a new light, allowing for the opposition between error and real intent to be the cornerstone of a rejuvenated Islamic theory' (*ibidem*), supposedly more suitable for the economic and social conditions of the 20th century. In order to achieve his purpose, al-Sanhūrī re-interpreted the original Islamic doctrine of the right of choice (*khiyār*) as a sophisticated theory of subjective intent versus error, with reference, in particular, to the (legal options of) *khiyār al-waṣf* (the choice due to the absence of a desired quality in the object), the *khiyār al-ru'ya* (the choice upon seeing the object), and the *khiyār al-ʿayb* (the choice due to a defect in the object).

As already seen in section 3.4.4, it is undeniable that a certain correspondence exists between the Islamic theory of *khiyār* and the Western doctrine of error, but, while the latter is focused on subjective intent – i.e. on internal perception as deceived by something – the former is related in the classical treatises to the objective qualities of the subject matter. In a revealing passage, Sanhūrī admits this problematic divergence and, implicitly, the challenge of reconciling civil law and Islamic law.

> Islamic law . . . has a clear objective tendency. Hence error, which is psychological and subjective, is not accorded a unified treatment [as in the civil law/French tradition]. The theory of error in Islamic law is fragmentary, being dispersed over its different categories. Here appears the right of choice due to the absence of a stipulated quality from the object, and there the right of choice due a defect in the object, both preceded by the right of choice upon seeing the object. At first it seems as if these notions are mutually independent, with no link between them. Yet, they all are closely related to the theory of error, as will be shown. In all these classifications, the main concern of the jurists is to safeguard the stability of the transaction and its property, in so far as it expresses the true intent of the contracting parties. For, its fragmentary character notwithstanding, the theory of error in Islamic jurisprudence is governed by two conflicting demands: the stability of the transaction and the respect for the true intent, with the latter finding its way amidst predominantly objective standards.
>
> (Sanhūrī, 1954–1959, *Maṣādir* . . ., Vol. 2, p. 111, quoted in Arabi, 1995, p. 158)

Sanhūrī's modernist reading, while recognising the objective tendency of *fiqh*, radically re-formulates the doctrine of *khiyār* in the light of the subjective nature of error in French law, linked to the 'true intent of the contracting parties,' as explicitly mentioned in the foregoing extract. A contradictory result in this reading, however, can be found in Sanhūrī's admission that in Islamic law '[i]f the terms of the sale – the actual words exchanged between the two parties – provide no evidence of a mistake, the contract of sale is considered valid, with no right of rescission. Thus if someone were to sell a ruby unknowingly, thinking that it is just a non-precious red stone, then the sale is legally viable' (Arabi, 1995, p. 161).

In fact, there might be a passage in classical *fiqh* favourable to Sanhūrī's modernist reading of *ghalaṭ* in the light of French civil law, taken from al-Kāsānī's explanation of the *khiyār al-ru'ya*, the choice upon visual inspection.

> The sale of an item which the buyer has not seen is not binding . . . because the *ignorance* about the qualities of the item affects the *consent* (*riḍā*) of the buyer, rendering it unstable. *The instability of the consent (riḍā) of the buyer calls for the right of choice.* For the buyer's objection to the sale due to the remorse upon seeing the object is permissible, allowing him to retract. The right of choice allows the possibility of retraction due to remorse upon visual perception of the object.
>
> (Arabi, 1995, p. 163; italics not in the original text)

As Arabi comments, 'this statement by al-Kāsānī is particularly significant as it lends support to al-Sanhūrī's claim that the subjective states of erroneous consent are accorded some weight by Muslim legists' (*ibidem*, p. 163, note 24); but, as immediately noted by Arabi, Linant de Bellefonds strongly rejects the interpretation of the passage as grounds for a general subjective theory of the mistake, since the error 'as legal cause for contract dissolution is mentioned by al-Kāsānī only in the discussion of lease and testament and not mentioned at all for the basic sale contract' (*ibidem*, pp. 163–4, note 24).

> [I]n the two thousand pages in 4° of the *Badā'i'* this conception of error as vice of the consent, doesn't seem to be repeated by al-Kāsānī; it is not found any longer in authoritative authors, regardless of the school they belong to, and it appears only in modern legal literature. It is incumbent then to bring things back to their right measure, namely that jurists as vigilant as the great doctors of Islam had evidently taken notice of the repercussions that error, in certain circumstances, might have on the consent of the contracting parties, but that, due to the particular structure of Islamic law, the issue did not seem to them of considerable practical importance and, in any case, not to warrant a solution which brings into prominence the notion of defective consent.
>
> (Linant de Bellefonds, 1965, p. 383; my translation)

In summary, if in drafting the Egyptian Civil Code of 1949, as well as the Iraqi Civil Code of 1951, Sanhūrī was able to incorporate 'the modern theory of error, reconciling it with Islamic law' (Arabi, 1995, p. 167), at the same time, 'al-Sanhūrī's construction, which transforms the peripheral consideration given to error by the classical Muslim authors into a full-fledged theory of *error as a formal source of legal right*, is a partial deformation of Muslim legal thought' (*ibidem*, p. 171; italics in the original text).

From the perspective of his activity as lawmaker, one should consider, in any case, that the faithful rendering of the original Islamic law was not Sanhūrī's objective: his main attempt, as noted previously, was to modernise the *substance* of Islamic law in the light of Western legal *forms*. In this regard, Sanhūrī's purposive re-interpretation of Islamic contract law can also be seen in the re-formulation of the Ḥanbalī doctrine of intention (*niyya*) as the counterpart of the French theory of cause as the 'subjective determining motive' for the contract, which finally results in rendering the Ḥanbalī meaning of *niyya* with the Islamic concept of *sabab*. As already shown (section 3.4.1), the two notions are radically distant from each other; in fact, *sabab* is never used in a subjective sense in the classical texts, since it indicates the divine 'immediate cause' behind the action. Thus, 'occasional causes of legal institutions' (*asbāb ash-sharā'i'*) are e.g. the contingent nature of the universe for religion; the schedule for prayer; the ownership of legal alms (*zakāt*) (Brunschvig, 1976, pp. 43–44); according to the Mālikī jurist al-Qarāfī (d. 684/1285), 'the marriage contract is the legal cause (*sabab*) of procreation' (quoted in Arabi, 1997, p. 203 note 8); and, in general, *asbāb ash-sharā'i'* are 'the objects or the circumstances to whose existence or appearance the legal institutions, the duties created or sanctioned by the Law, are linked' (Brunschvig, 1976, p. 44).

In his purposive approach, Sanhūrī's translates *sabab* into the (French) theory of the cause as the subjective determining motive for the contract.[26] More precisely, in accordance with his aim of combining Islamic and Western law in a unique framework, al-Sanhūrī equates the subjective approach of the Ḥanbalīs and the Mālikīs to the modern French jurisprudence of the cause as the *motif détérminant* of the contract, making no mention of the objectivism of the Šāfi'īs and the Ḥanafīs, where 'motive is so little taken into consideration that the sale of an object is clearly considered to be valid even if the ends it serves are illegal' (Chehata, 1969, p. 70, my translation; on the opposition objectivism/subjectivism in Muslim *fiqh*, see Chapter 3). Thus, the technical meaning of *sabab* as the 'subjective determining motive' or 'cause' for contract, a sense completely unknown to the classical jurists, was introduced by al-Sanhūrī in his project for the Egyptian Code of 1949 and clearly emerges in Arts. 136 and 137.

> Article 136. If the obligation has no cause (*idhā lam yakun li'l-iltizām sabab*) or if its cause violates public order or mores, the contract is invalid.
>
> Article 137. 1) Every obligation for which the contract mentions no cause (*sabab*) is presumed to have a legal cause unless there is evidence otherwise; 2) the cause mentioned in the contract is considered to be the true cause (*al-sabab al-ḥaqīqī*) until there is evidence to the contrary: when there is evidence of the falsity of the mentioned cause, the party

> claiming that the obligation has another cause which is legal must prove its claim.
>
> (Arabi, 1997, p. 201)

In relation to these articles of the Egyptian Civil Code, Sanhūrī explains that 'The cause, according to the New Law, is then the driving motive for [concluding] the contract (*al-bā'ith al-dāfi' ilā al-ta'āqud*)' (Sanhūrī, 1954–1959, *Maṣādir* . . ., Vol. 4, p. 28, quoted in Arabi, 1997, p. 201), a passage that testifies, again, to French legal doctrine as the backbone for Sanhūrī's education.[27]

It is worth noting that Sanhūrī himself recognizes explicitly that

> Islamic law is subject to two conflicting trends in relation to the cause [ulterior motive]: First it is a law with a marked objective tendency, giving weight to the expression of the will and not to the will as such, i.e. preferring the apparent, not the latent, will . . . [Šāfi'īs and Ḥanafīs]; on the other hand, Islamic law is a law in which ethical, moral and religious factors predominate, implying the significance of motivation, as the latter is the measure of the honesty and purity of intentions [Ḥanbalīs and Mālikīs].
>
> (Sanhūrī, 1954–1959, *Maṣādir* . . ., Vol. 4, p. 52, quoted in Arabi, 1997, p. 210)

Despite this, only the 'Ḥanbalīs are taken by Sanhūrī to represent the close association between pietist ethical and properly legal considerations in Islamic law' (Arabi, 1997, p. 221). In the end, by carefully selecting Muslim classical sources to modernise Islamic law, Sanhūrī acted in a very similar way to Ottoman reformers (see previous section), who dealt with the 'boundless ocean' of *fiqh* tradition animated by the 'search, at the price of very great efforts, for the pearls which are hidden there . . . [using] great experience as well as great learning in order to find in the sacred law the proper solutions' (Messick, 1993, p. 55) for their own Muslim contemporary societies. But, in doing so, 'the old "pearls" were fixed in the structural grid of numbered code articles, re-presented in an innovative abstract format that rendered the shari'a into something resembling the familiar form of "law"' (*ibidem*, p. 55). In the end, by re-locating the pearls from their own original habitat into a new one, not only was their *substance* but also their *form* radically transformed into a new textual polity for the Muslim world (paraphrasing McLuhan, 'the medium [of legal codification] shaped the message [of state power]:' see the start of section 4.3.1): a world animated by standards of state efficiency that imitate those of modern Western society.

If this conclusion can summarise the story of the Islamic contract in the state-centred world of Western modernity, the process of globalisation of investments from the second half of the last century has opened another chapter in the evolution of its city, where the realm of the *Codified Norm* has been replaced by the economic power of a global *Typewritten Market*.

4.4. *Typewritten Market*

The power of time in defining operative contexts for the Islamic contract has established a new space for commercial practice in recent decades: from the second half of the last century, the globalisation of capital flows has affected the economic, political, and social life of Muslim countries – as much as it has done for the rest of the world economy. Correspondingly, the realm of *Codified Norm* of Muslim states has become itself a *partial totality* (Bhaskar, 1994, p. 76), where the application of contractual rules is today radically affected by the business practice of the transnational *lex mercatoria*. Within this new context, as we will see, not only has the *ʻaqd* found another 'new life' (section 4.4.1), but its medium has shifted from state norms to Shari'ah-compliance certificates (section 4.4.2; the graphical variation used here from *Šarīʻah* to Shari'ah will be explained shortly). As a result, this transformation has given rise to a new textual polity, which can be described in terms of a *Typewritten Market* (section 4.4.3).

4.4.1. Global capitalism and the invention of Islamic finance: a new life for the ʻaqd between authenticity and contamination

Already at the start of the millennium, Ibrahim Warde could open a classic volume on the political economy of the Muslim world by asserting that 'Islamic finance can no longer be dismissed as a passing fad or as an epiphenomenon of Islamic revivalism' (2000, p. 1). In a very similar way, another seminal book on the subject, published by Frank E. Vogel and Samuel L. Hayes at the end of the 1990s, introduced the matter by noting how '[t]he dramatic growth of this unique form of commerce over the past twenty years coincides with expanding wealth in the Middle East and parts of Asia and with a turning away from secular Western practices' (1998, p. 1). In 2006, Mahmoud El-Gamal could repeat the same enthusiastic remarks: '[i]n recent years, financial activities conducted under the banner of "Islamic finance" have grown significantly in volume and scope, attracting significant attention worldwide' (2006, p. xi; for a general description of Islamic finance mechanisms, see Ayub, 2007).

While the Mit Ghamr Savings Bank, established in Egypt in 1963, is commonly referred to as the first example of Islamic banking in the modern world, the global dimension of Islamic finance started only during the 1970s and has developed till the present as an active segment of global capitalism, to the extent that '[t]he power of Islamic capital has generated numerous sites of legal contestation and negotiation, ranging from gateway financial centres, international law firms and transnational financial institutions' (Ercanbrack, 2015, synopsis).

Simultaneously, the literature on Islamic economics (which provides the theoretical background for Islamic financial operations: Cattelan, 2018) has grown exponentially; if Rodney Wilson could note in 1997 that '[t]here has been more written on Islamic economics in the last two decades than in the previous fourteen hundred years' (Wilson, 1997, p. 115; quoted in Warde, 2000, p. 40), the number of publications in the area have further multiplied in recent years. The creation of this *corpus* of literature has stood side by side with the growth of Islamic finance, giving rise to a global market whose financial transactions have very little in common with the practice of proprietary, credit, or silent partnerships that existed in Islamic medieval trade (for a precise outline of this reality, see Udovitch, 1970a).

Looking at this evolution, some noteworthy similarities can be found with what in the previous section has been described as the 'invention' of Islamic law (Buskens and Dupret, 2015). In a certain sense, just as a 'body' of Islamic norms (in a visual sense) did not exist before Western legal transplants and the start of the process of codification (since *fiqh* tradition was grounded on the acoustic space of the revelation), so a theory of Islamic economics and a practice of Islamic finance could not be found before the 1970s.[28]

If it is obvious that Muslim medieval trade worked within a social context completely different from the contemporary global market, the 'invention' of Islamic finance has followed a path of cultural hybridisation where the rules of *fiqh* contract law (in particular, the prohibitions of *ribā*, *gharar* and *maysir*: see section 3.5.4) are applied next to the global standards of conventional capitalism. Hence, contractual structures of classical *fiqh* (such as silent partnership, *muḍāraba*; full partnership, *mušāraka*; mark up sale, *murābaḥa*; lease, *ijāra*; and contract of manufacture, *istiṣnāʿ*) have been 're-clothed' to imitate conventional financial structures and adhere to a financial engineering mainly shaped according to common law. As she did with regard to the process of codification, the image of the *Arab Girl* dressed in Western fashion can offer here an anthropomorphic representation of what El-Gamal describes as 'Shariʿa arbitrage' (2006, p. 20), so summarising the current practice of Islamic finance in three steps.

1. Identification of a financial product that is generally deemed contrary to the precepts of Islamic Law (Shariʿa).
2. Construction of an "Islamic analogue" to that financial product. Examples includes Islamic home (mortgage) or auto financing – commonly using the Arabic-nominate contracts *murabaha* or *ijara*, as well as Islamic bonds or certificates commonly marketed under Arabic names like *sukuk al-ijara* or *sukuk al-salam*. In fact, an important step in executing Shariʿa arbitrage is finding an appropriate Arabic name for the Islamic analogue product, preferably one that was extensively used in classical Islamic legal texts. Differences in contract forms and language thus justify and lend credibility to the "Islamic" brand name.
3. In the meantime, an Islamic financial structure marketed under an Arabic name must be sufficiently similar to the conventional structure that it aims to replace. Sufficient similarity would ensure that the Islamic structure is consistent with secular legal and regulatory frameworks in target and origin countries (*ibidem*, pp. 20–21).

There is, without doubt, a marketing strategy, as well as compelling reasons of market regulation, behind the inescapable trade-off between efficiency and legitimacy (El-Gamal, 2006, p. 20) that belongs to Islamic financial products. At the same time, through the process of 'Shari'ah arbitrage,' the Islamic contract has found a new 'cosmopolitan life' in this new stage of its transformational practice. No longer anchored to norms codified within national boundaries, some essential features of the *'aqd* have been embodied in the global space that belongs to the practice of Islamic finance law. It is within this operative framework that, nourished by the forces of global capitalism and the ethical demands of Muslim élites and societies, Islamic finance and its law have emerged as a transnational market that transcends state frontiers and operates according to the peculiar dynamics of legal pluralism by connecting diverse networks of interests to multiple centres of norm production, application, and adjudication (on the subject, see, in particular, Foster, 2007; Pollard and Samers, 2013).

In this domain of transformative praxis, the new 'time' of the *'aqd* confirms a continuity-through-change that has always affected its practice (as we saw previously, the era of *Verbal Trade* started with the revelation changing the values of pre-Islamic society, and that of *Codified Norm* bore witness to its contamination by Western law). In particular, Islamic financial operations certainly repropose the appeal of a theory of property rights whose 'spiritual truth' derives from the ethical background of Islamic *dīn*, and that is mirrored in some 'secular rationales' that differentiate the Islamic market from the conventional one (on this point, see Cattelan, 2013).

Looking at the 'authenticity' of the *'aqd*, there are, in fact, three core elements that show the re-discovery (and vitality) of its legal tradition through Islamic finance; and namely, '(1) the centrality of the object in the transaction as something "real" ("tangible") to be traded; (2) the fundamental need for an equilibrium in the exchange; and (3) asset-backed risk and investment risk-sharing' (*ibidem*, p. 41; more extensively, pp. 41–46; on this matter, see also Cattelan, 2009). Each of these elements recalls central features of the Islamic theory of the contract that have been investigated in Chapter 3 and that the Islamic financial market has projected within the cosmopolitan space of global investments. Hence, with regard to the need for tangible goods to be traded (whose rationale lies in the 'real' connotation of the 'right,' *ḥaqq*, in Islam: see sections 2.4.4 and 3.5.3),[29] we can repeat here the words of Chehata.

> The decisive element of the legal relation lies in the object. The object takes place between the two persons who enter into a relationship through it. This relationship, of which the object is the specific term, is constituent of the right. The title that founds the right of the subject is the reason which establishes a link of belonging between him and the object.
>
> Once this relationship has been concretely realised, a state of adjustment and of equilibrium must rule: everything in its [due] place.
>
> (Chehata, 1968, p. 141, my translation; already quoted at section 3.6)

Second, the principle of the equilibrium between the countervalues immediately relates to the prohibitions of *ribā*, *gharar*, and *maysir*, examined in section 3.5.4. Hence, for the prohibition of *ribā* in terms of the need for a 'balanced unity,' 'equilibrium,' 'symmetry,' the passage by al-Kāsānī mentioned in Chapter 3 can further stress the need for this symmetry in the transactions of Islamic finance.

> Equality . . . is the aim of the contracting parties (*al-musāwāt . . . maṭlūb al-ʿāqidayn*). . . . The entirety of the sold object is to be considered equivalent to the entirety of the price (*kull al-mabīʿ yuʿtabar muqābalan bi-kull al-thaman*), and the entirety of the price equivalent to the entirety of the sold object. Any increment (*ziyāda*), whether in price or in the object which has no corresponding equivalent, would be an additional value without compensation . . ., and this is the meaning of usury (*ribā*).
> (al-Kāsānī, *Badāʾiʿ al-Ṣanāʾiʿ fī Tartīb al-Sharāʾiʿ*, quoted in Arabi, 1997, p. 208)

Last but not least, since '[t]he balanced and disclosed correspondence between tangible countervalues necessarily results in a favour towards asset-backed and equity-based financial instruments . . . [t]his preference [also] corresponds to specific risk strategies' (Cattelan, 2013, p. 44), where risk cannot be conceived as a commodity per se ('trading of risk is not admitted, and a number of financial instruments (that is, insurance, derivatives) that are widespread in the conventional Western market become invalid:' *ibidem*). At the same time, the remuneration of business participants 'cannot be determined *ex ante*, according to a predetermined ratio, but derives from a principle of risk-sharing in the profit (*mudaraba*) of the business, which may be extended also to the liabilities of the affairs (*musharaka*)' (*ibidem*, p. 45).

If the three essential elements of Islamic financial operations confirm the vitality of the Islamic *ʿaqd* – even beyond the boundaries of Muslim countries – this 'authenticity' has been contaminated by the contemporary textual forms through which it is granted; namely, 'the emphasis . . . on contract mechanisms and certification of Islamicity by "Shariʿa Supervisory Boards"' (El-Gamal, 2006, p. 1). The process of Shariʿah certification, as we will see in the next section, has radically transformed the idea of Islamic law when applied to the global economy through the canons of Shariʿah-compliance, with a shift in its social anthropology from the textual polity of *fiqh* legal texts in Muslim medieval trade (see end section 4.2.3), where actions were judged by rules legitimised by their own local context, to the realm of financial technology, where certifications own a legitimacy that is formulated context-less, and relies on some sort of 'dematerialised *Šarīʿah*' (Cattelan, 2021, p. 79).

This radical shift in the anthropology (and epistemology) of Islamic law – and so, of the *ʿaqd* – can be implicitly suggested by the graphical variation from *Šarīʿah* (that this book has employed with reference to *fiqh*) to the simplified transliteration 'Shariʿah,' in relation to the process of compliance (which will be used in the next section). In fact, far from being just a matter of style, this simplified transliteration, which is commonly employed both in international finance and academic literature, bears witness to 'a "transliteration" of Islamic finance into the semantic forms of Western modern law . . ., with a predominance of a business/legal language in Latin alphabet . . . instead of the moral/religious language of *Šarīʿah*' (Cattelan, 2021, p. 91, note 49).

4.4.2. *The textual polity of Shariʿah-compliance*

Dealing more in depth with the law of Islamic finance, a valuable starting point can be found in the *Encyclopedia of Islam.*[30]

> Islamic finance denotes financial transactions in compliance with Islamic principles. It is a business practice guided by Islamic law that has evolved in the context of global financial markets and is the most important application of Islamic contract law today. Moreover, it is the key area where the propositions of Islamic economics . . . are put into practice.
>
> (Bälz, 2014)

The contributor, Kilian Bälz, refers to Islamic law in various ways ('compliance with Islamic principles;' 'application of Islamic contract law;' 'the propositions of Islamic economics'). More precisely, after listing in the entry the general principles of Islamic banking (namely, (i) interest on loans is prohibited; (ii) speculation is unlawful; (iii) trading in debt is not allowed) and the contracts generally in use (i.e. *murābaḥa*, *mušāraka*, *muḍāraba*, *ijāra*, *istiṣnāʿ*), plus the issuance of *ṣukūk* (Islamic securities – certificates of investments, commonly called 'Islamic bonds'), he immediately specifies his definition in the sense of Shariʿah-compliance (see also Bälz, 2008).

> *Shariʿa* compliance – abiding by the prescriptions of Islamic law – is what sets Islamic finance apart from conventional finance. The review and certification process that creates the Islamic legitimacy for Islamic financial transactions and which constructs the normative framework in which Islamic banks operate is central to Islamic finance. Islamic financial transactions are normally reviewed and certified by a board of Islamic scholars (the so-called *Shariʿa* board), which renders an opinion (termed *fatwa*, in reference to traditional Islamic law).
>
> (Bälz, 2014)

Reading the *Encyclopedia*, it is evident that, although Islamic financial institutions identify themselves with Shariʿah-compliance (which 'creates the Islamic legitimacy' of their transactions), their claim to comply with Islamic contract law seems to be made as if no radical transformation would have affected the meaning of the concept over the centuries (Bälz suggests this historical variance when he notes that Islamic scholars' opinions are named *fatwā* 'in reference [in homage?] to *traditional* Islamic law'). But the normative space of Islamic finance cannot be properly understood, as remarked at the start of this chapter, without locating the Islamic contract *in-time* as a social (as well as anthropological and epistemological) construction. Hiroshige's *Bridge* (Figure 4.1) and Szymborska's *People* (who 'are subject to time, but they won't admit it:' see section 4.1 in this chapter) come back at this point with their epistemological power.

With reference to the *Verbal Trade* of classical Islam (section 4.2.3), this book has underlined how *fiqh* legal texts located *Šarīʿah* in context: the process of 'entextualisation' worked in a 'handwritten,' 'calligraphic' way and the social value of juristic solutions was grounded on rules that were legitimised by real-life situations. Moving now to contemporary times, how much 'material entextualisation' in Islamic contracts and securities arises from the process of Shariʿah-compliance? Is the *Šarīʿah* value of Islamic finance the same as *fiqh* rules or has the passing of time radically transformed the *ʿaqd*?

While the legitimacy of Islamic financial transactions is certainly grounded on (or rather, backed by) *Šarīʿah*, it seems to me that today's Shariʿah-compliance departs from the 'real,' 'right' (*ḥaqq*) of social relations towards a 'de-materialised *Šarīʿah*,' where the meaning of Islamic law is embodied in the validation of contracts rather than in human actions, and so it departs from the performance of Islamic *dīn* as Muslim *bíos* (see back, section 2.3). In this precise sense, if, in classical *fiqh*, actions were judged by rules legitimised by their *own* context, in the process of Shariʿah-compliance, the Islamic legitimacy of financial products is ratified through certifications *owning* a legitimacy that is formulated context-*less* (i.e. without a context). As a result, the Shariʿah-compliance process entextualised in Islamic contracts has replaced *Šarīʿah* as Text inscribed in the reality of Muslim *bíos*; correspondingly, in this new textual polity, the meaning of *ʿaqd* relates more to standardised products and securities rather than actual social interactions. One should also note that this shift reflects a much wider turn towards a rationalistic and purposive epistemology of Islamic law (through the *maqāṣid al-Šarīʿah*, 'the objectives of Shariʿah:' see Johnston, 2004), of which the process of Shariʿah-compliance is clear manifestation; not by chance, the reference to *maqāṣid* is widespread in Islamic finance, defining the meaning of Islamic law for individual action more in terms of efficiency than morality.

A move towards a de-materialised *Šarīʿah* has occurred in the social anthropology of Islamic finance within a textual polity whose paradigm 'text' is no longer the *Text* (the Qurʾān) but has split into standardised legal *texts* (the certifications by Shariʿah scholars embodying Shariʿah standards) and the contractual texts of Islamic transactions.

But what does this transformation imply?

It's difficult at this point to keep from commenting.
This picture ['Islamic law', *our* Hiroshige print] is by no means innocent.
Time has been stopped here.
Its laws are no longer consulted.
It has been relieved of its influence over the course of events.
It has been ignored and insulted (Szymborska, 1996, pp. 167–168).

Indeed, while, in global Islamic finance, the authority of 'Islamic law' is backed by the *Text* of *Šarīʿah*, it is, more importantly, embedded in Shari'ah-compliance *texts*, as both sociological and economic research has shown, while no longer echoed in the reality of Muslim *bíos*. For instance, a publication by Funds@Work (2010) has highlighted how the 'small world of Islamic finance' gathers a limited number of Shari'ah scholars whose signatures provide valuable (i.e. authoritative) certifications. Correspondingly, these signatures render valuable (i.e. economically profitable) Islamic securities: 'the choice of scholars hired to certify these securities matter for the market valuation of the issuing company' (Godlewski, Turk and Weill, 2014). In summary, within the space of Islamic finance, the world, where the meaning of Islamic law is inscribed, has become the financial world, a 'world of texts' and contracts, not of real people; financial products have replaced the social actions of actual *bíos*; Shari'ah-compliance has replaced *Šarīʿah*; technology has replaced the *Text*.

The three qualities of *fiqh* textual polity (see endnote 16) have disappeared in the world of Shari'ah compliance and have been substituted by: (1) a text-based approach to Islamic law in relation to contractual forms, not human actions; (2) the standardisation of context-less operations; and (3) uniform outputs that are functional to the efficiency of transactions management in the governance of Islamic financial institutions. Correspondingly, the (religious) *Truth* of *Šarīʿah*, as revealed in Islamic *dīn*, has been substituted in Islamic finance law by the (procedural) *truth* of (Shari'ah-)compliance, with a predominance of elements of legal and financial technology as the epistemological environment for its assertion (see section 4.4.3 in this chapter).

In fact, 'compliance' – from the Italian *complire*, 'to complete,' 'fulfil,' 'accomplish' – has no religious meaning and there is no Islamic legal definition of compliance. Instead, the notion belongs to the field of organisational technology: *Governance, Risk Management and Compliance* (GRC) is, today, a subfield of business administration with GRC defined as 'the integrated collection of capabilities that enable an organization to reliably achieve objectives, address uncertainty and act with integrity' (Mitchell, 2007). Hence, one can think of legal compliance as a tool of governance which aims to review, verify, and certify that the organisation's procedures and outcomes comply with the law in the broader sense (international, national, local legislation, codes, standards, and so on). Accordingly, Shari'ah-compliance has become today part of the technology of (Islamic) financial institutions, with a meaning that belongs more to the realm of governance rather than to (Islamic) law/religion.

Shari'ah-compliance reflects a governance technology where the value of transactions, contracts, and securities relates to standardisation; and, within this frame, the *Šarīʿah*-value of *fiqh* 'calligraphy' has been replaced by a dematerialised *Šarīʿah*, which is 'typewritten' in market-values. In brief, Islamic finance has given rise to a *Typewritten Market* as socio-anthropological space for the contemporary life of the *ʿaqd*.

4.4.3. *From* fiqh *legal texts to financial technology*

In one of his books, Italian philosopher and psychoanalyst Umberto Galimberti notes how today

> technology has become the environment . . . that constitutes ourselves in accordance with . . . [*its own*] rules of rationality . . ., functionality and efficiency. . . . But technology does not tend towards an aim, does not promote a sense, does not open scenarios of salvation, does not redeem, does not unveil the truth: technology [*simply*] functions.
>
> (Galimberti, 1999, synopsis; my translation)

Even the perception of contemporary *truths* (if not the *Truth*) is affected by the rationales of technology – as previously noted, the functionality of the *maqāṣid* purposive approach may be indirect proof of this claim in the epistemology of Islamic law (Johnston, 2004). What can we add to all this? Certainly, if Hiroshige's 'little picture' is 'by no means innocent,' neither is the meaning of 'Islamic law' – and then, of the *ʿaqd* – in Islamic finance.[31]

> For generations, it's been considered good form here
> to think highly of this picture [Islamic law],
> to be entranced and moved.
>
> There are those for whom even this is not enough.
> They go so far as to hear the rain's spatter [Islamic law's conceptual power],
> to feel the cold drops on their necks and backs,
> they look at the bridge and the people on it
> as if they saw themselves there,
> running the same never-to-be-finished race [the compliance that 'runs' *Šarīʿah*]
> through the same endless, ever-to-be-covered distance [the efficiency of technology],
> and they have the nerve to believe
> that this is really so [that Shariʿah-compliance equals *Šarīʿah*]
> (Szymborska, 1996, pp. 168–169).

If, at the beginning of this chapter, we imagined being in the rain, at the end of Hiroshige's *Bridge*, the race by the *People* of Islamic finance can illuminate, I believe, *their* meaning of 'Islamic law,' and thus of the *ʿaqd* in the textual polity of Islamic finance.

Just as Szymborska's *People* keep running *on the Bridge*, so Islamic finance actors keep asserting 'Islamic law' in a market where their presence *in-time* is immersed in a social reality dominated by an 'ever-to-be-covered distance.' Accordingly, their only option is a 'never-to-be-finished race:' as 'technology [*simply*] functions,' so Shariʿah-compliance locates their actions in a 'race' that 'runs' (in the sense of 'operates') *Šarīʿah*. In a nutshell, the 'Path' is no longer 'followed' (as it was in *fiqh*); rather, it is 'put to work.'

Although some may have 'the nerve to believe' that Shariʿah-compliance equals *Šarīʿah*, this section warns the reader about the radical transformation that the former implies for the social anthropology of Islamic law, and thus, the *ʿaqd* itself. While standardisation works as a law-making process where Islamic law is functional to Islamic finance operations, many Muslim believers, 'subject to [the] *time* [of financial/legal technology], . . . won't admit it.' Rather, they would prefer 'a way of expressing protest;' more precisely, Shariʿah-compliance as simulacrum of Islamic law. But, if Shariʿah-compliance belongs to the world of technology, so the reference to Islamic law and to the Arabic terminology of Islamic contracts (see El-Gamal, 2006: section 4.4.1) becomes a 'dialectical signature' for the market: a sign of community belonging to Islam in a world of legal/financial technology to which Muslim believers (as everybody else) are subject. Reduced to a procedural step in the governance of Islamic financial institutions, *Šarīʿah* (Shariʿah?) substantially 'works' in compliance with the standards that 'run' the market. As noted previously, the calligraphic trade of *fiqh* has been replaced by typewritten certificates, contracts, and securities, giving rise to a textual polity detached from actual social relations of Islamic *dīn* as Muslim *bíos*: in summary, to a *Typewritten Market* that embodies a de-materialised *Šarīʿah*, where the meaning of Islamic law *in-time* belongs more to legal/financial technology rather than to Muslim human action.

4.5. Human agency and the urban designs of the *ʿaqd*

Considering the transformative praxis of the *ʿaqd* in the history of the Muslim world, this chapter has offered a general overview of a continuity-*through*-change that has identified three ages under the names of *Verbal Trade*, *Codified Norm*, and *Typewritten Market*. This overview has concentrated on some distinctive features of each of these periods: instead of a precise account of the realities of the *ʿaqd* over the centuries, the fourth dimension (4D) of Bhaskar's dialectic has led our investigation to verify how 'the capacity for practical human *agency* to change the world' (Norrie, 2009, p. 12) has put *fiqh* contractual theories into practice. In this precise way, the change of contexts *in-time* has affected contractual norms – not only as an expression of human normativity but also as a manifestation of specific textual polities that have stratified in the evolution of the city of the *ʿaqd*.

If the urban design of Rome was mentioned at the start of this chapter as metaphoric representation of this stratification through history (see section 4.1), the third level (3L) of *totality* has been further developed here by moving from the static dimension of *being* to the dynamic nature of *becoming*, where '[t]he whole produces and enables its parts. . . . Structures too do not exist individually, but rather in their relationship with other structures constituting the whole. This generates the idea at the level of totality of holistic causality, which involves a causal relationship between structures in a whole' (Norrie, 2009, p. 16). Looking back at the three ages of the city of the *'aqd*, each of them can be dealt with as a ***partial totality***, contributing to the whole of the understanding of the Islamic contract in a narration where continuity prevails over division.

In this regard, focusing on the deep transformations (not only at a normative, but also at an epistemological and anthropological level) that the *'aqd* has experienced from the reality of medieval trade to those of state codification and global capitalism, its 'coordinates' can be commented on in relation to the variance of its textual polities (*fiqh*, codifications, and Shari'ah-compliance certificates). With this aim, the metaphor of the city of the *'aqd* that this book has employed finds some revealing correspondence with the fascinating analogy made by Brinkley Messick between shifting styles of writing and the design of cities in the Muslim world. Messick notes how, in the community of Ibb, legal documents were originally forged in the form of 'spiral texts;' that is to say, rotating the writing in a shape of a spiral, in a calligraphic practice whose 'space of knowledge'[32] radically changed with the incidence of state bureaucracy in commercial life from the second half of the 20th century.

> In a document from 1991, the text is entered on a contract form, which has printed margins and lines for text. . . . No rotation occurs in the orientation of the new writing; the text proceeds downward in regular horizontal lines, moving margin to margin until completion. In these contemporary documents the writing is constrained in a manner familiar to Western legal instruments; the spiral is harnessed and the lines are straightened and centered. These sorts of changes are also evident with typing, as in the shift from spiraling imamic letters to the standard margin and paragraph form of republican correspondence. The physical alteration from spiral to straight-ruled text is clear at a glance, but what is its significance?
>
> (Messick, 1993, p. 234)

'Physical differences between spiral and straight texts involve more than a simple matter of design, of curved versus not curved. . . . [In fact, they] are an important clue to differences in textual construction' (*ibidem*, pp. 236–237). By quoting Ernst Cassirer (1955, p. 84), Messick contrasts two modes of spatial organisation – the 'geometric' and the 'mythical' spaces (Messick, 1993, p. 237) – where the different relationship between form and content significantly resembles the differentiation made by McLuhan between, respectively, the visual and the acoustic space. The rational, abstract, and geometric space of the scopic regime of modernity (Jay, 1988; see section 1.3.3), with its assumptions of order, continuity, systematisation, contrasts an acoustic space made of 'curved' reflections, echoing a source that is replicated, where the form cannot be detached from the content, lacking in a centre (chosen by man) and in margins (artificially imposed by human rationality). As Messick remarks, '[a] lthough they apparently accomplish the same task, manuscript copies [spiral texts] and print copies [straight texts] work with differing technologies and epistemologies' (1993, p. 240).

Chapter 3 of this book focused on the construction of the *ʿaqd* in *fiqh* literature as a distinctive 'craft of place' (section 3.1), whose distinctive epistemology reflects the acoustic space of Islam (section 2.4.5). By locating this place *in-time*, this chapter has shown how much the ages of the *Codified Norm*, and later, that of the *Typewritten Market* have radically transformed the normativity of *Verbal Trade* of classical Islam: contractual rules (and texts) have embodied the visual logic of 'straight norms' and later the binary logic of 'certified norms,' as derived from the epistemology of financial and legal technology.

Correspondingly, the 'architecture' of the city of the *ʿaqd* has radically changed: construction techniques have been modernised according to Western standards (the legal transplants in Muslim countries) and the standards of global capitalism. At the same time, the urban design of the city has been transformed: the original 'maps' to the *ʿaqd*, as shaped by classical juristic schools (section 3.2), have been replaced by new (Western) coordinates. A passage that Messick refers to the town of Ibb, by comparing its urban evolution with the move from spiral to straight texts in Muslim societies, can describe the evolution of the Islamic contract as well.

> As was true of *madinas* from North Africa to Central Asia, the old walled town of . . . [the *ʿaqd*] was a labyrinth of closely packed multistoried houses on narrow and winding alleys and culs-de-sac. The new quarters, by contrast, are characterized by relatively straight-line, wide thoroughfares with some space left between the buildings. The growth of these newer parts of . . . [the *ʿaqd*] is governed, in theory, by a municipal zoning and building "code," which involves plans for the expansion of the town and endeavors to regulate standards of construction.
>
> (Messick, 1993, p. 246)

By narrating the changing realities of the Islamic contract, the *Arab Girl* would probably ascribe this meaningful depiction to the evolution of the urban design of her city, from 'a labyrinth of closely packed multistoried houses' (i.e. the labyrinth of plural opinions in *fiqh* tradition) to the impact of 'a municipal zoning and building code' (i.e. of state codification in the definition of contract rules). The global economy has put in force an additional layer of construction regulations by which the city of the *ʿaqd* is governed today: that of international standards and market certifications.

At the same time, as the physical layout of Arab towns shows, although old and new urban designs are recognisable as *different* spaces, they contribute to the history of the *same* city; if this chapter has a merit, it can be found precisely in its ambition to represent this unity-of-diversities for the Islamic contract, in relation to its transformative praxis.

Hence, if maps are narratives (section 3.2), the modern and contemporary evolution of Arab towns can mirror that of the new 'space of knowledge' (Foucault, 1970) for the *'aqd*: a space where Muslim actors have become used to *seeing* (the visual space of Western modernity), rather than *listening* (to the acoustic space of Islam).

> Within the sphere of formal knowledge, specifically within the discourse of the shari'a, the codification shift . . . had a structure parallel to that occurring between spiral and straight texts [as much as that from the labyrinth of alleys to linear streets in Arab towns]. In a manner analogous to the change in the form/content relation of spatial ordering in writing, the (casuistical) old discourse differs from the (abstractly rational) one. Whereas the former developed principles within cases (form following content), the latter elaborates principles independently of and prior to the cases to which they are subsequently applied (content following form). In the disenchanted thought of shari'a legislation, the old primacy of the concrete instance has given way to a new primacy of the rule. Having cut its ties to the older forms of human embodiment, the shari'a of the legislated code relies instead on an authority internal to the new discourse itself. The "straightened" (Bourdieu 1977: 169) thought that has appeared entails a changed character of knowledge, a new locus for truth, and a different relation to and among humans.
>
> (Messick, 1993, p. 250)

In the end, as the Conclusions will recognise, this book, too, is subject to this new space of knowledge, from which the understanding of the *'aqd* can no longer escape.

Notes

1 'This implies the irreducibility of perspective . . . and the necessity for continual *perspectival switches*, as one permeates a totality from an exponentially increasing multiplicity of angles, together with the necessity for rational *self-reflexivity*' (Bhaskar, 1994, p. 77; italics in the original text).

2 'Law in the books' and 'law in action' are classic categories used in the sociology of law to remark the distance between theory and practice – i.e. between the black letter of written law and the substance of living law (see section 1.3.1); in Chapter 1 this approach was already subject to criticism with reference to the assumptions underpinning Schacht's scholarship.

3 'Just as 3L has a special affinity with 1M, 4D has a special resonance with 2E, since agency, which is intentional causality, consists in absenting; that is, more specifically, the transformative negation of the given' (Bhaskar, 1994, p. 100).

4 I adapt here a passage referring to Islamic finance law taken from Cattelan, 2021, p. 76.

5 In this section of the book, I heavily draw from the article that I published in *Arab Law Quarterly* (Cattelan, 2021); I thank here the journal for the permission to reproduce (see also endnote 30).

6 Focusing his attention as an ethnographer on local papers produced in a distinctive geographical space, the town of Ibb (a provincial capital in Šāfiʿī Lower Yemen), with long-term field work conducted between 1974 and 1976, plus six further months of research in 1980, Messick studies handwritten documents as *vehicles* of a wide spectrum of personal and political relationships, with special regard to the hegemonic role of the text-makers in relation to their specialised legal and religious knowledge (which is vital to the interpretation, composition, and implementation, the 'embodiment' of *Šarīʿah* in the society of Ibb).

7 In her legal, historiographic research, Salaymeh underlines the need for a paradigm shift in dealing with Islamic law – a term that 'can be misleading because in actuality Islamic law is generated by multiple groups and institutions (legal polycentricity) and non-Islamic legal traditions coexist with Islamic ones (legal pluralism)' (2016, p. 3). It is good to note how, in introducing her book, Salaymeh states how the

> interplay between innovation and tradition has lasting echoes in Muslim jurisprudence. Generations of Muslim legal actors, historians, and leaders who succeeded the Prophet interpreted scripture and precedents in ways that simultaneously renewed and perpetuated legal traditions. They created a dialect of Islamic law; this book is an exercise in listening to its discourses.
>
> (*ibidem*, p. 1)

The 'echo' of the interplay between innovation and tradition shows some conceptual similarities with the approach taken in this volume; in Salaymeh's work, however, 'listening to the discourses of *fiqh*' does not imply any understanding of Islamic law within its *own* acoustic space, which is, instead, a core feature of this book.

8

> [T]here are several cases in which the early doctrine of Islamic law diverged from the clear and explicit wording of the Koran. One important example which has remained typical in Islamic law is the restriction of legal proof to the evidence of witnesses and the denial of validity to written documents. This contradicts an explicit ruling of the Koran . . . which endorsed the current practice of putting contracts into writing, and this practice did persist during the first century and later, and had to be reconciled with legal theory.
>
> (Schacht, 1964, pp. 18–19)

9 '[T]he jurists never modified their attitude toward written documents. . . . The personal word of an upright Muslim was deemed worthier than an abstract piece of paper or a piece of information subject to doubt and falsification' (Wakin, 1972, p. 6).

10

> The first is a movement from Text to text, that is, from law on the books to the document; while the second is from the world (as event) to text, from a specific human undertaking, such as a sale, to the document. Behind a given document text is the law, in front of it is the world: a document represents a bringing together of socially constituted and enduring legal forms and individually constituted and ad hoc negotiated terms.
>
> (Messick, 1989, p. 35)

11 Much of this section derives from another article that I published in *Arab Law Quarterly* (Cattelan, 2017); once again, I am grateful to the journal for the permission to reproduce.

12 I mention here, all together in the same sentence, the three 'fellows' whose methodological inputs have constantly influenced the development of this book (see section 1.3), so as to highlight their importance for a proper methodological approach to legal devices.

13 Horii refers, specifically, to Chehata, 1969, p. 56; Wichard, 1995, p. 87. See also Cattelan, 2017, pp. 253–254.

14 As Schacht explains, they can be seen as the

> use of legal means [external declarations] for extra-legal ends [illicit purposes] . . . The 'legal devices' enable the persons who would otherwise, under the pressure of circumstances, have had to act against the provisions of the sacred Law, to arrive at the desired result while actually conforming to the letter of law.
>
> (1964, pp. 78–79)

15 Schacht relates the historical origins of the field of *ḥiyal* to the teachings of Kufan authorities, prior to Abū Ḥanīfa; in particular, Ibrāhīm al-Nakhaʿī (d. ca. 96/717) and the already mentioned Šaʿbī:

> Schacht assumed that the Ḥanafī understanding of *ḥiyal* originated in connection with oaths. The *Makhārij* of both Shaybānī and Khaṣṣāf begin with a series of traditions from Kufan authorities prior to Abū Ḥanīfa, which form a basic argument for *ḥiyal* in general. . . . Schacht posited that either Abū Ḥanīfa or, more likely, Ibrāhīm al-Nakhaʿī (d. ca. 96/717), a famous Kufan jurist and theologian who plays a central role in these Kufan traditions, caused the notion of *ḥiyal* to move from the field of oaths into other spheres of the law.
>
> (Horii, 2002, pp. 318–319)

16 The textual polity of Muslim medieval trade can be summarised in relation to three essential features, each interconnected with the other: (1) a real-life approach to Islamic law in relation to human actions; (2) a particularistic casuistry as intrinsic nature of *fiqh* literature (on this point, see Chapter 2); (3) the elaboration of pluralistic solutions in context (see Cattelan, 2021, pp. 82–84).

17 I repeat here an extract from Chapter 3 (specifically at section 3.1) that I find particularly significant for the specific point of discussion.

18 I use here the term 'invention,' similarly to Buskens and Dupret, in the specific sense of 'the creation of a legal *corpus*:' for issues of translation of the label 'Islamic law,' see section 2.1 in this book.

19 There is no doubt, in fact, that

> [t]he positivist conception of Shariʿa as law was foreign to the understanding that Islamic scholars themselves had of the tradition that they transmitted. However, at present this view has become dominant to the extent that students at institutions for Islamic higher learning take courses in 'Islamic law' and 'Islamic legislation,' and that Islamists and other activists strive for the introduction of 'Islamic law' in Islamic states.
>
> (Buskens and Dupret, 2015, p. 32)

20 For other examples referring to the states of Kuwait, Bahrain, North Yemen, and United Arab Emirates, see Saleh, 1990, pp. 106–107.

21 Art. 127: 'The contract is non-existent if the subject-matter of the obligation is impossible to perform, the impossibility being absolute;' Art. 128: 'The subject-matter of the obligation should be determined specifically; it should exist at the moment of the contract; it should be determined as to its quality, its quantity and its genus in such a way that the contracting party should not be left in excessive ignorance which might lead to aleatory *gharar*;' Art. 129: 'The contract is considered valid even if the subject-matter of obligation is non-existent at the time of the making of the contract on condition that its existence is possible in the future and determined in such a way as to protect the contracting party against any ignorance liable to lead to aleatory *gharar*;' Art. 130: 'The subject-matter of the obligation should be: licit; in accordance with the public order and morals.'

22 He submitted the completed draft for discussion in 1942, and the Code was finally enacted seven years later.

23 By looking at al-Sanhūrī's work more in terms of legal comparison than of a radical reform of Islamic law, Ayoub interprets the Egyptian Civil Code as the result of al-Sanhūrī's objective to mark a delineation between the spheres of *dīn* (religion) and *dawla* (state). The key element of his project, using French comparative law as a method of legal inquiry, was a 'nationalist agenda of creating a unified legal order' where there was no 'future for Islamic law in the emerging legal state apparatus outside of civil law structures' (Ayoub, 2022, p. 133).

24 This work contains the course of lectures given by al-Sanhūrī in the Department of Legal Studies at the Arab Studies Institute, Cairo, in 1953–8.

25

> Between 1921 and 1927 Sanhuri pursued his doctoral studies at the University of Lyon. Towards this end, he produced two doctoral dissertations: the first, published in 1925, was entitled *Les Restrictions contractuelles à la liberté individuelle de travail* . . .; and the second, entitled *Le Califat, son évolution vers una societé des nations orientales*, was published in 1926.
>
> (Shalakany, 2001, p. 207; see all Part I: *Genealogical Introduction: Two Theses*, pp. 207–215)

26

> The word *sabab* has a number of meanings in modern Arabic, one of which is 'subjective motive': it can signify the cause of something (*al-ʿalam sabab al-ṣurākh*: the waving of the flag is the cause of screaming); but is also can signify, as in Sanhūrī's usage, the subjective motive behind the act (*ṭalab al-ʿilm sabab al-safar*: the desire for knowledge is the *cause* of travel).
>
> (Arabi, 1997, p. 201, note 3)

27

> The New Egyptian Civil Law adopted the modern theory of cause as a heritage from the previous Civil Law and from the practice of the Egyptian judiciary. The jurisprudence and judiciary in Egypt, prior to the promulgation of the New Civil Law, had already prepared the ground for . . . admitting the new fertile theory.
>
> (*Maṣādir*, vol. 4, p. 27, quoted in Arabi, 1997, p. 204)

28

> While there is no doubt that a centuries-old tradition of intellectual elaboration on social matters characterizes the Islamic civilization, from the ethical and legal dimension of the science of *fiqh* . . . to the contributions to sociology, history and economics by great thinkers like Ibn Khaldun, Ibn Taymiyya and Al-Ghazali, the origins of contemporary Islamic economic studies, as a collective enterprise of research achievements which is recognizable (as well as recognized) within academic circles, cannot be traced back beyond the '60s and '70s of the last century.
>
> (Cattelan, 2018, p. 4)

29 For a critical approach to the concept of 'reality' in the Islamic financial market, valuable insights can be found in Beeferman and Wain, 2016.

30 For this section, I have drawn heavily from my article, published in 2021 in *Arab Law Quarterly* (particularly, pp. 75–76, 84–88). I am grateful to the journal for the permission to reproduce (see also endnote 5).

31 Reproduced with permission from Cattelan, 2021, pp. 88–90.

32 Messick (1993, p. 231) refers here to a notion introduced by Foucault (1970).

References

Ahmed, S. (2016) *What Is Islam? The Importance of Being Islamic.* Princeton and Oxford: Princeton University Press.

Anderson, N. (1976) *Law Reform in the Muslim World*. University of London Legal Series. London: The Athlone Press.
Arabi, O. (1995) Al-Sanhūrī's reconstruction of the Islamic law of contract defects. *Journal of Islamic Studies*. 6(2), pp. 153–172.
Arabi, O. (1997) Intention and method in Sanhūrī's *fiqh*: cause as ulterior motive. *Islamic Law and Society*. 4(2), pp. 200–223.
Ayoub, S.A. (2022) A theory of a state? How civil law ended legal pluralism in modern Egypt. *Journal of Law and Religion*. 37, pp. 133–152.
Ayub, M. (2007) *Understanding Islamic Finance*. Chichester: John Wiley & Sons.
Bälz, K. (2008) *Sharia Risk? How Islamic Finance Has Transformed Islamic Contract Law*. Occasional Publications Number 9, Islamic Legal Studies Program. Cambridge: Harvard Law School.
Bälz, K. (2014) Finance. In: Fleet, K., Krämer, G. *et al.* (eds.) *Encyclopedia of Islam, Three*. Available at: https://referenceworks.brillonline.com/browse/encyclopaedia-of-islam-3. Accessed 15 April 2019.
Beeferman, L.W., and Wain, A. (2016) *Getting Real About Islamic Finance*. Cambridge: Labor and Worklife Program, Harvard Law School, May. Available at: https://lwp.law.harvard.edu/publications/getting-real-about-islamic-finance. Accessed 15 September 2021.
Bhaskar, R. (1993) *Dialectic: The Pulse of Freedom*. London: Verso.
Bhaskar, R. (1994) *Plato Etc.: The Problems of Philosophy and Their Resolution*. London: Verso.
Brunschvig, R. (1976) Théorie générale de la capacité chez les hanafites médiévaux. In: Brunschvig, R. (ed.) *Études d'Islamologie*, Vol. II. Paris: Maisonneuve et Larose, pp. 37–52.
Bourdieu, P. (1977) *Outline of a Theory of Practice* (trans. by Nice, R.). Cambridge: Cambridge University Press.
Buskens, L., and Dupret, B. (2015) The invention of Islamic law: a history of Western studies of Islamic normativity and their spread in the Orient. In: Pouillon, F., and Vatin, J.-C. (eds.) *After Orientalism: Critical Perspectives on Western Agency and Eastern Re-Appropriations*. Leiden and Boston: Brill, pp. 31–47.
Calder, N. (1996) Law. In: Nasr, S.H., and Leaman, O. (eds.) *History of Islamic Philosophy*, Part II. London: Routledge, pp. 979–998.
Cassirer, E. (1955) *The Philosophy of Symbolic Forms*, Vol. 2. New Haven: Yale University Press.
Castro, F. (1985) La codificazione del diritto privato negli Stati arabi contemporanei: appunti sulla circolazione dei modelli normativi. *Rivista di Diritto Civile*. 4(1), pp. 387–448.
Cattelan, V. (2009) From the concept of *ḥaqq* to the prohibitions of *ribā*, *gharar* and *maysir* in Islamic finance. *International Journal of Monetary Economics and Finance*. 2(3–4), pp. 384–397.
Cattelan, V. (2013) A glimpse through the veil of Maya: Islamic finance and its truths on property rights. In: Cattelan, V. (ed.) *Islamic Finance in Europe: Towards a Plural Financial System*. Studies in Islamic Finance, Accounting and Governance. Cheltenham and Northampton, MA: Edward Elgar Publishing, pp. 32–51.
Cattelan, V. (2017) Between theory(*-ies*) and practice(*-s*): legal devices (*ḥiyal*) in classical Islamic law. *Arab Law Quarterly*. 31(3), pp. 245–275.
Cattelan, V. (2018) *Theoretical Development and Shortages of Contemporary Islamic Economics Studies: Research Programmes and the Paradigm of Shared Prosperity*. Report Number 6. Istanbul: Research Center for Islamic Economics (IKAM).

Cattelan, V. (2021) *The Typewritten Market*: Shari'ah-compliance and securitisation in the law of Islamic finance. *Arab Law Quarterly*. 35(1–2), Special Issue *Islamic Finance and Contemporary Challenges*, pp. 74–91.
Chehata, C. (1968) Le concept de contrat en droit musulman. *Archives de Philosophie du Droit*. 13, pp. 129–141.
Chehata, C. (1969) *Théorie Générale de l'Obligation en Droit Musulman Hanéfite: Les Sujets de l'Obligation*. Paris: Éditions Sirey.
Comair-Obeid, N. (1996) Particularity of the contract's subject-matter in the laws of the Arab Middle East. *Arab Law Quarterly*. 11(4), pp. 331–349.
Duncan, D., Harrison, S. *et al.* (2019) *Babel. Adventures in Translation*. Oxford: Bodleain Library.
El-Gamal, M.A. (2006) *Islamic Finance: Law, Economics, and Practice*. Cambridge and New York: Cambridge University Press.
Ercanbrack, J. (2015) *The Transformation of Islamic Law in Global Financial Markets*. Cambridge: Cambridge University Press.
Foster, N.H.D. (2007) Islamic finance law as an emergent legal system. *Arab Law Quarterly*. 21(2), pp. 170–188.
Foucault, M. (1970) *The Order of Things*. New York: Vintage.
Funds@Work (2010) *The Small World of Islamic Finance: Shariah Scholars and Governance – A Network Analytic Perspective*. Available at: https://funds-at.work/wp-content/uploads/2018/02/Sharia-Network-by-Funds-at-Work-AG.pdf. Accessed 25 May 2018.
Galimberti, U. (1999) *Psiche e Techne: L'Uomo nell'Età della Tecnica*. Milan: Feltrinelli.
Godlewski, C.J., Turk, R., and Weill, L. (2014) *Do the Type of "Sukuk" and the Choice of "Shari'ah" Scholar Matter?* IMF Working Paper WP/14/147. Washington: IMF.
Hallaq, W.B. (2009) *An Introduction to Islamic Law*. Cambridge: Cambridge University Press.
Horii, S. (2002) Reconsideration of legal devices (*ḥiyal*) in Islamic jurisprudence: the Ḥanafīs and their "exits" (*makhārij*). *Islamic Law and Society*. 9(3), pp. 312–357.
Izutsu, T. (2002) *Ethico-Religious Concepts in the Qur'ān*. Montreal, Kingston, London and Ithaca: McGill-Queen's University Press (first published 1966).
Jay, M. (1988) Scopic regimes of modernity. In: Foster, H. (ed.) *Vision and Visuality*. Dia Art Foundation – Discussions in Contemporary Culture Number 2. Seattle: Bay Press, pp. 3–23.
Johansen, B. (1997) Formes de langage et fonctions publiques: stéréotypes, témoins et offices dans la prevue par l'écrit en droit musulman. *Arabica*. 44, pp. 333–376.
Johnston, D. (2004) A turn in the epistemology and hermeneutics of twentieth century *uṣūl al-fiqh*. *Islamic Law and Society*. 11(2), pp. 233–282.
Kamali, M.H. (1998) Sharī'ah as understood by the classical jurists. *IILM Law Journal*. 6, pp. 39–87.
Liebesny, H.J. (1975) *The Law of the Near and Middle East*. Albany: State University of New York Press.
Linant de Bellefonds, Y. (1965) *Traité de Droit Musulman Comparé, 3 Vols. Vol. 1, Théorie Générale de l'Acte Juridique*. Paris and La Haye: Mouton & Co.
Lydon, G. (2009) A paper economy of faith without faith in paper: a reflection on Islamic institutional history. *Journal of Economic Behavior & Organization*. 71, pp. 647–659.
McLuhan, M. (1969) The Playboy interview: Marshall McLuhan. *Playboy*. March, pp. 26–27.

McLuhan, M., and Fiore, Q. (1967) *The Medium Is the Massage: An Inventory of Effects.* New York: Bantam Books; London: Penguin Books.
Messick, B. (1989) Just writing: paradox and political economy in Yemeni legal documents. *Cultural Anthropology.* 4(1), pp. 26–50.
Messick, B. (1993) *The Calligraphic State: Textual Domination and History in a Muslim Society.* Berkeley: California University Press.
Mitchell, S. (2007) GRC360: a framework to help organisations drive principled performance. *International Journal of Disclosure and Governance.* 4(4), pp. 279–296.
Norrie, A. (2009) *Dialectic and Difference: Dialectical Critical Realism and the Grounds of Justice.* London: Routledge.
Pollard, J., and Samers, M. (2013) Governing Islamic finance: territory, agency and the making of cosmopolitan financial geographies. *Annals of the Association of American Geographers.* 103(3), pp. 710–726.
Rayner, S.E. (1991) *The Theory of Contracts in Islamic Law: A Comparative Analysis with Reference to the Modern Legislation in Kuwait, Bahrain and the United Arab Emirates.* Arab and Islamic Laws Series. London, Dordrecht and Boston: Graham & Trotman.
Said, E.W. (1978) *Orientalism.* London and Henley: Routledge & Kegan Paul.
Salaymeh, L. (2016) *The Beginnings of Islamic Law: Late Antique Islamicate Legal Traditions.* Cambridge: Cambridge University Press.
Saleh, N. (1990) Definition and formation of contract under Islamic and Arab laws. *Arab Law Quarterly.* 5(2), pp. 101–116.
Saleh, N. (1992) Are the validity and construction of legal acts affected by cause (*sabab*)? (A comparative study under Islamic and Arab laws). *Arab Law Quarterly.* 7(2), pp. 116–140.
Sanhūrī, A.R.A. (1952–1970) *Al-Wasīṭ fī Sharḥ al-Qānūn al-Madanī al-Jadīd* (*The Intermediate Explication of the New Civil Code*), 10 Vols. Reprinted in 1972, Cairo: Dār al-Nahḍah al-'Arabiyyah.
Sanhūrī, A.R.A. (1954–1959) *Maṣādir al-Ḥaqq fī l-Fiqh al-Islāmī, Dirāsa Muqārina bi-l-Fiqh al-Gharbī* (*The Bases of Right in Islamic Law, a Comparative Study with Western Law*), 6 Vols. Cairo: Jāmi'ah ad-Duwal al-'Arabiyya.
Schacht, J. (1964) *An Introduction to Islamic Law.* Oxford: Clarendon Press.
Shalakany, A. (2001) Between identity and redistribution: Sanhuri, genealogy and the will to Islamise. *Islamic Law and Society.* 8(2), pp. 201–244.
Stelzer, S.A.J. (2008) Ethics. In: Winter, T. (ed.) *The Cambridge Companion to Classical Islamic Theology.* Cambridge: Cambridge University Press, pp. 161–179.
Szymborska, W. (1996) *View with a Grain of Sand: Selected Poems* (trans. by Barańczak, S., and Cavanagh, C. from the original Polish version 1986). London: Faber and Faber.
Udovitch, A. (1970a) *Partnership and Profit in Medieval Islam.* Princeton, NJ: Princeton University Press.
Udovitch, A. (1970b) The "law merchant" of the medieval Islamic world. In: Von Grunebaum, G.E. (ed.) *Logic in Classical Islamic Culture, First Levi della Vida Biennial Conference, Near Eastern Centre, University of California, Los Angeles, May 12, 1967.* Wiesbaden: Otto Harrassowitz, pp. 113–130.
Vogel, F.E. (2006) Contract law of Islam and the Arab Middle East. In: *International Encyclopedia of Comparative Law, Vol. VII, Contracts in General,* Chapter 7. Dordrecht, Boston and Lancaster: Mohr Siebeck, Tübingen, and Martinus Nijhoff Publishers.

Vogel, F.E., and Hayes, S.L. III (1998) *Islamic Law and Finance: Religion, Risk and Return*. Arab and Islamic Laws Series. The Hague, London and Boston: Kluwer Law International.

Wakin, J.A. (1972) *The Function of Documents in Islamic Law*. New York: State University of New York Press.

Warde, I. (2000) *Islamic Finance in the Global Economy*. Edinburgh: Edinburgh University Press.

Wichard, J.C. (1995) *Zwischen Markt und Moschee: Wirtschaftliche Bedurfnisse und Religiose Anforderungen im Fruhen Islamischen Vertragsrecht* (*Between Market and Mosque: Economic Needs and Religious Requirements in Early Islamic Contract Law*). Paderborn: Fernand Schöningh.

Wilson, R. (1997) *Economics, Ethics and Religion: Jewish, Christian and Muslim Economic Thought*. New York: New York University Press.

Zysow, A. (1985–86) The problem of offer and acceptance: a study of implied-in-fact contracts in Islamic law and common law. *Cleveland State Law Review*. 34(1), pp. 69–77.

Conclusions

Ways of *saying* the *ʿaqd*

The story of the *ʿaqd* that this book has narrated is a story of continuity and change. It is also a story of non-identity, dialectics, and encounter.

Islam, the body of law, and the living text of *Šarīʿah*

Our voyage of discovery started from a fortuitous meeting with the *Arab Girl* at the gate of the city of the *ʿaqd*. The decadent picture of *The Almeh*, paradigm of the Western practice of Orientalism (Said, 1978), has been translated into a metaphor for the assumptions of Western scholarship in representing the nature of Islamic contract law.

Fighting against the daemons of the Western Temple of modernity (Chapter 1), this book has proposed an alternative path towards the understanding of the *ʿaqd*, grounded on a dialectics of non-identity (1M) (Bhaskar, 1993) in carrying the One Ring of law-religion. Through this methodological tool, the plural unity of Islam (Ahmed, 2016) has been located within an acoustic space whose rationales, departing from the visual rationality of the Western world (McLuhan, 1989), can offer an interpretative key to the logic of Muslim *fiqh* in the echo of divine will in the lives of Muslim believers. The replica of social life as an inherent purpose of *fiqh* in a balance between revelation, tradition, and reality (Calder, 1996) has been the pathway that this book has followed in the discovery of the Islamic contract. In turn, the absence of a *corpus* for the sacred law of Islam (Chapter 2) (2E) has defined the 'craft of place' for the city of the *ʿaqd* that we have visited through the multiple itineraries of the doctrinal traditions of *fiqh* jurisprudence (Chapter 3) (3L) and in a transformative praxis (4M) affected by an extended totality in contact with non-Islamic elements, the Western world, and global finance (Chapter 4). Within this transformative praxis, the continuity-through-change of the *ʿaqd* has been outlined in relation to the different ages of *Verbal Trade*, *Codified Norm*, and *Typewritten Market*, each typifying some essential characters of the nature of the Islamic contract *in-time*.

Moving from one era to the other, the absence of a 'legal body' for the *ʿaqd* in the time of medieval trade has been contrasted with to the 'invention' of this body during the codification period (section 4.3.1), paired with that of Islamic finance in the time of contemporary capitalism (section 4.4.1), in a mix

DOI: 10.4324/9781315145761-6

of continuity, contamination, and re-adaptation to changing contexts. In this regard, much attention has been dedicated, in this book, to the epistemological shift that has occurred in the Muslim world by moving from *fiqh* acoustic space (where humans could be understood in their ethical dimension 'only because the law as a particular manifestation of the divine Word constitutes them *by way of word*:' Stelzer, 2008, p. 169) to the visual space of written codes, and later, that of global commercial standards: a radical transformation that has deeply affected the urban design of the *'aqd* (see section 4.5; Messick, 1993, p. 246 ff.).

Looking back at the central assumption of this book – i.e. that the distinctive nature of the *'aqd* must be inferred from the interdependence between law and religion in Islam – a final reference to Messick can support the conclusions of our journey. Referring to the scholarship of Muḥammad b. 'Ali al-Šawkānī (1759–1834), the towering intellectual figure of early 19th-century Yemen, Messick underlines how in the Muslim world 'the shari'a, and Islam generally, survives not so much in concrete writing ("in the bodies of pages and registers") as through embodiment in the lives of individuals, in the living "text" they transmit and interpret' (1993, p. 43). Accordingly, '[a]cademic knowledges such as shari'a jurisprudence were understood to be embodied' (*ibidem*, p. 249) in the oral opinions of scholars, and only later registered in the books of *fiqh* literature. In a very similar way, as noted regarding the specificities of verbalism in Islamic contract law (sections 3.5.1 and 4.2.2), the Muslim world bears witness in its acoustic space to '[a] culturally specific paradox [that] informed the grounding of spoken words in written texts' (*ibidem*, p. 252).

> From the recording of Revelation to the documentation of property rights [and of contractual transactions as well], attempts to inscribe original speech, considered authentic and true, resulted in textual versions of diminished authority. . . . Associations of the spoken word with presence, truth, and justice, and of the written word with absence, falsehood, and injustice, held mainly in connection with the various authoritative texts of the discursive core. . . . At the heart of this "written tradition" stood a corpus of texts construed as recitations.
>
> (*ibidem*)

The paradox of a 'written tradition' built on a '*corpus* of recitations' is embodied in a movement where – by the 'reading,' *rectius* 'recitation' (*qirā'ah*) of the Qur'ān (section 2.4.2) – the dictum (*ḥukm*) of *Word* revelation proceeds to what is 'true,' 'real,' 'just,' and so 'right' (*ḥaqq*) in the Muslim *world* (section 2.4.4). Correspondingly, the human *word* itself becomes, in this acoustic epistemology, the echo of what was revealed; a 'living' text fostered by the transmission of *fiqh* tradition and 'embodied' in the actual lives of Muslim believers. Far from the representation of the 'body of God' in Christian religion (see Chapter 1), the Temple of Islam gives 'body to God's *Word*' in the actions of human beings. Hence, from the divine Word to the dimension of worldly transactions, *fiqh* tradition in medieval Islam acted as a 'tool of mediation' – a 'surface of reflection' for the Message – in an interplay of ideal-real where contractual rules were necessarily linked to local, contextualised realities. In summary, the 'local knowledge' (Geertz, 1983, p. 167; see also section 3.1) of the *'aqd* was 'embodied' in the real lives of Muslim believers, with the Law being multiplied in a ramified echo – the polyphony of the *Word*-in-the-*world*. In this context, the *'aqd*, as factual performance of God's will (section 3.6), could be *said* in multiple, divergent, plural ways in the tradition of *fiqh*, as it is the result of the action of *listening to* the revelation – the reality of Muslim lives being the specific arena for its polyphony.

However, as noted in Chapter 4, the acoustic space of *Verbal Trade* was later substituted by the transplant of Western visual rationality (the *Codified Norm*, expression of the cultural encounter with the modern state, replicated in Muslim countries) and later the epistemology of capitalism (the *Typewritten Market* of global Islamic finance).

The One Ring of law-religion and the return to the *Arab Girl* (and ourselves)

Both at the end of Chapters 1 and 2, the reader was invited to wait for the final destination of our journey, not in the discovery of the 'place' of the Islamic contract, but rather, of a new way of *saying* it by *listening to* the echo of the Islamic revelation.

Indeed, if, in the Islamic tradition, spoken words are associated 'with presence, truth, and justice,' in contrast to written words (the place of 'absence, falsehood, and injustice:' see the foregoing), the acoustic epistemology that has fuelled our research, on the one hand, implicitly *negates* the recipe of Marcel Proust's 'only true voyage of discovery,' which 'would be not to visit strange lands, but to possess other eyes, to behold the universe through the eyes of another' (Proust, 2006, p. 657). To explore the city of the *'aqd*, an alternative medium of understanding grounded on the need for *listening* rather than *seeing* must be followed: not the 'eye,' but an oral-aural medium.

On the other hand, the cultural connotations of Western visual epistemology (McLuhan, 1989) have been essential for the practice of translation, comparison, and contextualisation in this book, without which its research could not have been undertaken. If *non-identity* constitutes the core of dialectic (Bhaskar, 1993), that process of *negation* was specifically required to embrace the *totality* of the Islamic contract in its divergences and multiplicity (Ahmed, 2016), as well as the recognition of its *transformative praxis*, moving from *The Two Towers* (Ch. 3) to the bridge of Babel *in-time* (Ch. 4). In this respect, as we have seen, if the *'aqd* was a specific societal discourse in Muslim medieval trade, the invention of modern Islamic law (Buskens and Dupret, 2015) 'decisively repositioned [*Šarī'ah*] within nation-state frameworks' (Messick, 1993,

p. 253), from the 'bodies' of Muslim believers to the *corpus* of 'the codified and legislated form of law' (*ibidem*), where the primacy of the *eye* as medium of understanding prevails.

Considering all this, a final homage to the *Arab Girl* can sketch the ultimate meaning of our research.

To the extent to which her 'improper body' has been 're-phrased' in the acoustic space of Islam – negating its visuality as an expression of Western culture and a representation of Orientalism –, we should be aware that the visual code of modernity, against which we have fought, has been paradoxically re-affirmed in the pages of this book. The absence, falsehood, and injustice of written words have 're-placed,' in this book, the presence, truth, and justice of spoken words, not only through the tools of comparison (and thus the necessary dialectic between the *positum* of Western law and the *absence* of *fiqh*) but also through the very medium through which the contents of this search have been communicated (that of written pages). Reflecting the same paradox, the reader may rightly complain that all of Chapter 3 has been structured in the form of a 'body' that was *absent* in the tradition of *fiqh*.

These apparent fallacies, however, can be resolved (and justified) in the light of the dialectical perspective to which our research has been devoted.

It is well-known that the trilogy of *The Lord of the Rings* concludes with the One Ring being destroyed, the Hobbits returning to the Shire after the great battle of Middle-Earth, and the various human kingdoms united under Aragorn. But each story has its own ending, and the story of the *ʿaqd* has quite a different one. If the non-identity of law-religion requires that the One Ring should not be destroyed, but rather, carried again (and again) in comparative studies, the traveller, immersed in the culture of Western modernity, cannot escape from the canons of visuality in narrating, from a dialectical perspective, the acoustic story of the *ʿaqd*.

Far from being a declaration of defeat to modernity, it seems to me that this conclusion can offer an implicit invitation to the reader to engage in further reflection about *ourselves* and the *others*. In the end, if the city of the *ʿaqd* that this book has explored can itself be 'read' as a cultural construct, as was the *Arab Girl*, 'listening to' its contents (i.e. by actively engaging with the rationales of an acoustic space) may render its message in the language of Islam: a language of presence, truth, and justice for the Muslim believer.

Fully adhering to the fourth dimension of Bhaskar's dialectics (4D), the transformative praxis that implies 'the capacity for practical human *agency* to change the world' (Norrie, 2009, p. 12), my wish is that this search will contribute to a process of *becoming* in the representation of Muslim societies, grounded on a better understanding of the Western pre-assumptions in 'looking at' this world through the visual perspective of modernity. In the constellation of opportunities that the *non-identity* East-West can open up, not only will *re-orienting* the *ʿaqd* towards 'listening' to the law and religion of Islam offer a more precise account of the rationales underpinning *fiqh* tradition, but it will also provide the travellers with better ***orientation*** within their visual culture, by locating their own 'map' in the space of modernity.

Knowing ourselves better through the *'aqd*, in this dialectical process of self-discovery and becoming, may be the most precious gift that the *Arab Girl* has given to her guests. A Ring that the reader should keep as a memory of this journey and a lucky charm for future adventures.

References

Ahmed, S. (2016) *What Is Islam? The Importance of Being Islamic.* Princeton and Oxford: Princeton University Press.

Bhaskar, R. (1993) *Dialectic: The Pulse of Freedom.* London: Verso.

Buskens, L., and Dupret, B. (2015) The invention of Islamic law: a history of Western studies of Islamic normativity and their spread in the orient. In: Pouillon, F., and Vatin, J.-C. (eds.) *After Orientalism: Critical Perspectives on Western Agency and Eastern Re-Appropriations.* Leiden and Boston: Brill, pp. 31–47.

Calder, N. (1996) Law. In: Leaman, O., and Nasr, S.H. (eds.) *History of Islamic Philosophy.* London and New York: Routledge, pp. 979–998.

Geertz, C. (1983) Local knowledge: fact and law in comparative perspective. In: Geertz, C. (ed.) *Local Knowledge: Further Essays in Interpretive Anthropology.* New York: Basic Books, pp. 167–234.

McLuhan, M. (1989) Visual and acoustic space (from McLuhan, M., and Powers, B.R. *The Global Village.* New York: Oxford University Press). Reprinted in Cox, C., and Warner, D. (eds.) (2004) *Audio Culture: Readings in Modern Music.* New York and London: Continuum, pp. 67–72.

Messick, B. (1993) *The Calligraphic State: Textual Domination and History in a Muslim Society.* Berkeley: California University Press.

Norrie, A. (2009) *Dialectic and Difference: Dialectical Critical Realism and the Grounds of Justice.* London: Routledge.

Proust, M. (2006) *Remembrance of Things Past* (trans. by Moncrieff, C.K.S., and Hudson, S.), Vol. 2. Ware, Herts: Wordsworth Editions.

Said, E.W. (1978) *Orientalism.* London and Henley: Routledge & Kegan Paul.

Stelzer, S.A.J. (2008) Ethics. In: Winter, T. (ed.) *The Cambridge Companion to Classical Islamic Theology.* Cambridge: Cambridge University Press, pp. 161–179.

Glossary of Arabic terms*

ʿadl justice [3.3.3; 3.6]

al-aḥkām al-khamsa 'the five legal/religious qualifications' [in general, 2.4.4; in relation to the contract, 3.3.2]; see also *ḥukm*

ʿaqd (pl. *ʿuqūd*) contract; more in general, legal 'bond,' 'tie,' binding act [see, in particular, 3.3; 3.3.3; 3.4.3; 3.6]

ʿaql human reason, intellect, rationality [2.3; 2.4.4; 2.4.5; 3.4; 3.5.2; 3.5.4; 3.6]

ahliyya legal capacity [3.3.1; 3.3.2]

ākhirah the Hereafter [2.3]

ʿayn (pl. *aʿyān*) specific thing, property *hic-et-nunc* [3.5.3]

bāṭil (of legal act) void, null, inexistent, invalid [3.3.2]

bayʿ contract of sale, exchange [3.4.2; 3.5.4]

dayn (pl. *duyūn*) debt, credit, obligation [3.5.3]

dhimma legal personality [3.3.1; 3.5.3]

dīn religion (gathering aspects of obligation, direction, submission, and retribution), correct Muslim lifestyle, Islamic *bíos* [2.3]

dunyā (earthly) world [2.3]

faqīh (pl. *fuqahāʾ*) Muslim legal scholar, jurisconsult, expert of *fiqh* [2.4.1; 3.2]

fāsid (of legal act) voidable, defective, invalid [3.3.2]

fatwā legal opinion given by an expert of *fiqh* [3.4.2; 4.4.2]

fiqh normative understanding of the revelation; Islamic law; the science and knowledge of *Šarīʿah*; Muslim jurisprudence [1.3.3; 2.4.1; 2.4.2; 2.4.3]

furūʿ (al-fiqh) the 'branches' of substantive law [1.4; 2.4.1; 2.4.3; 2.4.5]

ghalaṭ (vice of) mistake [3.4.4; compare with 4.3.2]

gharar risk, hazard, uncertainty, speculation [3.5.4]

ḥadīth (pl. *aḥādīth*) tradition from the Prophet [2.4.2]

ḥalāl not forbidden, permitted, allowed [2.4.4; 3.3.2]

ḥaqq (pl. *ḥuqūq*) right, in the sense of what is 'true,' 'real,' 'just,' and therefore is 'right' according to the revelation [2.4.3; 2.4.4]

ḥarām forbidden [2.4.4; 3.3.2]

hiba gift, donation [3.3.3; 3.4.1; 3.4.2]

ḥīla (pl. *ḥiyal*) legal device, stratagem [3.4.3; 4.2.3]

ḥukm (pl. *aḥkām*) rule, qualification, God's command, decree, status of the action, judgement [2.4.3; 2.4.4]
ʿibāda (pl. *ʿibādāt*) act of worship (*fiqh al-ʿibādāt*: see Introduction, endnote 2) [1.1; 2.3; 2.4.2; 3.4.3]
ibāḥa doctrine of permissibility [3.4.2]
iḥsān virtue, internalisation of the faith [2.3]
ījāb offer (as constitutive element of the contract) [3.3.3; 3.5.1; 3.5.2; 4.2.1]
ijāra (contract of) hire and lease [3.4.2; 4.4.1; 4.4.2]
ijmāʿ consensus among scholars as source of law [1.4; 2.4.2]
ijtihād effort (of the legal scholar to understand the revelation) [1.3.3; 2.4.4; 4.2.3]
ikhtilāf divergence of opinion, disagreement [2.4.4; 2.4.5]
ikrāh duress (as vitiating factor of the contract) [3.4.4; 4.3.2]
ʿilla (pl. *ʿilal*) (divine, efficient) cause for the event [2.4.4; 3.4.1; 3.5.4; 4.3.2]
iltizām obligation [4.3.1]
īmān faith [2.3]
irāda will [2.4.2; 3.4.3]
Islām surrender (to God) [2.3]
isnād chain of transmitters of a tradition of *aḥādīth* [2.4.2; 2.4.5]
istiḥsān juristic preference
istiṣnāʿ (contract of) manufacture [4.4.1; 4.4.2]
jāhiliyya (age of) ignorance before revelation [2.4.5; 4.2.1]
kalām speculative theology [2.4.3]
kasb acquisition, performance of the action [2.4.4; 3.4.1; 3.5.1]
khalīfah (Muslim believer as) God's vice-regent [3.4]
khiyār (pl. *khiyārāt*; also *ikhtiyār*, pl. *ikhtiyārāt*) choice, preference, option as an element of the contract [3.4.3; 3.4.4; 4.3.2]
madhhab (pl. *madhāhib*) juristic school, religio-normative doctrine [2.3; 2.4.3; 3.2]
maḥall recipient of the duty; location, place (for responsibility) [2.4.2; 3.3.1; 3.3.2; 3.5.3]
majlis meeting, contractual session [3.5.1; 4.2.2]
makhārij Ḥanafī doctrine of 'exits' in allowing legal devices [4.2.3]
makrūh disapproved [2.4.4; 3.3.2]
māl (pl. *amwāl*) property [3.5.3]
mandūb recommended [2.4.4; 3.3.2]
manfaʿa (pl. *manāfiʿ*) proceeds, use, usufruct [3.5.3]
maqāṣid al-Šarīʿah objectives of Islamic law [4.4.2]
maqṣūd (pl. *maqāṣid*) motive, aim, purpose [compare endnote 16 at Ch. 3 with 4.3.1]
maysir gambling, game of chance [3.5.4]
milk ownership [3.5.3]
muʿāmala (pl. *muʿāmalāt*) commercial/worldly transaction (*fiqh al-muʿāmalāt*: see Introduction, endnote 2) [1.1; 2.3; 3.4.3]
muʿāwaḍa (pl. *muʿāwaḍāt*) civil/commercial bilateral transactions [3.3; 3.5.4]

mubāḥ neutral, indifferent [2.4.4; 3.3.2]; also licit [3.5.3]
muḍāraba silent partnership [3.4.2; 4.4.1; 4.4.2]
mukallaf (believer who is) fully responsible [2.4.3; 2.4.4]; the person who is fully capable [3.3.1; 3.3.2; 3.5.1]
murābaḥa mark up sale [4.4.1; 4.4.2]
mušaraka full partnership [4.4.1; 4.4.2]
nikāḥ (contract of) marriage [3.3.3; 3.5.1; 4.3.2]
niyya intent, motive, intention behind the action [3.4.3]
qabūl acceptance (as constitutive element of the contract) [3.3.3; 3.5.1; 3.5.2]
qarḍ (contract of) loan [3.5.4]
qaṣd *animus contrahendi* [3.4.3]
qimār gambling [3.5.4]
qiyās analogy, analogic reasoning [2.4.2; 3.4.1; 4.3.2]
Qur'ān the Book, the recitation-text of the revealed Word [2.4.2]
raqaba substance of the thing [3.5.3]
ribā unlawful gain, illicit enrichment, increase, excess, quantitative disequilibrium, interest [3.5.4]
riḍā individual consent, assent, approval [3.4.3; 4.3.2]
rukn (pl. *arkān*) essential element (of the contract) [3.3.2]
sabab (pl. *asbāb*) cause, empirical circumstance for the action, for the occurrence of the duty [3.3.1; 3.4.1; compare 2.4.4 with 4.3.2]
sadd al-dharā'i' principle of 'blocking ways' in relation to the permissibility of legal stratagems [4.2.3]
ṣaḥiḥ valid (legal act) [3.3.2]
ṣakk (pl. *ṣukūk*) certificate of investment in the Islamic financial market [4.4.2]
ṣarf (contract of) monetary exchange [3.5.4]
šarika partnership [3.4.2]
Šarī'ah the 'way to water;' the Right Path to be followed by Muslim believers for salvation; revealed divine Law [1.3.3; 2.3; 2.4.2]
šarṭ (pl. *šurūṭ*) conditional element of the contract [3.3.2]; (attached) stipulation [3.4.2]
ṣīghah external expression, manifestation of the intent [3.5.1; 3.6]
ṣūra form through which the contract is expressed [3.5.1]
sunna recommended (of legal/religious act) [2.4.4; 3.3.2]
Sunnah Tradition of the Prophet [2.4.2]
tabarru'a (pl. *tabarru'āt*) gratuitous, liberal act [3.5.4]
tadlīs fraud as a vitiating factor for the contract [3.4.4]
taklīf divine injunction [3.3.2]
tarāḍī agreement, mutual assent, mutual consent [3.3.2; 3.3.3; 3.5.2; 3.6]
taṣarruf act of disposal; capacity of disposition [3.3.1; 3.3.3; 3.5.3; 3.6]
ummah community [2.3]

uṣūl (al-fiqh) 'roots,' principles of knowledge, *fiqh* legal methodology [1.4; 2.4.1; 2.4.2]
wājib obligatory [2.4.4; 3.3.2; 3.5.2; 4.2.1]
wujūb legal/religious duty [3.3.1]
zakāt alms-tax [2.3; 4.3.2]

Note

* More detailed explanation of the term can be found in the sections of the book specified in squared brackets.

Index

Note: numbers in *italics* indicate a diagram or a figure

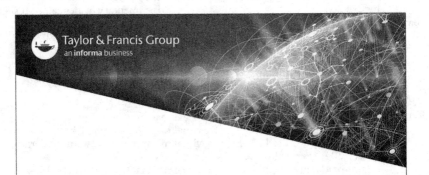

Printed in the United States
by Baker & Taylor Publisher Services

Printed in the United States
by Baker & Taylor Publisher Services